The A List

Launched to mark our forty-fifth anniversary, the A List is a series of handsome new editions of classic Anansi titles. Encompassing fiction, nonfiction, and poetry, this collection includes some of the finest books we've published. We feel that these are great reads, and the series is an excellent introduction to the world of Canadian literature. The redesigned A List books will feature new cover art by noted Canadian illustrators, and each edition begins with a new introduction by a notable writer. We can think of no better way to celebrate forty-five years of great publishing than by bringing these books back into the spotlight. We hope you'll agree.

ELEVEN CANADIAN NOVELISTS

INTERVIEWED BY GRAEME GIBSON

LIST

Excerpts from several of these interviews appeared on *CBC Anthology*

First published in 1973 by House of Anansi Press Ltd.

This edition published in 2014 by
House of Anansi Press Inc.
110 Spadina Avenue, Suite 801
Toronto, ON, M5V 2K4
Tel. 416-363-4343
Fax 416-363-1017
www.houseofanansi.com

Distributed in Canada by
HarperCollins Canada Ltd.
1995 Markham Road
Scarborough, ON, M1B 5M8
Toll free tel. 1-800-387-0117

Distributed in the United States by
Publishers Group West
1700 Fourth Street
Berkeley, CA 94710
Toll free tel. 1-800-788-3123

House of Anansi Press is committed to protecting our natural environment. As part of our efforts, the interior of this book is printed on paper that contains 30% post-consumer recycled fibres, is acid-free, and is processed chlorine-free.

18 17 16 15 14   1 2 3 4 5

Library and Archives Canada Cataloguing in Publication
Gibson, Graeme, 1934–, author
Eleven Canadian novelists interviewed by Graeme Gibson
/ Graeme Gibson.

Issued in print and electronic formats.
ISBN 978-1-77089-814-1 (pbk.).—ISBN 978-1-77089-816-5 (html)

1. Novelists, Canadian (English)—20th century—Interviews.
2. Fiction—Authorship. I. Title.

PS8081.G5 2014   C813'.5409   C2014-902671-4
                        C2014-902672-2

Library of Congress Control Number: 2014907273

Series design: Brian Morgan
Cover illustration: Michael Cho
All photographs: Graeme Gibson
Text design: Alysia Shewchuk
Typesetting: Laura Brady

Canada Council   Conseil des Arts   ONTARIO ARTS COUNCIL
for the Arts   du Canada   CONSEIL DES ARTS DE L'ONTARIO

We acknowledge for their financial support of our publishing program the Canada Council for the Arts, the Ontario Arts Council, and the Government of Canada through the Canada Book Fund. We acknowledge the financial support of the Government of Canada through the National Translation Program for Book Publishing, for our translation activities.

Printed and bound in Canada

INTRODUCTION
by Graeme Gibson

Eleven Canadian Novelists — published in February 1973 — was very much a creature of its time. The late sixties and early seventies had seen a remarkable growth of new, often experimental Canadian writing. This was followed by the appearance of small independent publishers, many of which had writers as editors or helpers.

Anansi was one of these presses. Notable among others were Quarry and Coach House, founded in 1965, and Oberon in 1966; then came Anansi and Mel Hurtig in 1967, Sono Nis in 1968, and New Press in 1970. On the whole these were avante garde and/or nationalist houses that produced a remarkable range of significant and often challenging writing.

Dave Godfrey's collection, *Death Goes Better with Coca-Cola* (1967), was Anansi's first prose fiction. Then, in 1969, Anansi published six novels and one collection of stories, all by previously unpublished book writers. In the two following years it produced two collections of stories and fifteen novels, including work by Austin Clarke, Matt Cohen, Marian Engel, and Roch Carrier. Two-thirds of the seventeen titles were by new writers. According to *The Canadian Encyclopaedia*, in 1969 Anansi produced a third of all novels published in English Canada.

Between 1968 and 1971, poets such as Allen Ginsberg, George Bowering, Joe Rosenblatt, and Michael Ondaatje joined the house. Anansi also published important non-fiction, including George Grant's *Technology and Empire* and Northrop Frye's *The Bush Garden*. In response to the Vietnam War, Mark Satin's *Manual for Draft-Age Immigrants to Canada* appeared in 1968. That this book sold 65,000 copies, mostly by mail, highlights the desperation of draft-age Americans.

By the early seventies there was a literary ferment from Newfoundland to British Columbia in both English and French writing. With the reviews of Bill French and Kildare Dobbs and others, critical attention significantly improved. The Canada Council and Ontario Arts Council had supportive and creative officers. Partly because of all this energy, writers living abroad, such as Mordecai Richler and Margaret Laurence, returned to Canada. Given that a mere five Canadian novels were published by Canadian houses in 1960, there had been a quantum leap: these were indeed heady times.

A critically important and remarkable man was CBC broadcaster and editor Robert Weaver. Not only did Bob feature Canadian writers and poets in the influential radio shows he hosted and created, but he also founded *The Tamarack Review*, edited many literary anthologies, and created the CBC Literary Awards. A very smart and genuinely modest man, he was tacitly accepted as the Godfather of CanLit.

To my good fortune, Bob engaged me to interview a couple of writers for "Anthology," his flagship CBC program. The "couple" turned into eleven, and then thirteen. The last two, Norman Levine and Mavis Gallant, were unfortunately too late for this book.

At the outset, I intended to talk with a representative batch of novelists who were between the ages of thirty-five and forty-five, but that category quickly collapsed. Weaver and I didn't insist upon it, we merely drifted away from it: somebody appeared in town unexpectedly or our attention was caught by a new book or, on the negative side, it became impossible to interview someone we'd planned on.

I don't recall the order in which the interviews occurred, but I do know that I thoroughly enjoyed each one. Apart from Mordecai, who was in Montreal, I interviewed the others in the old CBC building on Jarvis Street. I first met Margaret Laurence and Alice Munro in one of its ancient but very effective burrows. They came one after the other, Jack Ludwig, Marian Engel, Timothy Findley, and all the rest, and they seemed to come with a sense of personal optimism, but also an optimism that must have been fed by the palpable energy of Canadian writing. Whatever it might have been, there was a curious camaraderie, one that perhaps had something to do with our ongoing concern with a writers' union. Eight of us were present at the founding of the Writers' Union of Canada in November 1973, and at least one other joined later.

It must be said there were many strong and interesting writers back then: nobody would have found it hard to suggest others we could have included. Inescapably this leads to a collective regret. Although entitled *Eleven Canadian Novelists* the book depends almost exclusively on writers from Central Canada. That was a result of our country's size, the reality of the CBC budget, and the fact writers then did not travel as often as we do now.

I don't remember when Bob suggested turning the interviews into a book. Nor do I recall how we proceeded, apart from Anansi being the publishing choice. However, I do remember very clearly that the woman hired to transcribe the tapes turned out to be hard of hearing: as a result, she relentlessly translated "The House of Anansi" into "The House of Nazis" throughout the entire text — which is not what we had expected.

Undaunted, I finally took black-and-white photos of each writer in order to complete the book. Over the years I've occasionally returned to their faces: Mordecai Richler and Margaret Laurence are inhaling cigarettes, Symons is scowling, Tiff Findley and Matt Cohen are pensive and Marian Engel is watching something off-stage with considerable interest. These particular writers are gone now, but they and the rest who survive played most significant and entertaining roles in the remarkable development of Canadian literature.

Interviewer's Note

THIS BOOK BEGAN as a series of interviews taped for broadcast on the CBC. The first was done almost three years ago, the last in October 1972. The idea of putting the interviews together as a book came from Robert Weaver, who has provided advice and encouragement throughout.

I've been trying to determine what logic there is, or has been, in the selection of the writers. At the beginning I intended to talk with a representative batch of established novelists who were, arbitrarily, between the ages of thirty-five and forty-five; but that category quickly collapsed. Rather than deciding not to insist upon it, we merely drifted away from it: somebody appeared in town unexpectedly (someone whom I'd perhaps been wanting to meet), or our attention was caught by a new book or, on the negative side, it became impossible to interview someone I'd planned on. Clearly there are many strong and interesting writers in Canada: nobody will find it hard to suggest others who could have been included. A book like this would have to be much larger to provide more than a small representative sampling of the people who are currently working as serious prose writers here.

Hopefully, what *Eleven Canadian Novelists* can do is introduce the reader to something of what these particular novelists, as professionals, feel about their art and craft and, at the same time, reveal some of their experiences and attitudes as people and as inhabitants of this country. Although the interviews were far from being formally structured — "conversations" might be a better term for them — I tended to repeat certain key questions about writing as a pursuit, an activity, and I was continually being surprised by the variety of the answers. If one generalization about writers emerges from the interviews, it is the impossibility of making generalizations about writers. My other questions were directed more specifically to the work of each individual author.

Reproducing a taped interview verbatim produces, as we soon found, results which are sometimes incomprehensible on the page: the logic of speech is not the same as the logic of the written word. In view of this fact these interviews have been lightly edited, always after consultation with the writers themselves: though we've tried to keep the tone as conversational as possible.

— G. G. 1973

LIST OF INTERVIEWS

MARGARET ATWOOD

FICTION
The Edible Woman
Surfacing

POETRY
The Circle Game
The Animals in That Country
The Journals of Susanna Moodie
Procedures for Underground
Power Politics

NON-FICTION
Survival

MARGARET ATWOOD was born in Ottawa in 1939.

What is it about the novel that is opposed, say, to poetry or the film script that you've done, what is it about the novel you like?

I don't know. I don't think it's a positive attraction towards the novel — it's just there are things you can't do in any other form. Things you can't do in poetry unless you want to be E. J. Pratt and write very long narrative poems. You can't have characters, you can't have very involved plots — it's a whole different thing. Poems are very condensed, and a film script isn't a primary form for a writer — it's a secondary form. It's a primary form for a director.

Are novels less personal?

No, no, it has very little to do with that. It's more a question of how much room you have. You have a lot more room in a novel to move around, and you can build a much more complex, I won't say complex because poems can be very complex, but you can build a larger structure.

Perhaps you never think this way, but do you think of yourself differently as a poet than as a novelist or . . . .

Of myself?

Yes, when you're working.

I don't think of myself at all when I'm working. I think of the thing I'm doing, and obviously I think of the novel as a different kind of thing than a poem . . . it's a lot more hard work. It's physical labour in a way that poetry isn't. You can write a poem very quickly, and then it's done, and you've had everything, all possible satisfactions and engagements with the thing condensed into a short period of time. The equivalent for that with a novel is when you get the idea or when you get a few of the key scenes. But the problem then is sustaining your interest long enough to actually sit down and work it out, and that is difficult for me because I don't like work, I don't like working. I will do anything to avoid it, which means that in order to actually finish a novel I have to isolate myself from all distraction because if it's a question of a choice between the work and the distraction, I'll take the distraction every time.

What about a collection of poems, like Susanna Moodie, *where in fact you do have a character?*

Yeah. That assumes that I sat down with the conception of a character and wrote the thing through from Chapter One through the middle to the end; but they came as separate poems and I had no idea when I began that I was going to end up with a book of that size. It wasn't planned that way. I wrote twelve at first and stopped and thought, you know, this is just sort of a long short poem, twelve short poems, that's it. And then I started writing more of them, but I didn't know where it was going. I don't write books of poetry as books. I don't write them like novels.

With a novel presumably you know where you are going when you begin?

Not entirely, but I know there is enough of a skeleton so we'll end up with a book of a certain length.

How do you write novels? I mean, you write quickly, I gather.

I write them in longhand, which is very bad. I wish I could write on a typewriter — it would save a lot of trouble. I do write very quickly, but under a lot of pressure. I try to work through something like ten pages a day, which of course never happens. . . .

Do you write the first draft of a novel pretty well in one spurt?

Well, I don't know. I've only written two, actually I've written three, the first one didn't get published, and the first one took a long time because I had a job, I didn't have uninterrupted time and it took me about three months. With *The Edible Woman* I went through the first draft in about a month and a half. And the other one, *Surfacing* — when did I finish it? last summer? there's no sense of time — it got interrupted, I wanted to write it through and I did get something like a first draft. But then I had to go off and work on the film script, and not until I was into something like the third draft did I have a straight period of time.

You do a fair amount of rewriting then?

Yeah, a lot. I think the pressure is to get the thing down in some form or other so that it's out there and then can be worked with.

Do you enjoy writing?

Do I enjoy writing? I guess I would have to, wouldn't I, or I wouldn't do it.

Well, you said you hate . . . .

I don't like the physical thing and I don't like the sort of willpower involved in making sure that your sentences are sort of okay, and that you haven't repeated the same word about nine times on one page. That sort of busy work is editing. I enjoy the initial thing. I don't enjoy the tidying up very much because it's like work.

Okay. What is the writer's, the novelist's role — do you think he has a role?

I don't know. I'm sure he has lots of roles, but I very much object to other people telling me what my role is in any area of life whatsoever. I think people define their own roles, and my "role as a writer" may be entirely different from somebody else's. Somebody else may feel that his role is to write a novel about being saved for Jesus Christ and the novel should convert people, or that what he should be writing is a novel about how to get rid of the Americans. I don't see writing as having quite that kind of function. I think if you are going to save souls or save the world, you should be a preacher or a politician, so I don't see my role in any one-to-one relationship with society. I think anybody who does is deluding himself. Books don't save the world.

Does a writer have any responsibility to society?

Does society have any responsibility to the writer? Once society decides it has responsibility to me as a writer, I'll start thinking about my responsibility to it. You know, I think its general attitude towards me when I started to be a writer was that I was crazy or somehow undecorous, and if society regards me like that, I don't see that I have any particular responsibility towards it. I think that's society's attitude towards anybody when he's first starting. But if you become successful, then it's an okay thing for you to be doing, because as we all know, this society pays a lot of attention to success. But that is not a respect for writing per se as a legitimate activity, that's a respect for success, which is a different thing. It would have the same respect for you if you were a successful used-car salesman.

Do you think this is particularly Canadian, our response to writers?

No, it's American. . . . I think this is getting better, but one always sees things in terms of one's struggling youth to a certain extent, and that was certainly the case with mine. I could count on the fingers of one hand people whose attitude towards what I was doing was positive. The rest were either incredulous or negative.

Do writers know something special, say in the way physicists or astronomers or sociologists do?

Do they have a body of knowledge that is transmittable? No. They have presumably a skill with words. Apart from that they can be very different from one another. They don't necessarily share any body of knowledge, any viewpoint, any psychological pattern, although sometimes they try to. There's a certain amount of pressure on them to see themselves in terms of society's idea of what the writer should be. You know, you should go to Paris and drink a lot, or you should kill yourself, you should be Lord Byron or T. S. Eliot or something like that. . . . I think they have common problems, but that's different. That may shape you to a certain extent, having problems in common.

Do you mean problems professionally or personally?

Professionally. I mean what they do entails a certain kind of problem, such as how do you write and make enough money to live? How do you get published? Are publishers fair to writers? How to get your books distributed? How do you deal with your audience, supposing you acquire one?

Do you feel kinship with other writers?

With some, yes, with others, no. Just because a person is a writer is no guarantee that I'm going to like them or like their work or have anything in common with them at all. I don't think people get a gold star on their forehead for being a writer. I think also there seems to be no connection whatsoever between whether I like someone's work and whether I like them. I can like someone's work very much and not get on with them at all, and the reverse.

What do you like most about your own writing, your own work?

Doing it. After it's done, you mean? Looking at it as an object? I don't know. I don't tend to like it very much after a certain point, and I think that's maybe a healthy sign, that is, if you get too stuck on your own earlier work, it probably means there's nothing else new coming along that you're interested in. I think the book you always like best is the one you're about to write. And what you think about the ones you have written is what you did wrong, or how you would do it if you were going to do it over again, or whether you ever would do it over again.

Who do you write for?

Oh, oh . . . who do I write for? I think I wrote for — once upon a time I thought there was an old man with a grey beard somewhere who knew the truth, and if I was good enough, naturally he would tell me that this was it. That person doesn't exist, but that's who I write for. The great critic in the sky.

This feeling you have — it presumes some standards?

Oh yeah, but I don't always know what they are. . . . I would say that's a personification of some ideal or perfection which is unattainable, but various human beings can embody certain parts of that, and they'll come along and if it's somebody whose opinion you really respect, that's part of it, and you never know where those people are. You may never meet them, but if you don't have the faith that they are out there somewhere, then you'd stop writing.

Do you feel part of a tradition?

Yes.

Now is it particularly a Canadian tradition or . . .

Yes. I can only talk about poetry because the Canadian tradition in novels isn't old enough or there isn't enough of it to really . . . Yes, I guess it is sort of there, but you have to go searching a lot more for it than for the poetry one. I think it has partly to do with when I was born and when I started writing. I think that if I had been born in 1920, there wouldn't have been a tradition for me to feel part of, or it would have been one that was hopeless or inaccessible. I started writing in 1956 roughly, and that was in high school, and we sure weren't getting any Canadian literature in high school then. We got one E. J. Pratt poem in grade thirteen, that was the extent of it. And even that was not presented as Canadian, it was just sort of there, not explained, along with *Hamlet*. And I didn't know that people slightly older than myself were around and writing until I got to university, and until I got to the second or third year. So my early poetry is all fairly strange. It all reads like Wordsworth and Lord Byron. But when I did discover Canadian writing, it was a tremendously exciting thing because it meant that people in the country were writing, and not only that, they were publishing books. And if they could be publishing books, then so could I. So I then read a lot of stuff, and I was lucky enough to know somebody who had a fairly extensive library of Canadian poetry, which I read from beginning to end, so that by the time I was about twenty-one I had certainly found my tradition. I was talking with P. K. Page a couple of years ago, and she said that when she was writing there wasn't any Canadian tradition, they were all turned on to people like W. H. Auden, you know, your models, the people that you were learning to write from, were all in other countries, and that isn't true of me. I learned to write from people in this country.

And that carried over when you came to the novel?

I don't know, it wasn't there in the novel. Novels have only been . . . no . . . people have only started to write novels in the same way, I mean with the same profusion and the same confidence, if you like, in this country during the last seven years, and they weren't doing it when I was learning to write, and I always wrote both poetry and prose. It's just that the prose took a while longer to get published, and that says something too, because people weren't publishing novels either at that time. The novel thing is a much more recent development.

Have you any idea why it's happened in the last ten years or seven years?

There's always a connection between what people write and what they read; and what they read depends partly on the availability of publishing facilities. That is, if what they are reading is all imported novels about New York, or about London, England, nobody in this country is going to feel that they can write a "real" book unless they go to those places, and even then they can't really write a real one because they aren't from those places. So when you don't have a publishing industry in your own country that is publishing stuff about the country, you are automatically defeated because you have no audience, you have no models. You are a kind of amputee, and you have to either go away and write as an exile or you can go away and write as a fraud, but you can't stay there and write real books about a real place, because it somehow . . . there's no input for it, and there's no outlet for it.

There tended to be for the short story, didn't there, during the twenties and the thirties?

Yes, there were magazines and the CBC and a lot of people wrote short stories as a result, but novels were another thing. Very seldom was one published, and very seldom did it acquire an audience. Historical romance is another story, and things like *Jalna* and *Anne of Green Gables*. Those were different, you could write those if you wanted, but if you had other ambitions, you were doomed to paralysis.

Perhaps that's why there were so many one-book people writing.

Yes. Sure they wrote their book, they put everything into it. They got no feedback, and they gave up, and I would too. So what I'm saying is that I think the increase in the number of good novels has something to do with the growth of the Canadian publishing industry and places like Oberon and Anansi, if you like, and New Press.

All right, we were talking about advantages and disadvantages of being a writer in Canada. Are there any advantages?

Oh, tremendous. All that I've been saying about this is changing very rapidly, obviously. It's almost reached the stage where there are more publishing companies than there are good writers. Also,

I found this when I lived in the States, because there is no long-standing tradition, because there are no huge giants hanging over you, you're very free. You don't feel you're competing with Herman Melville or William Shakespeare, you know, the thing is wide open, you can do anything, although I think the desirable thing to do is to find what in the tradition is usable and use it.

Do you feel we finally have to measure ourselves against "giants," people like that?

Okay. There are two things. One is how good the book is, and that's got nothing to do with your country or anything else. The other thing is what is in it? You can take any body of material — let's just take the western as an example — and you can use the tradition and you can make a good one or you can make a bad one, using essentially the same kind of thing, so you learn to write really from two directions; one is the formal direction and the other is the sort of social mythology direction. And I think that the formal thing you can learn from anyone who happens to plug into your own formal direction, you know, he could be from Mars, it wouldn't matter, if he was doing something you found formally interesting; but if you're trying to use somebody else's social mythology, you're doomed. You know, if you try to write like an American, if you try to write like an Englishman, and you aren't one, you will just produce a piece of plastic. No matter how formally skilful you are.

Good.

We've been so cut off from our social mythology that we hardly know what it is; that's one thing that has to be discovered. The other thing you have to do, and you don't learn it from "Canada" necessarily, is how to be a good writer, how to do the thing you're doing in the best way possible.

Because we don't have within our own tradition "giants," for want of a better word, is there a danger that it's too easy for us to make an impact or too easy for us to . . . .

You can be as good as everyone else fairly easily, but to be really better, that is harder.

And I presume this is one of the reasons that there are so few sort of international Canadian writers at this point?

No. That has to do partly with the book publishing industry. I don't know whether one's being known in other countries has anything to do with the goodness of one's writing. It may certainly have to do with the taste of the people in that country and what they are willing to believe. You can write a mythology about your country which is absolutely fraudulent, like we could write about Mounties and huskies and living in igloos and things, and that would be pretty fake right now for Canada, but people in Germany would probably think it was super-duper because that is their image of what goes on over here. You're asking how does one become a classic? Well, you don't know for two hundred years anyway, do you? But how one gets published in other countries, that's a whole different story.

You see it primarily then as a publishing problem?

Well, it is certainly partly a publishing problem, and one of the problems with it is that there are no agents in Canada. If you are a Canadian and want an agent — and having an agent is half of getting published "internationally" — then you have to go outside the country to get one. I think that if the government really wanted to do something, it could set up a literary agent in this country. But they'd have to get someone almost superhuman, because it would have to be someone who would know the scene in New York and know the scene in London and live in Toronto. I think that may be changing too. People are becoming more aware of what's happening here, but of course you must remember that for a long time Canada was just regarded as the sticks, not only by people outside the country, but by people in it.

A slightly different kind of question. Does writing demand a particular kind of selfishness?

Everything demands a particular kind of selfishness. If you're asking is the kind that writing demands different from everybody else's kind, I don't know. There again, that assumes that writers have personalities in which you can identify an X factor common to all. And I'm not too sure that is true. Partly my suspicion of questions like that is the wish to avoid romantic stereotypes of the writer. You know, all writers are crazy, or they're all geniuses or some nonsense like that; and to say that all writers have a peculiar kind of selfishness seems to me to fit in a bit with that. But you sort of have to go into a room and shut the door and say: Go away, everyone, because I'm going to write, and you get very annoyed at people who interrupt you, but I don't know whether that's selfish. It seems to be just a kind of condition. You know, if you were a watchmaker and somebody interrupted you, you would probably be just as aggravated if you dropped your dial or whatever.

In what way is writing important to you?

Oh, every way. Do I have a choice of ways? In what way is it important to you? (*laughter*)

All right. All right. How did you start writing?

How did I start? I started writing when I was five. . . . You should read my novel about the ant.

You began with novels at five?

Novels and books of poems, in which I made the book first and
filled in the poems later. I already was into publishing. (*laughter*)
Then I had a sterile period between the age of nine and the age of
sixteen, and that's sort of a blank in my life as far as writing goes.

What sustained you as a writer?

My next book. (*laughter*) I think it's sort of a . . . what keeps me
going as a writer? That's a very mysterious area. I don't really
want to find out. There are a lot of things that I just would rather
not know about writing, because I think that if you get too curious about it, and start dissecting the way you work and why you
do it, you'd probably stop. Maybe not. Anyway, that's one of my
superstitions.

Can you make a living from your writing?

Yes.

From your writing itself or spinoffs from it?

Not just from poetry, although if I lived very frugally, and ate
nothing but onions and wieners . . . But if you throw in novels and
short stories, then I could.

You must be one of the few writers who can do that.

I'm talking only in terms of the last couple of years and the next
few years ahead. That depends on your writing a book every year,
which I can't do. So it's not that clear a thing, but I think if every
other source of income was taken away from me, I could probably
manage to exist.

Have you encountered any particular problems as a woman writer?

In getting published?

In sort of growing up and thinking of yourself as a writer, getting published, criticism, the response of other writers, just the whole. . . .

Sure. I don't think they are typical. I think that at the time I started writing, since writing was such a freaky thing in itself, and since very few men were doing it either, it wasn't that I was a woman who was writing that people found peculiar, it was that anybody at all was writing. For so long writing was regarded as a freak thing to be doing, and in a frontier society what is important is work and building houses and bridges and things like that. And writers are viewed as irrelevant or redundant. Men writers overreact to that, and define writing as a really male thing to be doing. And if you're a woman doing it, that really threatens their position, considering they've gone to all this trouble to tell anybody who sort of scorns their activity that what they're doing is really very hairy-chested. The reviewing thing is something else; the fact is that there is no critical tradition that the reviewer or critic can draw on for treating the work of women seriously. I think it's better in this country than in the States, and looking back through *Letters in Canada*, you don't find much of that garbage about feminine sensibilities, but in your run-of-the-mill review it often comes up, though not so much in connection with my own work because they can't really do that easily. What you get instead is the other side of the coin. If people can't say you have a watercolour feminine sensibility, they'll say something like "she thinks like a man." I mean, they seem to find it very hard, if they want to say something that's good, to say that it's good and also admit that the writer is female. They seem to feel that they have to make you an honorary male if they're going to say you're good. So there's that.

What else? Certainly not with publishers. Publishers are in business to make money, and if your books do well, they don't care whether you are male, female, or an elephant. I've seldom had any of that kind of thing from any of my publishers.

What about the response of other women; do they try to categorize you or. . . .

Well, of course now that Women's Lib has come along, it's very curious. I think that back in the days when what you were supposed to do was pay attention to the diapers and the washing of dishes, I was a threat to other women's life positions. I think now I tend to get made into a kind of hero, which is just as unreal. It makes me just as uncomfortable to be — well, it's the same thing, it's turning me from what I am as a writer into something I'm not.

Another general question, hopefully the last one: what do you think are your major preoccupations as a novelist?

I don't know. We're talking as though I've written ten novels. I've only written two, and one that didn't get published.

That's three, and you're going to write another one.

They're all so different from each other that I can't really talk about it. Also I think it's the sort of thing that critics do, and although I'm willing to talk about somebody else's preoccupations and do critical studies of them, I'm not at all willing to do that on myself. I think that other people should do that if they're so disposed, but I don't want to make myself the subject of my own criticism.

Okay. Let's talk about your two novels. There seem to be two kinds of problems and each novel emphasizes one of them. The first one is the alternatives that are open to people, and specifically women, and that's in The Edible Woman; *and the second is the destructiveness of society, or in some cases the mere banality of it or the irrelevance of it, but in Surfacing, your second book, it's the evil of it — and in both novels there's the question of how to survive, given these two problems. Does that seem, generally, a relevant assumption?*

I guess so. I mean, the last thing you said, about how to survive, is certainly true.

Marian in The Edible Woman *is confronted with a frequently silly, irrelevant kind of social situation, like her fiancé is not up to her in any way, her job isn't up to her in any way, and there don't seem to be any alternatives in the lives around her, and what she's got to figure out is how to escape from this trap she finds herself in, survival in that way. The protagonist in the second book has a much more fundamental need to survive.*

Here we're getting into the whole thing of critical analysis of one's work. You know I can say certain formal things: *The Edible Woman* is an anti-comedy, and *Surfacing* is a ghost story. (*laughter*) That sort of determines not only what happens in the book but the style.

Let's pause here. What do you mean by an anti-comedy? The Edible Woman *is an anti-comedy?*

I think in your standard eighteenth-century comedy you have a young couple who is faced with difficulty in the form of somebody who embodies the restrictive forces of society and they trick or overcome this difficulty and end up getting married. The same thing happens in *The Edible Woman* except the wrong person gets married. And the person who embodies the restrictive forces of society is in fact the person Marian gets engaged to. In a standard comedy, he would be the defiant hero. As it is, he and the restrictive society are blended into one, and the comedy solution would be a tragic solution for Marian.

Okay, let me come back to the society thing. In The Edible Woman, *it seems to me that society is really unreal or irrelevant. It's the object of Marian's wit and her considerable kind of objective humour, which keeps coming through. But in* Surfacing, *it has become evil, society has become an evil force.*

Yeah.

The protagonist of Surfacing, *who in a sense has gone through all of Marian's experiences, but has lived them out, the marriage. . . .*

Oh no. The marriage isn't real. She made it up.

But she's lived through it in her head, I mean she's lived through the implications of it in a way that Marian hasn't. And there's another thing which I found in Surfacing *which intrigues me, and that's guilt. That protagonist of* Surfacing *says at one point, when she's talking about the dead heron: "The trouble some people have being German I have being human"; and she also, a bit later, talks about the cruelty of children, the cruelty that she partakes of. . . .*

It all comes back to original sin, doesn't it? I think if you — this is too complicated to talk about. (*laughter*)

Yeah, well let me put it. . . .

It depends on whether or not you define yourself as intrinsically innocent, and if you define yourself as intrinsically innocent, then you have a lot of problems, because in fact you aren't. And the thing with her is she wishes not to be human. She wishes to be not human, because being human inevitably involves being guilty, and if you define yourself as innocent, you can't accept that.

Why does she define herself as innocent, or how does she define herself as innocent? Is it need because of. . . .

I think ever since we all left the Roman Catholic Church we've defined ourselves as innocent in some way or another. But what I'm really into in that book is the great Canadian victim complex. If you define yourself as innocent, then nothing is ever your fault — it is always somebody else doing it to you, and until you stop defining yourself as a victim, that will always be true. It will always be somebody else's fault, and you will always be the object of that rather than somebody who has any choice or takes responsibility for their life. And that is not only the Canadian stance towards the world, but the usual female one. Look what a mess I am and it's all their fault. And Canadians do that too. Look at poor innocent us, we are morally better than they. We do not burn people in Vietnam, and those bastards are coming in and taking away our country. Well, the real truth of the matter is that Canadians are selling it.

You seem to imply in the book that there are two kinds of people. There are the Americans, not based on nationality, but based upon a kind of approach — like hunters, because the people which they mistake for Americans turn out to be Canadians, and they're the ones that killed the heron. Is there a distinction? Are there the two types?

Are you asking me or are you asking the book?

I'm asking you about the book.

I think in both of the books you have a choice of thinking the central character is crazy or thinking she is right. (*laughter*) Or possibly thinking she is crazy and right. To a large extent the characters are creating the world which they inhabit, and I think we all do that to a certain extent, or we certainly do a lot of rearranging. There is an objective world out there, I'm far from being a solipsist. There are a lot of things out there, but towards any object in the world you can take a positive or a negative attitude, or, let us say, you can turn it into a positive or a negative symbol, and that goes for everything. You can see a tree as the embodiment of natural beauty or you can see it as something menacing that's going to get you, and that depends partly on your realistic position towards it; what you were doing with the tree, admiring it or cutting it down; but it's also a matter of your symbolic orientation towards everything. Now I'm not denying the reality, the existence of evil, some things are very hard to see in a positive light. Evil obviously exists in the world, right? But you have a choice of how you can see yourself in relation to that. And if you define yourself always as a harmless victim, there's nothing you can ever do about it. You can simply suffer.

And the protagonist of Surfacing, *does she do more than identify herself as a victim?*

At the end she does. She refuses to identify herself as a victim, that's step one. (*laughter*) Only if you stop identifying yourself as a victim, you know, fated by powers that be, can you act.

Right. Then she says at one point, too: "If I had turned out like the others with power, I would have been evil."

Yes, but you have to think of where in the book she says that.

Yes, it was at the beginning, yes.

Yes. That's a refusal too. I mean, the other thing you do, if you are defining yourself as innocent, you refuse to accept power. You refuse to admit that you have it, then you refuse to exercise it, because the exercise of power is defined as evil, and that's like people who refuse to get involved in politics because it's dirty.

So at the end when she says that she must be a survivor — is that her phrase? something to the effect that she mustn't be a victim? — so is she accepting then the responsibility of some power?

Of action.

Of action, which is a kind of power.

Sure. Every time you act, you're exercising power in some form, and you cannot predict the consequences of your actions entirely. You may hurt someone, but the alternative to that is closing yourself up in a burrow somewhere and not doing anything ever at all.

Which is what at one point she tries to do. Now, is Marian's revolt, let's call it that, against the situation she has found herself acquiescing to — is that a comparable kind of thing? Is she asserting herself in the baking of the cake and offering it to Peter?

I don't know, nobody's ever been able to figure that out. *(laughter)* When writing the film script, we had long conversations on just exactly what that means. Obviously she's acting, she's doing an action. Up until that point she has been evading, avoiding, running away, retreating, withdrawing.

Hiding under the bed.

Yes, to begin with; secondly in refusing to eat; and she commits an action, a preposterous one in a way, as all pieces of symbolism in a realistic context are, but what she is obviously making is a substitute for herself.

Again in Surfacing, *the protagonist says: "but I was not prepared for the average, its needless cruelties and lies. My brother saw the danger early, to immerse oneself, join in the war or be destroyed. There ought to be other choices." Are there any other choices?*

We'll put it this way. You're standing on the edge of the lake, right, and you can do three things: you can stay standing on the edge of the lake, you can jump in and if you don't know how to swim you'll drown, or you can learn to swim, supposing you want to have anything to do with the lake at all. The other thing would be to just walk away, but we will suppose that this is the entire universe.

One of the things that happens to both of them, but more clearly to the woman in the second book, in the popular phrase, is alienation or isolation, the deadening of sensibilities. I think it's towards the end of Surfacing, *she says: "Language divides us into fragments; I wanted to be whole." Is this her attempt to be inhuman or to be non-human or to be like an animal or a plant?*

The ideal thing, let's think in terms of real life, the ideal thing would be a whole human being. Now if your goal is to be whole, and you don't see the possibility of doing that and also being human, then you can try being something else. . . . There are great advantages in being a vegetable, you know, except you lose certain other things, such as the ability to talk. Life is very much simplified. (*laughter*) If you think you're a watermelon, you don't have to do anything, you can just sit around. The ideal, though, would be to integrate yourself as a human being, supposedly. And if you try that and fail, then you can try being something else for a while, which he does.

By the end of both books, the women seem to have come a long way towards being human beings.

Oh I don't know . . . (*laughter*) . . . does anyone ever achieve it? If you define human beings as necessarily flawed, then anybody can be one. But if you define them as something which is potentially better, then it's always something that is just out of reach.

In Surfacing *there are the surveyors, there are the hunters, there. . . .*

You're getting far too serious about all this, what is all of this analysis for?

The people out there. (laughter) What I'm trying to get at is the implication that there are two kinds of societies in Surfacing *— that there are the hunters, the people who kill the herons.*

The people who kill.

The people who kill. One of the assumed definitions is that the Americans, not a nationality, but a state of mind, are the killers. And there are other people who aren't.

Okay, let's think of it this way. If the only two kinds of people are killers and victims, then although it may be morally preferable to be a victim, it is obviously preferable from the point of view of survival to be a killer. *(laughter)* However, either alternative seems pretty hopeless; you know, you can define yourself as innocent and get killed, or you can define yourself as a killer and kill others. I think there has to be a third thing again; the ideal would be somebody who would neither be a killer or a victim, who could achieve some kind of harmony with the world, which is a productive or creative harmony, rather than a destructive relationship towards the world. Now in neither book is that actualized, but in both it's seen as a possibility finally, whereas initially it is not.

Okay, just one more question, regarding the unacceptable sort of roles, the unacceptable things open to your characters in both books. There aren't many things in society which give anybody enough, and in many cases they're filling in time. They're just doing things. It's a kind of busy-work living, and the men tend to be either pompous, like Peter, a kind of meticulous pomposity, or they're like Joe in the second book, who is an observer. Then if you scratch them, beneath the surface you find a sense of failure and a sense of being threatened.

Yes. I don't think that's very unrealistic. (*laughter*) Let's say that I think of society in two ways: one is simply the kind of thing that Western Industrialism has done to people, and the other is the Canadian thing, where men particularly have been amputated. Women haven't been amputated as much relatively, because absolutely they've been amputated a lot more, but they didn't have as far down to go and Western Industrialism hasn't changed their lives that much. They still have some kind of connection with their own bodies, and the celebrated woman's role, although many people may find it, you know, aggravating, still is something to do. If you can't think of what you are supposed to do, you can always have a baby, and that will keep you busy enough. But some guy who is doing nothing but punching little holes in cards all day, he has no connection with himself at all, and guys who sit around on their asses in an office all day have no contact with their own bodies, and they are really deprived, they're functions, functions of a machine.

And they tend to feel themselves as failures, at least the characters in your books, well, particularly Joe. And David.

In a way. They tend to blame that on other people.

And they feel put down by women.

Yeah, sure. It's all true. I mean, it doesn't seem to me to be any great insight on my part. (*laughter*) It just seems to be a state that is fairly widely acknowledged. And all the things that you've been talking about are really just sort of the jam on the sandwich, because for me, the interesting thing in that book is the ghost in it, and that's what I like. And the other stuff is there, it's quite true, but it is a condition; it isn't, to me, what the book is about.

Your protagonist has returned looking for her father, and at one point she says that one of the things about her father was his ability, his quite remarkable ability, to give the illusion of peace. She grew up during the war, not knowing about the war, and her mother and father had been able to give this illusion of — I think the word she used is peace. And her return, and the whole ghost thing, seems tied in to that. Peace and being in touch with the land.

That's all true, but it's much easier for me to talk about the formal problems involved in writing a ghost story, which I've always been fascinated by. You want to talk about ghost stories? *(laughter)*

She sees her own ghost, doesn't she?

There are various kinds of ghosts you can see. You could have just a simple, straightforward ghost story in which somebody sees a ghost which has no relation to them whatsoever. You could have a sort of primitive myth in which dead people are as alive as living people and they're just accepted, nobody is too surprised by it because it happens all the time. Or you can have the Henry James kind, in which the ghost that one sees is in fact a fragment of one's own self which has split off, and that to me is the most interesting kind and that is obviously the tradition I'm working in. But I wanted to write a ghost story for the same reason that I'd like to make a good horror film. I think that it's an interesting area which is too often done just as pulp.

I'd like to relate the ghost, the fragment of self that is split off, to the society that is overwhelming her and isolating her, the victim thing. Because in some sense the father, the ghosts that she perceived, were not victims.

That's true. And they aren't evil ghosts.

And having perceived them, she is somehow stronger.

I haven't worked this out, again it's like the cake in *Edible Woman*, you know, I just can't be that analytical about my own work. I could give you all kinds of theories as to what I think they're doing in there, but my guess is really as good as anybody else's. I know by the logic of the book what they are doing, but I don't have a whole bunch of theories about it. They exist. You can make of it what you will.

She's accused at one point of disliking men, this is in Surfacing, *and for an instant she wonders, but then she says: "Then I realized it wasn't men I hated, it was the Americans, the human beings, men and women both. They'd had their chance, but they turned against their gods."*

Everybody has gods or a god, and it's what you pay attention to or what you worship. And they can be imported ones or they can be intrinsic ones, indigenous ones, and what we tend to have done in this country is to use imported gods like imported everything else. (*laughter*) And if you import a god from somewhere else, it's fake, it's like importing your culture from somewhere else. The only sort of good, authentic kind of a thing to have is something that comes out of the place where you are, or shall we put it another way and say the reality of your life. We were talking about books earlier. If you think that what you have to be doing is writing about New York City, and you don't live there, or if you go there and try to pretend that you've always lived there, you can't do anything authentic; and I think that Christianity in this country is imported religion. The assumption of the book, if there is one, is that there are gods that do exist here, but nobody knows about them. Anyway, this gets us into metaphysical realms. The other thing that the imported gods will always tell you to do is to destroy what is there, to destroy what is in the place and to make a replica of the god's place, so that what you do is you cut down all the trees and you build a Gothic church, or imitation thereof. And I think that the authentic religion that was here has been destroyed; you have to discover it in some other way. How that fits in with the book I don't know, but I'm sure it has something to do with it.

We were talking about the irrelevance of society to the people living in it. In some sense, we're pushing it, but in some sense they're godless. . . .

They have gods. The gods are — I think a kind of futile adjustment is probably the god. It used to be success. It used to be the individualist kind of thing where you went out and stomped on everyone and made a million dollars, but that isn't even the god anymore. I think the god is probably fitting into the machine.

Somebody else's machine.

Yeah, somebody else's machine. Again I think people see two alternatives: you can be part of the machine or you can be something that gets run over by it. And I think there has to be a third thing.

AUSTIN CLARKE

FICTION
The Survivors of the Crossing
Amongst Thistles and Thorns
The Meeting Point
When He Was Free and Young and He Used to Wear Silks

AUSTIN CLARKE was born in Barbados in 1934.

I'll start with a couple of general questions. How did you start writing?

I should say, Graeme, that I started writing before I knew I was going to be a writer. I remember as a little boy in Barbados writing a rhyming poem, you know, AB AB, I think is the scheme you would use for that, on a chap, on a younger fellow. I was in love with his sister and his name was James, and he had bandy legs, so this was called "The Ballad of Bandy Legged James," and the influence was obvious, you know the famous thing, "Reading Gaol" is one and there's another famous ballad, I can't remember the name, but this went on and went on and went on, I couldn't stop it, you know, and that's the first thing I remember. Now I was always entranced by books, just looking at books, and I remember, when I was much younger than the instance I gave you, sitting down and wondering how a man could write a book from the beginning to the end, and when he got to the end remember what he had written at the beginning, because naturally one should want to know this, so I got myself some paper and stuck them together and I wrote a book by Austin Clarke. I wasn't Austin Clarke in those days, I was A. A. C. Clarke, you know, my initials in the English system, and I didn't actually write anything in the pages,

I just had a series of hills and valleys, you understand what I mean, and that is all. But your question is much more serious than that, you mean how did I begin to write, that I'm known now. . . .

What happened next, after that, if that's the beginning?

What happened next? Well, I came up here to go to the university and when I was at the university I wrote some poems. Actually no, the poems had been written in Barbados, because I was writing for the school magazine as most schoolboys do, and the poems were shown to an editor here, an English chap at Trinity College, and he liked them and gave me the poetry prize. I was a poet in those days, poetry prize. I was telling my wife recently that it was five dollars; she insists that it was ten dollars, and we got engaged on that ten dollars and bought a bottle of gin and had a hell of a party with that ten dollars and then I never thought very much about writing, until I dropped out of the university and was living in what is now the horrible Yorkville Village. In those days it was a slum, Hazelton, and I thought that I would be the successor of this Englishman who wrote *The Lady's Not for Burning*. Who is that? Christopher? It's gone. Anyhow, I wanted to write like Eliot, and I wanted to write like this man, but then, you know, I was — money problems, you know.

Do you write any poetry now?

No, I don't, I don't at all.

What is it about the novel and the short story that attracts you?

Well, I was about to say that I went into the novel after having failed in poetry and verse and plays. I was very influenced by Eliot, I studied Eliot at college in Barbados, and I went into this having failed in the other field. For a while I didn't know whether it was the best thing to do. There was no way of telling, and of course in our business one tells whether one has made a right decision if the product is sold, if an editor accepts it, then you feel you are successful, which may not be the case, you see what I mean. I know in my own case I will probably stick to prose, you know, the novel and the short story, I never will write any verse or poetry.

What about the difference between the story and the novel for you? Is it a different impetus at the beginning? When does a story turn into a long story or a novel?

I have never been able really to explain these things even to myself. And when people ask me, it causes me to think and perhaps to rationalize, you know. But let me see if I can do some of that now. I would say the short story to me is like an interruption in a period of my daydreaming, because I spend most of my time daydreaming, that is to say that I am gathering these stories as I live, I mean even now, you know, talking to you, I can see behind you, I can see two people there behind you, in the studio, and this is registered. At the moment of conception, to use that arrogant term, in other words when I feel so uncomfortable about daydreaming that I have to stop and write down what I have been daydreaming about, that is when I write the story. Now the novel is naturally more difficult. I'm not saying the novel is more difficult to write than a short story, I think the short story is much more difficult to write than the novel, because in the novel one can do a certain amount of jiving — if one has made a mistake, one can correct it, but not in the short story, certainly not the best short stories. I would think about the novel for quite a long time, about the structure of that novel. In the short story, structure comes out with the story, you see what I mean. Now you know a story of mine that was read very well by Bud Knapp: *When He Was Free and Young and He Used to Wear Silks*. The title suggests something strange, perhaps nonsensical, is going to be said in this story, so it was the kind of story where I found myself trying to justify the title. So that story flowed in and out, but there is still some structure there, of course; whereas in a novel like *The Meeting Point*, for instance, I suppose we can get to *The Meeting Point* sometime. In *The Meeting Point*, I was very influenced by Coltrane, John Coltrane.

You talk about that at one point. Sam talks about one of the records at one point in great detail. . . .

Sam Berman. I was also very influenced by Beethoven's Sixth, used to hear it every day on the CBC, and I played Beethoven's Sixth I would say for five months and practically learned it by heart, because you see in *The Meeting Place*, I tried to capture, I tried to show that — I think this symphony of Beethoven's has three movements, it might have four, but I think it has three, anyhow the book is divided into three. Let us say it has three, and I felt that this piece of music I was listening to of Coltrane's was a very complicated centre (*laughter*) meshed into this, so when the classical music changes, you got a little insertion of the jazz, you see what I mean. I don't know if it worked, I'll tell you this now, I don't know if it worked, but this was a case where I consciously tried to structure the book along the lines of two pieces of music I particularly liked, and one could say it failed or not, but it was an interesting thing to do.

Do you find music the natural sort of analogy for prose?

Yes, I do, yes, I do.

Prose the analogy for music perhaps.

Yes, yes. You know, I'm beginning to think that I'm becoming less intellectual in the sense of using this, and more gutsy, you know. Like, I'm working on a story now and I find if I don't hear music in the words, I can't end the sentence, in other words, like Coltrane or any other kind of musician, you know when he has come to a logical conclusion of a phrase, you know in his music. I would be so bold as to say that I am more fortunate than you are in the sense of dialect, that I have the Jamaican, the Trinidadian, the Barbadian. . . .

Plus the hip talk.

Plus the hip talk, yes. You of course are exposed to all these, but I'm saying that I get more groove out of these, more easily, and of course you have your own dialects like Rosedale and things like this, but in itself that way of speaking is very musical. That way of speaking is actually like Shakespeare, you see. Now I don't know if anybody has ever said this before, but that West Indian way of speaking, particularly Jamaican, and Barbadian, the way they handle words, is very much like Shakespeare and not too far from the Bible. When you talk about music now and prose, you have to go and listen to Martin Luther King, the late James Baldwin, Flip Wilson in some of those skits he does about the church, and you see how the Bible and what you might call black American speech, it's so close to Martin Luther King, you know, that famous thing, "I have a dream," and that's the only worth of the speech, the quality, you know, not the content.

There is this tremendous musical quality in your use of dialect. I find a great stylistic sense even when it isn't dialect. What about style and content or form and content for you in your writing?

I will tell you something now. Look, I have never really been able to analyze literature that way, you know. I did Literature in college in Barbados and I did Political Science and Economics here, so I was spared the university critic exam on English, right? Probably for the worse or for the better, but the thing is I have never yet been able to look at my work in this way. I don't know what form is. If you had me up against a corner now, I could get out easily by saying: Well you know, Graeme, being a black man and having come from Africa, the African sense of culture and art is quite different from the Western, so we wouldn't consider form separately from content. For instance, when the cat in Africa makes a statue of a prince from a piece of wood as tall as this microphone, the head takes up three-quarters of the material, and the legs and the thorax, the rest of the body, take up the other third, and I don't think he would be able to tell you well why he has the head, you know, three times bigger — was this man really so monstrous? In other words would you say now that this man was an intellectual, that he used his head more than he used the rest of his body?

No.

The man would not. It's just that this is the way it came out, and I think this is probably the purest animal — I may be wrong, this could be really authoritarian, but I'd say this certainly is the purest expression of art when one just does it and one. . . .

What about craft then, the role of craft?

Craft, as you know, it. . . .

As a writer, you learned your craft. . . .

I learned my craft from writing compositions under an Englishman, he'd say: Clarke, write a composition on a clock, you have half an hour, and then tomorrow, write a composition on a pin, and then write composition on a picnic, you know. . . .

Yes. This kind of thing you found very useful as a writer?

Very useful, plus six books of Ridout, I think that's the way you pronounce it, I suppose in this country you might say Ridou. . . . We were trained in English — split infinitives, you know what I mean, we were trained. . . .

Could you teach grammar?

Oh yes, oh yes. I could teach, oh yes, plus Latin, I studied Latin and then the training continued when I worked as a reporter in the north for the great Lord Thomson, the *Timmins Daily Press* and the *Northern Daily News*, and then I used to make a hustle here in Toronto for the *Globe and Mail* and I wrote for the three papers, freelancing, and you see craft is sweat. Craft is when I sit down and I'm still daydreaming in front of the typewriter and I just write what comes into my head, you see, and I correct it; and craft too is letters, I write a huge amount of letters. I write letters every day to people.

Do you have any novels that haven't been published?

Oh yes. I have.

Or not going to be published in the immediate future? I know that you have a sequel to Meeting Point.

Yes, part two to *Meeting Point*. . . . *A Second in Trinity* is going to come out sometime soon.

Do you have other ones that you have put away?

Yes, which I wouldn't show to anyone.

You think they're unredeemable, those books?

Oh, irrevocably. (*laughter*) I wouldn't show those. I would probably come on strong later on, say this is my first work, and send it to some man who wants to buy that kind of junk, but I wouldn't show it to anybody.

How many are there?

Two.

Did you write them before Crossing?

Yes, I wrote those books in the first or second year of marriage, when I was still Christopher Fry, that's the man I was going to be better than, Christopher Fry. When I was trying to write like Christopher Fry with a little colouring of T. S. Eliot, and taking into consideration Dylan, you know, Dylan Thomas — I wanted to be like the three of these people, so I wrote these two books then and apart of course from inexperience, the books were doomed to failure because I worked from an outline. I had my outline done very well and then I would write a chapter or a paragraph and it had to fit the outline, you see what I mean. So that it was just a waste of time.

What's the writer's role in a society?

In society? That, Graeme, is being more arrogant, I think, than is necessary. I don't think that the writer or the artist really can have this kind of role as a citizen or as an influential citizen, a role that is going to influence society more than the role of the mason or the Italian who makes the subway, you see what I mean. I don't like to say "the arts" anyhow, I mean "the arts" sounds so funny, what the hell are the arts? I feel badly that people don't regard me as a serious writer, you know, sometimes. But then I say to myself: well, why should they? I mean, why should they? I'm making some money writing books. All I hope about my influence is that I would bring a little bit of happiness, you know, to people who read these, so I'm more concerned now with introducing in my work a certain amount of mirth, to use that old English word, mirth and girth, you know. (*laughter*) But the role of the artist, I feel, you see, in societies that are culturally developing, somebody up there all of a sudden thinks that the artist ought to have some role, that the artist ought to be a man who is going to look at the society and try to fashion the society in some way. I don't think that the artist should have any greater role than honesty, you know, truth to his work. Sincerity. I feel that if you say the role of the artist, the role of Austin Clarke the writer, is to show society where society is wrong, you know what I mean — I think that detracts from my being an artist. I would think so.

But you don't believe that you have any particular role other than to do what you're doing.

No, no. But now we come into a very serious thing now. The black man in this kind of society, where the black man who makes it or looks as if he makes it is singled out as a representative of the race, you see, there I would say that I have a definite role. I have a role that reassures blacks that they can make it too, because you see it is only important for blacks in that kind of situation to have an idol or image or mortal like me, because the situation tends to be a bit disillusioning, you see what I mean. But in a situation like in Barbados, or in Africa — well, I'd better stick to Barbados, because I know that better — in Barbados and the West Indies the artist is even more disregarded than he is here in this country, and I would go so far as to say that in Barbados I am more disregarded as an artist than I am here, because you see certain psychological things are working for me here, so that's why I can't come on so strong and talk about the role of the artist. But I know my role as a black man. It is very single.

I would think there are problems in being a black writer. If you don't have any role in society as a writer, you must as a black man now feel tempted or feel the responsibility to have some role, to do something about the situation of the black man.

Well, I don't want you to get too confused on this role thing, because I see where that could go, you know. I'm not trying to shun the problem. Let me begin by quoting one of our exceptionally good writers, Naipaul, V. S. Naipaul, who has written books titled *Miguel Street, The Middle Passage*, well, lots of good books, *The House for Mr. Biswas, The Night's Companion, Mr. Stone and the Night's Companion* . . . V. S. Naipaul in this book *Middle Passage* said: Race certainly cannot be the basis for any serious literature. Three years ago I would have said: Naipaul, you're talking a lot of damn nonsense, you know. Having lived in the States now, having taught the literature written by black Americans, I see that in that literature, apart from the very few exceptions, Baldwin in one book, and I don't mean *Another Country*, I mean his first book, an excellent book, *Go Tell It on the Mountain*, Richard Wright in some of his books, and Ellison of course, the master of them all, *An Invisible Man*, apart from those examples, perhaps Meville Kelly, some alias stuff of LeRoi Jones, who is now known as Imamou Imali Brethout, Gwendoline Brooks, you get a body of literature which I call vindictively ritualistic, in which, to use another term from my other life, in which the cycle in existentialism you see is working so hard that you must agree with Naipaul that certainly . . . Well, look, I don't have to come on so strong — I'm saying this: black people in a society, if they're segregated, certainly cannot have a total vision of the society. It's as simple as that. If the vision they're going to exploit or if the vision they use in their artistic endeavour is restricted, and if the artistic disposition and the artistic facilities and what you call the craft is not developed, then certainly one is going to get a situation where the writing is going to be as jaundiced as the view that is outside this artistic thing we're talking about. You see what I mean. But if you look at America now, where you see that all of the recent works with very few exceptions are talking now about this race problem, in a way that is not the important way to talk about race, though there is nothing wrong with talking about race, you know, Senghor and Aimé Césaire, those people, brilliant poets, talk about it, but what I'm saying now is where you get these people talking about race as a reaction, you see what I mean, it is all right to talk about black people, if you can describe black people as beautiful people, positive people, you know, but if you talk about black people as a reaction . . . Let me give you a better example, that one's probably too jumbled. I was watching television yesterday, just by accident, American television, and we talk about images now, and one could consider what I saw as the same thing as somebody writing it down. Now there was this cat who comes on — I'm not only talking about images, I'm talking about the idolization of certain images which are really not characters, but which are myths or roles. This cat came on, you know, with a bottle in his hand and he was beautiful and he was groovy, drunk, you see. Then a minister came on, then you had another black cat who was on dope, he came on. Then you had the heavy black cat from Ivy League, three-piece and this kind of shit, you see what I mean. Now they were stereotypes, so that's what I'm talking about. One has to be careful.

Careful to avoid propaganda or rabble-rousing or being locked into a kind of political arm of. . . .

Of course. Yes, of course you must, or you are going to get yourself into some difficulty here for the simple reason that nowadays, and I'm very conscious of this as a teacher of this thing, nowadays one has to be very careful in the definition of literature.

Do you have any pressure on you because you don't write more specifically about, say, race problems, because in fact you're writing about people?

No, no, there's no pressure on me. I couldn't operate, you know, with pressure. I wouldn't tolerate pressure. But I should also say, Graeme, that I write a lot of articles which would probably satisfy that requirement. But apart from that — you see, the thing is this, this is the problem I get into. I'm sure now that years ago, when I wasn't published in America, that was the reason: my work was not fitting into a model which the publishers and the prevailing mood demanded — so far as blackness and racialism were concerned, there was no way of dealing with me, see? In other words, and this I think is important because the West Indian in America is a bit of a problem for the same reasons, he does not have the same ritualistic sensibilities, certainly not the moment he arrives in America. I mean, he might be educated into feeling the same way, but he doesn't have the same ritualistic sensibilities as the black Americans, and, you know, one isn't quite sure where to place him, and I would say that the American literary establishment, if there is such a thing, probably isn't quite sure where to place the West Indian writer.

Let me change and ask you in what way is writing important to you?

Simply because there is nothing else I can do, and nothing else I want to do. I can't give you any other answer.

Do you think writers know something special about the world, say like physicists do or like anthropologists or like lawyers?

You see now this is where we tend to disagree. I think you have come from a tradition where the writer approaches an elitist kind of position in society. I've come from a tradition where the writer is an ordinary person. I would like to think so. I would like to think of myself as an ordinary person. Now I would say that the special knowledge that the writer has is simply knowledge that accumulates, is an accumulation. Here's a man who spends or should spend most of his time daydreaming or looking out the window or writing or something, and it seems to me that when you sit down eight hours a day doing one thing, after eight years you must accumulate some knowledge, you know what I mean? Now I feel that just because society is structured so that people go to certain other people for their opinions, one would tend to come to me for opinions of some kind of humanitarian nature. But I might be a bastard, and if I am asked to advise or to give an opinion in these humanitarian matters because I'm an artist, well, people don't know that at heart this has nothing to do at all with what I am like. It can be very misleading. That's why I don't think one should really trust what the writers are made to say any more than one should trust what any intelligent man is made to say.

You say you've spent eight years doing something which means you're going to accumulate knowledge of some kind. What kind of knowledge is that, you say it's humanitarian — is that from observing others or observing yourself or. . . ?

Observing others, observing oneself. I think that I know people very well. Now you see you've put me in a position where I'm talking about myself, and I don't usually talk about myself. I think I'm pretty kind-hearted. Nowadays it doesn't really matter to me what kind of man the man is, you know. I feel that because I'm a man, I would automatically give another man a chance, you see what I mean, not that I would enter any kind of relationship if I knew that it was not going to work, but I would give the man a chance, so that in other words I would be free enough that both of us could see the possibilities. That's the kind of knowledge that one gets. One gets to know people. One understands that most people are beautiful, and the rest of it is just tensions, pressures that they can't deal with. Because very few of us, you know, Graeme, see that's why I'm not criticizing you too much for regarding yourself, and me for that matter, as members of some elite —

I didn't say I did. I'm not. . . .

I think you would have come to that, to that elitist thing because we are writers. But I was going to say that very few people, since we are in Canada now, let us just talk about Canada, I feel very few people in Canada are mentally equipped, and when I say mentally equipped I mean stability, health, et cetera, to deal with the problems in this world, or in this country, and many people are going crazy. Now it is possible that we both are crazy, but we could get our therapy free in the sense of sitting down in front of a typewriter, you see what I mean. We don't have to go and hire a psychiatrist to do this kind of thing. That's what I'm talking about. So that when I look outside at people, I look outside on a beautiful scene now, I shouldn't say beautiful but an interesting scene across the street from where I live. I look outside and there's this woman, a young woman, and she is my age and obviously separated from her husband. He's a young man. He comes on Sundays in a little red Volkswagen, parks the Volkswagen in front of the house or round the corner, and goes for the children. She hands him the children through the window — they live on the ground floor, you see — and there's no conversation that passes between the two. One then sees this man trying to protect these children in an overprotecting way. He goes away, the woman remains home. One can't even say that when he goes away she has men coming in, because one doesn't see that. She doesn't. You see what I mean? He comes back with the children and she takes the children through the window. On other days she's taking the children through the door, the front door, you see. But there's still no conversation passing, you know. So then, seeing this, one has got to make judgments on this, right? Now you can make many judgments. But I don't make judgments. I'm saying before I can make a judgment, let me find out why.

Now do you try to find out why, or does it become a story and then it becomes a why for you? Obviously a story would begin for you.

Yes. Okay. Okay. Now if I were writing the story, it would depend on the particular time that I was thinking about the character of one of the two. If I was going to make the woman the main character, it would depend on the particular time in my daydreaming when I have fallen in love or out of love with this woman. If I have fallen in love with this woman in the sense that a writer falls in love with the character, or even in an ordinary sense, then I would probably make her a very nice woman, not irredeemably nice, you see what I mean, but I wouldn't put any other characteristics or bricks in the structure of her characterization. So that one could say, well probably she is not so cool, or she is or she isn't all right, see what I mean, so that I would have in a story to understand the why, you see.

Is writing a process of understanding, I mean a way that you try to understand?

Yes. In my stories I have found, I shall also say, another influence. I started writing when everybody was interested in psychology and psychoanalysis, you know. I never had the need to be psychoanalyzed, I've always regarded myself as rather healthy, though I am told that if I make that kind of statement I am not very healthy (*laughter*) but I have always regarded myself as very healthy. Anyway, another part of my influence is psychology. Well, I tell myself it's psychology, so that my stories, if there is any seriousness at all in my stories, the people in my stories must do things that are psychologically correct.

Instead of being thematically correct or something like that?

Yes. In other words they must behave like people, and there must be reasons, you know what I mean. In other words, before I could write the story of this woman and her estranged husband, I would have to find out what made her put the children through the window. I would also explain what putting the children through the window means to him, not to me, because it could mean something else to me, you see. I would then go about making him take these children in this protective way. I would follow him in the car, I would make him give the children an extra ice cream, which one would do because he's compensating for something.

Now when you say you have to understand why it is that she hands the children out the window, are you concerned with that woman across the street or, when she becomes a character, is it just the character you're interested in?

I'm concerned with her.

With the actual woman?

Yes.

And so when you write a story, there are real people, then, people whom you know, in your stories?

In some cases, they are. Like that woman, if I wrote that story, the woman that came out in the story would not be only that woman next door, you see what I mean, but they are pieces of real people. Then of course one gets this question: is it intellectually conceivable that a writer create a character, aspects of which do not exist at all? You see what I mean. So one would have to say, well, this piece reminds me of her and this piece reminds me of my wife, et cetera. You know.

Right. Okay, does writing, do you think, and perhaps my point of view is being revealed here, does writing involve a certain kind of selfishness?

I don't understand how you use selfishness.

For example, are there some things that you wanted to write about people that you haven't written because you thought it would hurt them? Or have you really ever been in a situation where you've been tempted not to write something, but have written it? You know what I'm saying?

Give me a cigar, Graeme. You're asking me about five different questions here. Let me begin by saying that I . . . You see, I've become so academic, I always say, 'Let me begin by saying,' and it's obvious that whatever I say first is what I begin by saying, right? Anyhow, only recently have I been able — I shouldn't say have been able, only recently have I written stories about people that are close to me, people I love, and when I did this, I said, 'My god, Clarke, you're running out of material,' because I had never done this before, and I think that I did this as a possible way of exploiting further the dimensions of what you might call experience. You know what I mean, and I probably came to it because I read the biography of this woman, Fitzgerald's wife, Zelda, where he had used her. I thought it was mean on his part, but of course one can't even say that. I mean, why is it mean on his part to have used his wife, and yet to have produced such beautiful work, you see. So one can't say that. Now that probably comes to your question of selfishness. I would say the writer must be selfish for the simple reason that if he is going to be a serious writer, most of his time must be taken up by this. I don't mean selfish in the sense that he tramples on friends, but I find, looking back over my life, that I have not trampled but I have more or less stepped on the corns of many people in the sense that I did not have enough time to go back or to make another telephone call and say, "Well look, I'm sorry, I did this because, you know . . ." I was really thinking about that, which to my mind becomes an irony in a relationship, because then there ought to be no need for it, you know, but then, selfish, I don't know whether I could call myself —

No, I didn't mean necessarily just you, but this writer's thing, the writer's role. And what you're saying is that it does demand a kind of selfishness.

I think it demands extreme loneliness, to the extent now that I find I behave differently when I get out of my writing role, I want to talk, and not only am I talking, but all the characters that I've been dealing with, you know, are talking, a great loneliness. Yes, I suppose yes, and a great amount of selfishness. That's what I was saying to you.

MATT COHEN

MATT COHEN was born in Kingston in 1942.

What qualities do you like best in your own work?

It seems adequate when it has clarity, when the voice out of which it is written seems authentic, which is not all of the time, by any means. And those are the times when a lot of things come together, and I have access to various centres at once and can move freely among them and keep a completely accessible surface.

When you say the voice is working, is that a voice centred in a character or in an overview?

In an overview. For me to be satisfied with my own voice is very difficult. I don't feel right unless it has a certain distance, but it also has to be immediate, and getting those together at the same time is a problem.

When you say the voice has to be at a distance, is this an objectivity you're talking about in dealing with the substance of the book?

No. Distance isn't exactly the right word. My ambivalence to what I'm talking about has to be included in it, and in my novels I have different ways of dealing with that, and I wasn't always completely satisfied with how I did it; but both novels were partly determined by my need to keep back, to be honest about my ambivalence.

Okay, can you talk more specifically about the ambivalence? Would you say that it appears in Korsoniloff, *the first novel?*

Korsoniloff is ambivalent about his own existence, and about his own identity, also about whether he liked or disliked people. But the main area of ambivalence was taking place in his relationship with the reader via the journal, where the only way he could satisfy himself was at every point to undercut himself. Everything he tried to do had to undercut itself at the same time, or he couldn't get it on the page.

Is the ambivalence in Korsoniloff *the same kind of ambivalence that is in, say,* Johnny Crackle Sings? *Is it a constant within you, or does it have to do with the intent of the novel, or the demands of the novel?*

I'm not very ambivalent. I have a lot of ambivalent feelings about writing, but the fact is I do it consistently. I didn't do it for a long time, even when I wanted to do it, that was just a destructive whim, and I suppose that could happen again; but in *Korsoniloff,* the character was paralyzed by his ambivalence, and that was a very unsatisfying way for me to write, because I didn't feel as paralyzed as the character was, and I wanted to have more fun writing. In *Johnny Crackle,* the ambivalence is more cultural. I think ambivalence is just a general pattern of energy almost, of attachment to things, and so I'm at least free to express it in any one of all sorts of ways. In *Korsoniloff* it was via paralysis, in *Johnny Crackle* it was much more cultural. In the short stories, it's just by juxtaposing a lot of things at the same time, and by using dialogue which is, I think, of the three, the one I feel best about.

Can you tell me a little more about the cultural ambivalence in Johnny Crackle Sings?

Johnny Crackle was a person with one set of values who took on, entire, a second set — the American pop mythology. It was in that second context that he made his own identity (even his name), felt at home, excused his own life. But finally, because it was artificial to him, he had to throw it off, to return to what was authentic, alive, for him. So, at least for him, it was impossible to swallow whole the American myths — not for intellectual reasons, but because they were foreign to his own experience.

He went back to the land in some sense, didn't he?

Yes.

I want to ask you a couple of more general questions and then I'll come back to the book more specifically. In what way is writing important to you?

One way that writing is important to me is that it maintains my sanity. During the winter I really thought I was going to go insane. It's interesting — on the other hand, I don't really want to go insane. I don't just think, well, that would be an interesting experience, I should go through it. I feel the same way about meat grinders. When I am writing well, the stakes are very high because my writing doesn't just reflect my life, often my life reflects my writing by this time, and one way for me to grow is to grow through my writing and then it will bounce back into my life and behaviour. So it's part of the process of me staying alive and growing. As an external activity, it is the most interesting one to me that I've been able to come up with. It's also important to me because it gives me an entrance into the reality arena, which I want, and I've no particular illusions about a lot of people reading my books and changing their lives, but it is a means for me to articulate my own world and externalize it rather than having to turn in against myself. And I am afraid of my own self-destructiveness, so I look for ways to externalize rather than internalize.

So it's an objectification of all kinds of things for you.

Uh-huh, and it's also a means of objectification that allows a great deal of play, and I'm much more interested in play than work in a lot of ways. I enjoy it more.

How did you start writing?

Well, when I was six, I wrote a short story on a boat when we were crossing the Atlantic Ocean. I'm not quite sure why I did that, probably to show off. And when I was in high school, I got bored with poetry and . . . I'm sure it's a very common experience, and one morning I woke up and wrote about ten poems in a row, and I thought: Gee, anyone can do this. Of course, they were terrible. That wasn't the point. I could do rhymes and stuff. After that I wrote on and off for four or five years, and then stopped entirely.

Why did you stop?

When I was twenty-one, I graduated from college and won a writing prize for short stories, and it was enough plus a bit of savings to go to Europe for a few months. I ended up living in this barn for six weeks all alone, and there were various gypsies around who were supposed to be hostile. I didn't speak French very well, so I wrote a lot. I wrote a long epic poem and I was working on a novel, and when I went back to London, I got an offer of publication for the novel, and there was a sort of a whole set-up, people were going to subsidize me, et cetera. I got really scared, and I felt very unready for it, and I was very unsure of what I was doing, so I just . . . I came back to Canada and went to graduate school and just shut down.

What happened to that novel?

Burned it. I burned everything I have written before I was twenty-five.

Did you burn it when you came back to graduate school or subsequently?

Subsequently. It wasn't a good novel particularly. I got about seventy pages done or something. But it was very frightening to find out that it was so easy to write at least a mediocre novel.

Did you find that any period in your life, say like childhood or something, was particularly useful to you as a writer? Do you come back to certain periods, or do you see it in that kind of sense?

I think the period that I fed most directly off is a period in my mid-twenties, of about four years, when I just acted absolutely impulsively in any situation I was in, and consequently I had a lot of different experiences, and I experienced a lot of fairly strange states of mind which I seemed to be able to deal with at the time. So that was the big learning period for me, and it matched up with earlier periods, but it's the lens through which I get to the earlier stuff.

Primarily in your mid-twenties, then. Some people have mentioned puberty, for example, as a particularly intense time, and others have kind of early memories that come back, but yours tend to be in the middle twenties.

Yes. I have a fairly good memory of my life. I don't have big periods that are blocked off to me, but I never really acted with a great deal of freedom until I was in my twenties.

Do writers know something special about the world, or about life or whatever, say like physicists or sociologists?

It's a confusing question because I'm not sure whether physicists et cetera do know something special or whether they simply share some sort of language.

Okay. Have you felt lonely as a writer, not as an individual, but as a writer, lonely in a way that in a different cultural situation could have been avoided?

I never thought it could have been avoided. I think I've had quite fruitful associations with other writers and editors, when it was possible for me to be open to it, and there's been an awful lot of times when it wasn't possible for me. I think that was inevitable. I think with all writers that's true — though sometimes they try to mask it through literary communities — and I think it will continue to be inevitable, but there are periods when I've gotten really a lot from other people.

You're talking in terms of editorial work or a response to manuscripts. Is that when you're open, or is it more on a kind of personal, give-and-take level?

There's three main things that I've gotten from other writers and editors. One was when I started writing again when I was twenty-five or twenty-six . . . 1968. I was really encouraged to do so. I'm not sure I would have if I hadn't been. And the second thing was that publishing with different publishers, and having that open to me, really freed me from feeling very dependent on feedback. And then the third thing was this winter, people pushed me to write the short stories and to put away a draft of a bad novel I'd done, and that was really valuable, because I could have just stayed mired in that for years.

Do you consider yourself a "Canadian" writer? I mean, do you think of yourself in these terms?

Well, I think in some ways I am, by sociological circumstance. Often I think that Canadian writing is either . . . there is some combination of regional writing and high Tory Anglican Toronto, and that's not me. I think I'm a regional writer, and that's obviously the Ottawa Valley. I've lived there a lot and I got a lot from it, but with these two, also common to "Canadian," is a lot of conservatism, not closedness to change but conservatism as it is meant in Canada; and I am not a conservative. I just am not, and so I perceive those things and I'm interested in them, but I'm not of them.

What do you have in mind when you say conservatism in Canada?

Two attitudes, really. The first is that the physical is sacred — that things, at least in this world, begin and end in our own bodies. But what that is supported by is a Christianity which requires an elite of those who know and rule. And then the first attitude becomes a second: that what *is* is sacred . . . then the details are unacceptable.

Are there any obvious advantages or disadvantages in your own experience to being a writer or becoming a writer in Canada?

I think it's been easier to publish in Canada at the particular time that I happened to start writing. It was probably a hell of a lot harder ten years ago. I think this is because there was a period of ferment, a lot of openness to new writers and not a need to compete with or duplicate old writers, or for that matter to jump on them. There was a kind of freedom, free forum, which I think is probably really unique. And I think the disadvantage has probably been that there has been such a cultural emphasis on Canadianism that at times I was taking Canadian literature almost too seriously for my own good.

Too seriously for your own good in what way? What is it about Canadian literature that taking it seriously can be detrimental?

Well, most Canadian literature up to the last few years is, in terms of its formal structure, conventional, even boring, and it just happens that one of my areas of strength is to be able to play with formal structures. So at times my input got limited by the fact that I was reading Canadian writers, and now I've started to read Canadian writers and non-Canadian writers, because I don't want to just . . . I've a very scientific attitude towards that kind of thing sometimes, and if someone else has done it, there's no reason why I should do it. But I can learn from what they've done and go on from there.

When I was growing up, my own experience was that it was very difficult to believe that one could be a writer in Canada, because they simply didn't seem to be that available, they didn't seem to be around. Maybe this was because we weren't taught Canadian literature in schools, and the existence of writers as individuals was something that I didn't discover until I was thirty. Do you have any sense of this?

Absolutely. I didn't even consider the possibility of being a writer in Canada when I was growing up, because it didn't seem like a possibility that one could consider unless one happened to be independently wealthy. I didn't know how the "writers" got there and there was obviously only room for two or three and they were doing it, and I wasn't sure I wanted to do that anyway. It's only in the last six months that I have thought of myself at all as a writer.

What did you think of yourself before? What did you think about the activity before?

Oh, I thought it was writing, but I didn't think it was a long-term role. It was a matter of holding out against economic impossibility.

Okay. What is the writer's role, the novelist's role, although we'll include short stories as well — the fiction writer's role? Does he have any responsibility to society or . . .

Well, there are certain ideas that society takes from him, that have to do with what is real and what isn't real — questions of ideology. I think people really use novels almost like etiquette books, to see, well, what it is that people do, to know what is permissible, to know at what point they have to start worrying, et cetera.

Things to do with behaviour in society?

The relationship between the individual and society, sexual propriety, the amount of violence that is permissible in relationships, and I guess anti-social behaviour as opposed to social behaviour, what is politically acceptable. One of the things that novels do in a society is to explicate what is considered normal. Sometimes they wouldn't appear to be that way, but I think that's one of the things society expects of novels, maybe they're a little bit ahead of the time, though I think most novels tend to explicate what is conventional. I think people use them that way, whether or not it's a part of the writer's intent. I think some writers should write about what is actually happening, because an awful lot of what is actually happening in a country is invisible. Because I don't consider the news as really the news, like we hear the news over the radio or television or read it in the papers, but just reading it has nothing to do with anything. In some ways it does, but it is not the news for the people who are reading the news. It is not their news at all. They're cut off from their news completely.

And so you think that the role of fiction is, at least for some fiction writers, to give the news?

Absolutely. That's one possible role.

Whom do you write for?

What audience, or *if* an audience? I'm very unclear if I have an audience, or, if I do, who it is. Partly I write for myself and partly I write for an audience of non-writers. I do hope that there are people out there who are reading it and so I should try to be clear. I do feel some vague responsibility to the hypothetical audience, but I have very little sense of its existence in detail.

I mean, are there certain people who, when a book comes out, say certain things and you feel you've reached this hypothetical audience? We're not talking in terms of numbers, although numbers are nice.

I felt with *Johnny Crackle* that I reached more of my audience than with *Korsoniloff.* A few people made interesting comments about the book, and having a few people make interesting comments means a lot more than no people making interesting comments. (*laughter*) So I felt that the book must somehow have presented itself in such a way that it was possible for the reader to get something out of it.

Okay, a different kind of question. How do you work? I mean, how many words on a good day, how does the day go when you write?

The rules are always changing. When I wrote *Korsoniloff,* I worked almost every day, and between one and two pages a day was the norm. Occasionally it turned out to be three or four, and more often it turned out to be less, but I worked pretty well every day. I just started at the beginning and went right through to the end, once I had an idea of what I was going to do with the book. *Johnny Crackle* was totally a free-for-all. I wrote it in cars, in hotel rooms, sitting under tents. I'd give it up for a couple of months and start writing it again, and it varied anywhere from a couple of sentences to ten pages in a day. The short stories was a really intense period. I did most of them in two and a half months. I worked about ten hours a day, and I would write anywhere from a paragraph to fifteen pages.

Do you find it difficult to begin in the morning, or do you go to it joyously?

I'm not too joyous in the morning. (*laughter*) Quite often I don't even wake up in the morning. I write late at night rather than in the morning. Usually after four or five hours of being awake and letting that go down, I start writing.

Do you enjoy writing?

Oh yeah, I really enjoy it. I also hate it, but I'm indifferent to that.

Do you make your living as a writer?

I make my living in my role as a writer. I don't make my living from royalties. I come closer to making my living from advances than from royalties. (*laughter*) Which is why publishers go broke — that's not true, of course.

Does being a novelist or writer demand a particular kind of selfishness?

Yes. One is remaining true to something which may have nothing to do with other people, and that's a fairly weird input into intimate relationships, and I guess it's selfish in some way, because in your relationship with someone, everything is not up for grabs, which is supposed to be the condition of the truly open relationship.

Does the prospect of the time when you no longer can write as well as you would like frighten you?

I've never been able to write as well as I would like.

Well . . . the prospect of the time when you no longer want to write or can't write, does that frighten you?

I see two possibles. Scenario Number One is that I gradually become a wino, or my brain turns to jelly from acid, my cock falls off, or any one of those things, and I can no longer write, and you know it's really tragic, and I get all bundled up and I read my books every night, but it's hopeless, and I'm just a has-been, sort of a whole boxing career trip, make a movie about it or something. Scenario Number Two is that I write these fantastic books which I'm really pleased with, but I become detached from them, and go and sit under the Bodhi Tree and help old ladies across the road and smile at children and no longer have a need to do such an eccentric thing as writing. I've no idea how to decide which one it is.

Okay, let's talk a bit more specifically about the books. There's an obvious thematic progression from Korsoniloff *to* Johnny Crackle Sings. Korsoniloff *never really resolves his duality. He endures it in a sense, but it seems he's vaguely threatening and he's vaguely threatened, whereas Crackle goes through it. There's a phrase, a very similar phrase that appears in both books.* Korsoniloff *speaks of striving towards "ground zero" — he hasn't achieved ground zero, and Johnny Crackle gets into "condition zero." What is the value of zero?*

That's the point where there's no resistance to the external world. That can be total catatonia, because that's the simplest way of having no resistance to it, by not reacting to it. The point of the whole condition zero concept is that it's necessary to become free from obsessions and habits in order to move on, to grow. It's almost impossible that Korsoniloff would ever make it, at least I couldn't see him getting past that. He could, you know, have more acceptable solutions to himself, and even his duality was constantly shifting, but he could never decide whether to move outside him-self — or whether he thought it possible. His only area of freedom was self-preservation.

A sense of suicide and also the possibility of doing it to others is almost a third persona, isn't it? At the beginning of the narrative Korsoniloff's only accomplishment is the complexity of his contradictions. Is that the thing that condition zero will free you from . . . the complexity of con-tradictions?

Yes. Because in condition zero there is no self. But Korsoniloff, at least, was open to his own conflicts instead of just repressing them, pretending that he is all right. That is what is interesting about him.

In what sense is it interesting? Is it also valuable for him as an individ-ual, or does it just make him interesting as a character?

I think it would make him a more interesting human being to be with, and it was necessary for him as a person, I should think, to have some existence of his own. It was necessary for him, so we can't give him credit for having thought of it, but it gave him a possibility. It meant that he could confront the possibility of not being like that, and that is absolutely essential.

Yeah, he did have a sense that things could be different for him, while at the same time it becomes fairly clear that another area of him, another of his persona doesn't know what's happening at all. Is it Gail at the end? She said he didn't know what was happening, and he agrees with this.

Gail to him represents the kind of unified wisdom of the lady who reads tea leaves; he does not really understand what she says. He only understands that he has to agree to it.

But she's right, isn't she?

Oh, absolutely.

When he was studying philosophy, he discovered all he was really doing was writing down what other people had said and it became clear to him that he didn't want to do that, but there's never any real alternative for him in his mind. He just stayed on with the teaching, and it gets to where at one point he's calling students stupid, so even that isn't working particularly well.

Well, I think he hopes that by living out a more instinctual life, he will accumulate a set of experiences which will allow him to create a new world for himself and a new personality which will derive from his immediate perceptions as opposed to more abstract kinds of knowing. But because he's always only half-experiencing things, that never happens. . . .

Even when he is attempting to be instinctive, he is watching himself attempting to be instinctive, which is self-defeating.

It's an infinite-regress thing.

All right. So at the end, then, he's endured in some way, he's managed to maintain his complexities, and he just throws away a line at one point which seems to me to be important in terms of both books, when he says about the dead man's float, "anyone could learn that in a few minutes." And yet he's always seemed content with the dead man's float — just lying on the water with his face in it.

And watching himself do it.

What about madness? It's a possibility in both novels, I mean it's an actuality in both novels although not a clinical matter necessarily. Is it redemptive, I mean Johnny Crackle when he arrives at condition zero?

He is, as you say, catatonic or whatever, there is madness there, but it is clearly redemptive of experience.

Yes, it is redemptive in his case.

Would it have been for Korsoniloff?

Yes. For Korsoniloff, yes, for all people, no, but it might have been just the thing for Korsoniloff. And what he was essentially doing was shoving it aside. Crackle was able to go through it. That doesn't mean that it's everyone's job to go through a schizophrenic episode in order to come to themselves. It's not the sort of thing one could ever recommend to someone.

No, it's sort of a structural thing in the book, or a thematic thing. With Korsoniloff, his self-consciousness and his refusal really to go all the way, even when he is pursuing experience, he is putting off the crisis, he is avoiding the implications of so many things in himself. I mean, they go through his head and he is becoming progressively more violent in his potential. When at the end he thinks of shoving Gail off the balcony, or there's the episode where in his imagination he shoots the old woman and is covered with blood — in some sense he is not confronting the inevitable drive in him that Crackle acquiesces in or even pursues. Crackle does it with dope, doesn't he?

He does it with dope and he doesn't have so much violence to confront in himself.

Korsoniloff's also incredibly hostile towards Tonker — there's almost no one in his life that he wouldn't consider wiping out at one point or another.

Tonker threatens him because he's so literally material — his most obvious quality is quantity — a huge, fleshly creature, stuffing food into himself. A really grotesque fraternity graduate.

And just in passing, there are a number of fat people, very fat people in your work. There's the guy that keeps falling up the stairs in one of the stories. . . .

Harold, the elephant.

The elephant, a really threatening grotesque figure, and also the fat lady in the Columbus thing, but she's different, because she's worked to put that fat on her, and it's well toned, so she doesn't have the same disgusting quality to her.

I often use fat people to talk about the physical side of existence. And also I'm interested in them, the whole phenomena, because I'm so thin, it just seems like another way of being, to have this incredible mass to move around, it fascinates me and so I write about it.

There's a whole question of shedding, you know, of getting rid of patterns or habits. It's in Korsoniloff again when he talks about other people and says: "they long for escape, but act only to secure themselves in their own chains." Would you see that, say, as a general problem facing your characters? to get out of that bind?

Uh-huh. Although for Korsoniloff it was really an unresolvable problem, because he was able to experience things in different ways at times. He could take himself that far, but he could never move the centre of his life, and that's what's really important, to be able to move the centre of your life.

What I'd like to find out is to what extent the patterns, the methods, the impulses, those things which enslave, come from the individual and how much it has been done to them.

I think an awful lot of it has been done to them by a society that really encourages finding a particularly strong definition of self, and makes mobility and forming oneself really difficult through guilt and the economic substructure and the school system and just so many different things. What one is encouraged to do is something that you define rigidly from the beginning, just be really persistent, marry once, keep your good friends ever since grade two, et cetera, be the same for as long as possible, that is what one is supposed to do, and when you try not to do it, you run into all sorts of things which are external to you. On the other hand, one is hooked into oneself by one's desire for approval and by the capacity to be upset or freaked or made anxious by the things that one runs into, so in a sense it's like deciding which is more responsible, it's just the Buddhist view versus the political view, Koestler called it the Yogi and the Commissar, and I think they're both totally compelling and there's no reason to decide between them.

This sort of problem of entrapment and enslavement really adds up to the definitions of self that one is handed and accepts?

One side of the problem of attachment is the self, in that it requires particular kinds of self to be attached, but the other problem of attachment is in reality, as we use reality, because there is a physical world which demands certain specific things for survival, and no matter how you organize it, unless you just want to be hooked up intravenously or something, and there are other various social organizations possible for survival — all of which have some sort of rigidity.

What about nature? It does not have an obvious role in Korsoniloff, *but it becomes fairly explicit in* Johnny Crackle Sings, *that nature is obviously a way out for Johnny. Before his first recording date, he's really very nervous when suddenly after all this time it looks like he's going to make it and he doesn't quite know what the hell is going on and he feels very threatened. He goes to the island and he spends about a week or ten days walking and sitting and coming back and playing cards periodically with his friend Lew. Now that is obviously a fantastically supportive thing for him. He comes out of it no longer afraid, just curious. . . . What about the role of nature?*

Writing *Korsoniloff*, I was trying to deal with the view that human beings are divided into their head and their body, and that their problem is to get it together. So instinct equalled nature in some way. But I wasn't too concerned with the role of actual physical nature — the planet. Korsoniloff's perception of the details of city nature and country nature weren't too different in mode. For Crackle, actual physical nature is something to which he could really connect, and placing himself in that environment was really redemptive. Even when his mother left when he was sixteen, and he went to live on Lew's farm, it was always a redemptive thing for him. It was a means by which he could exist authentically and grow.

At the end would he be able to . . . do you think he is now in a position where he will grow potatoes or babies or whatever?

Yes, though that wouldn't necessarily be enough for him.

He wasn't after "enlightenment," though, was he?

No, enlightenment was a false goal for him. He was after shedding a certain mythology, and that happened, and it happened in a . . . you know, in a real way, so it was done. I think his life had really improved by the end of the novel and it was possible for him to live a real life. I think Lew's life had been almost destroyed . . . because he had not been able to generate enough energy to individuate himself from what Johnny was going through, and so finally Johnny used him and he let himself be used.

I want to try to bring together a question on or related to nature. Nature is available to Johnny Crackle as a source of strength, and it's something that he returns to at the end. It is not available to Korsoniloff. Is that a way of seeing the difference between the two of them?

Yes.

Does it have anything to do with the fact that Korsoniloff is an intellectual and Johnny isn't?

It does in the sense that for Korsoniloff to become an intellectual represented a rejection of his past, and his past had included nature. Crackle didn't have to reject his past to become what he was. He just had to lay something on top of it.

All right. Nature has another role for Korsoniloff too, because his mother drowns, and so . . . is nature in some symbolic way destructive for him?

Well, sure it is for lots of people in the sense that the idea of nature is hostile, and it's something to be afraid of; you can drown or trip and break your leg, et cetera. That's not one of Crackle's worries — he doesn't relate to it in that way.

The dead man's float and his mother's drowning. This is vague, but is there any way of seeing Korsoniloff's problems, his relationship . . . I mean, you talk about the separation of the head and body which Crackle loses, partially through dope, partially through just a drive, and Korsoniloff never loses it, in fact in some ways it's even stronger at the end than at the beginning, because having gone through these things, he's still self-conscious about "now" in some way. What I'm trying to say is, does his problem come from a real separation from the natural world? He feels guilt about his mother's death in some funny way, can this be related to nature?

I think that his separation from the natural world is a symptom of his problem — it's one of those symptoms that reinforce the problem because it's such a central symptom, so it's both cause and symptom. At first it's symptom. He's separated from the natural world because he's separated from himself, and going on a bunch of hikes wouldn't help him. Although there is one place in the book where he gets into the habit of driving up north and just sitting at times, so it does have some limited access to him. And at every point where Korsoniloff has a sort of a little good thing happen to him or tries to make some connection outside that will get past himself, it's always with the physical world, like Gail — he's very physical with Gail, you know she's not dumb, but it's being able to be just sort of two animals together, not in the usual sense . . . two living beings together . . . two-legged animals. The problem with Korsoniloff is that his problems are greased but not changed. Nature greases it for him.

All right. You didn't really respond, I think, to the question of whether . . . you said intellect is a symptom . . . let me ask the question again. He is an intellectual; he is almost a mockery of an intellectual in many ways, in a kind of humorous way, but it's a very destructive way. I mean to say, is the university a measure of Korsoniloff's more desperate straits?

Yes. The university demands a consistent self-destruction and abstraction that's fairly unique, a very high level compared to what most other life courses demand.

The whole educational system, then, is the process of adapting to forms, eh? Is that what happens to Korsoniloff?

Yes, because you have to take as real what is totally unreal, and in order to do that, you have to destroy what is real in yourself.

Okay, let's leave the novels now and say some things about the short stories. Have you been writing short stories from the beginning or did you come to them recently, say for this collection, Columbus and the Fat Lady?

I wrote occasional short stories from the beginning, but intensely only for this collection.

What got you into writing stories as opposed to novels?

I wanted to experiment with different things, and the novel was too cumbersome a form to experiment with. I wanted speed and facility, a certain kind of speed and facility, and I'm very attracted to some of the formal things about short stories, because they're short, and so that was a good way to do it. I also wanted to try things that I had never tried, which meant that I thought I would have to be throwing out an awful lot of what I did, and so if I was going to throw it out, I thought I'd rather throw it out after a couple of weeks than after a couple of years, and my idea was to write one a week for three months, and I thought I'd probably have to throw them all out. I just thought it would be a good thing to do.

In the stories, as also in the two novels, there's an interesting playing with so-called reality and potential reality or daydreaming — on an obvious level, daydreaming. Episodes which obviously don't happen on any real level in the story have the same kind of value, in some cases more value than events which do happen. Now can you talk at all about the attitude that this reflects?

Yes, I think what are at stake are the categories of fantasy and reality, and whether they're really different, and what reality is rooted in and how one decides what is real, and there's been a real progression in my writing on that question. Korsoniloff could barely accept fantasies as being real, not that he did not have fantasies, but he could barely deal with them at all, it's kind of a chaotic area. In *Johnny Crackle*, the schizophrenia between reality and fantasy was there instead of the schizophrenia of personality. But there was a counterpointing; with the stories, the counterpointing was not dependent on whether it's fantasy or reality — it's dependent on the kind of patterns or juxtapositions that are happening. So obviously I've decided that in some sense fantasy and reality share really a lot, and that the things they share are often much more important than their differences. As far as I'm concerned in my writing now, I draw almost no distinction between the two. There can be so-called fantasy experiences which are unreal, or they can be real, and the same with reality experiences. It all depends on how one is connected to it.

And stylistically or technically, this is highlighted by, say, repetition. Scenes will begin with a statement, and will work their way out, and then you'll return to the theme where that scene first began — sometimes almost identically — and then work it out in a slightly different way.

Yes, it will be different when it's repeated, because meanwhile other things have happened which have made it different, and in one sense that's a comment on the relationship between fantasy and reality, that fantasy changes reality; fantasy therefore must be real. I think I'm just fascinated by the idea of coming back to the same point, and what it means to come back to the same point. In *Korsoniloff*, it means paralysis; in the stories, it means energy, and it's really interesting. They could have the exact opposite meaning.

What about some of the specific stories? I'm interested in the Columbus story, when Columbus is alive in the present in a freak show. His experience seems to me to be very much in the tradition of both Korsoniloff *and* Johnny Crackle, *but he is really stuck and he ends up at a freak show. Johnny Crackle ends up on a farm and Columbus ends up in a freak show.*

Yes, the freak show represents the maximum freedom to which Columbus can aspire. He's a victim in a lot of different ways, he frees himself of the Old World to some extent, simply because he was a victim there and hoped for something better. It's a very complicated story for me — it's also about science and the rational world that succeeded the medieval world. Reason existing as flight from chaos, both in the obvious chronological way and in the sociological way; the new middle class who were interested in reason and science gained some sort of stability and freedom. But Columbus becomes a victim of his own flight. There's no way out for him.

As there isn't in some sense for Korsoniloff?

There is a way out for Diego. I imagined a whole novel of him taking off with the girl. . . . But for Columbus — he can just suffer in an interesting way.

Another question. One of the things I like best about Johnny Crackle Sings *is that the human dilemma that the characters find themselves in, the need to strip things away, to shed, in Johnny Crackle had real substance in the world and in his own life, whereas Korsoniloff never got out of his head, and while he did have relationships, they didn't have the kind of substantial reality that they have for Johnny Crackle. The same is also true of, say, someone like Galahad in* "Too Bad Galahad," *continually pursuing the Grail in its various guises and he in his various persona, and the same thing with Columbus; they are both of them somehow locked again almost in Korsoniloff's world, separated from real world experience.*

I don't know. Columbus was incredibly open to experience. Just because he couldn't experience himself in the disguise of a flower child or something like that didn't mean that he wasn't open to experience. So he was not cut off from the world at all. His problem was more in the other direction.

I'd like to ask a question having to do with where you are now, I mean with the sense that you're moving towards another novel. What is the attraction of the novel as opposed to short stories?

Part of it is simply the space and the freedom. Short stories are very finicky; one has a lot of freedom, but they are also very finicky, so short, you have to round off all the edges. If you don't, then you have to not round off all the edges in an interesting way. The novel is the much more energetic form, I think, it demands a lot more, but interaction with it produces a lot more. Also, for some reason, I just think that the novel is a form that will endure, not in its present particulars necessarily, but I think it's something that will endure because of the kinds of time things that jump out of it. I think it's a time thing.

And the fact that you can do whatever you want with it. . . .

A novel has so much happening in it to the characters that it really doesn't matter what the last sentence is, which is a lot different from most short stories.

Okay, just a general question: what do you see yourself doing next? As a writer.

My next novel?

Or do you see it as a novel, do you have a real sense of what it's going to be?

Well, I am working on a novel that may or may not come into existence. It's a novel about a conflict between nature and the city, but nature already acted upon by the city, I mean the city in sort of general terms, I suppose; and about the kinds of changes that people are going to have to go through as they recognize that the life sources of the roots to which they think they can turn are already altered and destroyed. I don't have the kind of optimism that lies behind some of your questions about nature and the sense that nature is something that is always there. I mean obviously the real world, there is always a physical real world there, no matter what you do, but what's happening to the real world outside of Toronto, to that natural real world, is that it is being permeated in so many different directions by all sorts of new economic considerations and by machines and by all sorts of manipulations, manipulated almost as much as the city street is manipulated, so that it's really unclear, when one goes out and looks at the grass and the trees, whether one's performing a worship of ritual of the archaic or . . . well, or what. In the novel I will try to deal with those things.

MARIAN ENGEL

FICTION
No Clouds of Glory
The Honeyman Festival

MARIAN ENGEL was born in Toronto in 1933.

Do you think writers know something special about the world like, say, a physicist?

I find that a tempting theory and I always turn that down inside myself, because I think that way madness lies. I've been talking to people recently who say novelists are prophets; they're just playing with words, but even if it's an interesting theory and a very small one, it makes me uncomfortable. I don't think that novelists are entirely special, and I don't think one can both theorize and create. One of the things fiction writers can do is lay out the cards a little differently so that the pattern can be more clearly seen, and then the logical development from that becomes prophetic. In other words, I don't think they know anything that anybody else doesn't know. They see differently, and their job is devising different methods of seeing. Not making intellectual theories.

You can teach someone to be an anthropologist, though not necessarily a good one, but can you teach someone to be a writer?

If I thought so, I'd be teaching at the writing school at York University this summer. Writers teach themselves to be writers. The only thing you can do is to make them read a lot. Otherwise it seems to me the basic ingredients are perseverance and a kind of vision, not necessarily a standardized kind; but there is something, some way of seeing, that makes people into novelists. A great familiarity with prose, good prose, is necessary, because you don't want to go and invent the wheel, do you? And a wide range of experience, and if anybody is in a writing school, of course he is not out getting that experience.

You have two novels published. Do you write anything other than novels?

I'm always writing something. I'm a compulsive writer. I've written a lot of short stories. I don't really consider myself a short story writer, but once or twice a year I get a good idea, and I've got a very convenient character now that I write short stories about. This character is a social anthropologist called Ziggy, and gradually Ziggy is becoming a big deal and I'm enjoying him very much, and he goes into short pieces. I don't think he'd make a novel; not a novel for me, because the short stories are really somebody else's short stories entirely. I don't know why the genre doesn't fit me in any special way, but it fits Ziggy superbly, so I've written a lot of stories about Ziggy — he's had three wives.

You say the short stories are really somebody else's, the novel is yours. What is it about the novel that attracts you or what is it that makes it yours?

Well, I think the tendency . . . You know, if anybody makes anything, he generally makes the thing he likes best. You see children doing this: If they like rhymes best, they make up rhymes. If they like stories best, they make up stories.

Okay, I'll rephrase the question. What is it with the novel that you like best?

Oh, the bigness and the challenge and the complexity, and the looseness. You know, there are no rules, no rules at all. There are critics who would like to be able to find rules, and there are critics who make up rules, but there are no rules except what comes off and what doesn't.

The prophetic we began with . . . I'd like to come back to that, because the whole question of why the novel continues to exist and in fact thrive in many ways, despite the predictions about its death . . . you say it has something to do with the prophetic. Can you elaborate on that?

This is John David Hamilton's theory, not mine. We were sitting around one night talking about writers and he was talking about Mailer's war novels and how they seemed to relate to Vietnam now and we were saying what is it in the novel that makes a novelist sometimes a prophet, a good one, and of course my . . . a great temptation in these situations is to say: aaah . . . I'm a prophet! And so I had to suppress that in myself and think of some reason for this, but I really think that there is a way of predicting behaviour by seeing people's characters, that's simply what the psychologists do. I think any sort of clever person who knows a fair amount about human nature can say: That is that sort of person, he will do that sort of thing. And I'm sure Mailer did this about the United States.

Okay. Another general question: what do you like best about your work so far?

I like some of the prose, some of the rhythms are right. The little words are put together in a way that satisfies me. Generally, when I go back to things, I'm just embarrassed by them. I'm beginning to be very embarrassed by the first novel, because I'm not really the person who wrote it anymore and it's so flat-footed. Except there are some things I like in it. There is a passage that, you know . . .Europe is a place in people's minds, I like that very much. But I suppose I'm most interested in the poetic effects in those two books because that's what they mostly are, they're not strung together on any big framework.

Is language, then, the unifying force for you as a writer?

I think it was at some point. I've done a lot of novels. I'm rather stupid and I had to teach myself to write novels by writing many of them, and I see those two books as rather special ones because they're the ones that got published and they're quite different from the others I was working on, which were much more Victorian, and they were worked out in terms which I didn't really believe in. I think your straightforward Victorian novel still exists as the detective novel, and there are some very fine ones being written, but serious work can no longer be expressed in those terms. Why? Because the form is too much of a straightjacket, even though there's always somebody shouting that we need characters in fiction, your old-fashioned round characters as opposed to your flat characters. Well, characters have become cute, decorative. We no longer see things that simply. Sociology has taught us that no novelist can hope to put down characters in the accurate terms that a sociologist or an anthropologist can, or any of these people with a battery of computers. One individual simply cannot learn enough about another individual to do it that way. It's great fun making up characters, but it seems an easy game in relation to modern sociological information. Therefore I think you have to really do what you find you can do. All writers do what they can do rather than what they would like to do, but you also . . . I think one of my solutions is to make words work for me. To make word patterns and people patterns.

What about the problem of becoming, you know, in some way public? Do your friends tend to be writers? Do the people you know, the people you have in your house, tend to be novelists or poets?

My husband is a broadcaster; it's working out in our lives that old friends are the best friends, and many of these are people we went to university with. We were in the group that turned out the university newspaper and literary magazine, the dramatic society and debating society, and those people tend to be either teaching at universities or in politics or both, or writers of some sort. One of our best friends is a songwriter, and I have fascinating conversations with him. There's your word-smithery again.

Right. Do you feel the need for, or do you find, the kind of community here, which feeds you as a writer?

Community of people?

Yes. Let me ask the question another way. Do you think it's important that writers have a community of artists around them in order to help them work or to make their work better?

No, I don't think so. It's a loner's job and only loners do it, and what good is a bunch of loners in a room?

When there's a bunch of loners, say in Paris, at the same time, and there's a kind of historical magic associated with that, do you think that is nonsense?

Oh, it's very pretty for the outside world, but I bet you Hemingway was getting to know the jockeys and Duff Twysden's crowd, and Fitzgerald was getting to know the socialites, and they weren't really together with each other. All the Hemingway and Fitzgerald encounters seem to have been minor tragedies. Now, some writers are more sociable than other writers and relate to people in less competitive ways. The Hemingway–Fitzgerald thing fascinates me because it was so competitive. Certainly Hemingway was. They had their antennae out in different directions, so that I'm sure they never really related to each other except when they were talking about their publishers and their agents and their mutual friends, but when it came to actually experiencing anything, you know, the Hemingway and the Fitzgerald version of the same experience is completely different, so therefore their encounter was only valuable for outsiders who looked at it or read about it and thought how pretty.

So it doesn't much matter to you here in Toronto whether there are other people writing or not?

Well, it matters that there should be an intellectual community, that matters dreadfully, but as far as knowing other writers and novelists, I've always found that very difficult, because there's very little shop to talk, except agents.

Does being a novelist demand a particular kind of selfishness?

Oh yes. It's a very selfish thing to do. Selfish — what is selfish? All right, you write out of your own self, therefore you cultivate that self, you cultivate your own ego like a little flower in a pot, you water it and you tend it and of course this rather gets in the way of other people's lives, so again I think you have to . . . oh, you know, I'd like to be a big character who'd just let my ego rip, and the awful thing is maybe I am . . . but I think we all try to soft-pedal that to make it tolerable for the people we live with.

Another way of looking at selfishness . . . surely there are the people who see or want to see something of themselves in the book. Does this ever create problems with people around you, do they feel they have been done badly by or does this ever enter your thinking at all?

There's a certain hang-up about spouses. I don't think I have ever put anything of Howard into a book, and I don't think I ever will, he's sort of stay-off-the-grass. It's not his idea — it's mine. I just wouldn't write about him ever, because that destroys the relationship, I think. Certainly in *The Honeyman Festival* I was very careful not to make the husband anything at all like Howard.

Do you find that there are other situations, say when there is somebody, or even part of somebody, and you'd really like to use them?

Well, they say nobody ever recognizes himself in a book, that's what Hugh MacLennan used to say, and I think this is false but very comforting. I think people have been very much on the lookout to see whether there were any actual people in *The Honeyman Festival* who related to anyone else. . . . People don't understand fiction in this country.

In what way?

They seem to have run into a whole tunnel of disbelief now, and I'm not talking about just my own book, because if they said that about my own book I could say, I'm a failure, I haven't convinced people that this is a fiction. But they seem to say this about a lot of other books too, and there's an almost sick desire to make every novel a *roman à clef* and the flashy current concept of the non-fiction novel maddeningly confuses the whole issue, and people are really, I find, very keen not to believe that there is such thing as imaginative creation.

Yes, and there is a tendency to say your books are very personal, which is not the same thing as being non-fiction. What about the business of the personal in fiction? Do you think perhaps in some ways the distinction between fiction and non-fiction has been blurred?

Oh, it's been blurred, and it's certainly been blurred in a popular way because, you know, half of the novels on the bestseller list frankly derive from certain characters. There was one that was supposed to be Frank Sinatra, for instance, and everybody bought it and read it, because they wanted to believe that this man was Frank Sinatra. So the novel that is partly biography finds great demand. That doesn't mean it is a good thing. It's merely gossip.

But coming around to the serious novel, though; if in fact the forms of the Victorian novel no longer apply to the serious novel, the art novel or whatever the hell you want to call it, and the rules don't work anymore, that means the writer is thrown back increasingly upon a personal view of the world.

Yes. And on himself, simply because the kind of things people want to know about, and the kind of information that we have to build up because of psychology and sociology and anthropology, things that are meaningful because they go beyond the social sciences . . . these we could not possibly know unless we had derived them from our own experience. I'm doing an interesting new book now and trying to lick this problem in certain ways.

Can you talk about how you're trying to lick it?

Yes, because I think it will be published eventually — well, it may never be, but it's still an interesting academic problem. The book is well established, so it's safe to talk about it. I set it for myself, because after doing *No Clouds of Glory* and *The Honeyman Festival*, I got very uptight about using too much of myself. I also felt that I was becoming diminished, my own reality was becoming diminished, and I still find myself eating obsessively — do you do that too? When I'm really putting it out on the page, I go into the kitchen and eat and eat and eat and eat. . . .

No, I drink. . . .

Yes, well I do too, but I often got very worried about this problem and I said no more big women for me, just to finish that, so I did a novel from a man's point of view, and I ran through that in about a year when I was doing a lot of reviewing. It's a bad book, because I kept losing my balance. I was reading too many other people and not being able to write like myself. And maybe I'll straighten that out, it will come out someday because it's quite a good book, but unfocused. And then I started doing the one I'm doing now, which is set in Cyprus, where we used to live. I still don't know whether to make it literally Cyprus or to make Cyprus a never-never land or to create a whole new never-never land. I had to do it from a woman's point of view simply because in a society which is completely sexually divided, where the woman's role and the man's role is worked out very clearly according to a pattern that was laid down a thousand years ago, a woman's experience is very different from a man's.

Now I want to talk about being a writer in Canada. Do you think there are any specific problems or advantages in being a writer in Canada?

Oh yes, of course; there are problems and advantages. You're working in an English-speaking world — that's an advantage; but you're in a small segment which isn't, in a literary way, let's face it, highly thought of outside. The Americans dislike our work less than the British do, but "Canadian" isn't one of the big happy designations as far as literature goes, and Canadians, though for some odd reason they buy poetry, don't buy novels in great enough quantity to support a writer. Sometimes I feel it's ridiculous, sitting in the midst of a desert producing a product nobody wants, especially when a friend phones and says, "Isn't it marvellous you have a book out, I put a nickel reserve on it in the library." It's hard to survive — to think well enough of yourself to continue — in this atmosphere. To illustrate that point: Last year I was in the hospital for something dreary, bored stiff, not very sick. The only interesting part of the experience was the Romanian house physician, with whom I talked quite a lot, about a lot of things . . . the Middle East, and Queen Marie of Romania, things like that. Finally he said (we were speaking French), "What do you do?" and I said, "I'm a novelist." And he said, *"C'est un beau métier."* Just like that. *"C'est un beau métier."* It's a good trade. And I felt an awful gush of ex-loneliness: nobody here, none of my own people, could say anything like that, anything so comforting. It's a good trade. Not having people around who talk like that is very lonely. But if another novelist said it, it wouldn't feel as good. On the other hand, the last five years have shown that people are really pulling themselves together on the matter of identity and they seem most flatteringly to be recognizing that writers will help them with their identity crisis. And since we are more conservative than the States and younger than England, we can still do some traditional things and get away with them. Robertson Davies can write *Fifth Business* and succeed with it, because we aren't sure enough of our own literary judgment to praise each other in international terms. It's also peculiar that though the short story is getting harder and harder to market in the States, there are two quite good markets here — *Chatelaine*, and Robert Weaver's *Anthology* program.

Here's a general question. In what way is writing important to you?

In what way? (*laughter*) That's a big one. I write. I've always written. It's a kind of tic. But I shouldn't admit this because another thing people seem to be interested in about writers is this writer-thing: the artist as freak, sideshow. I have a theory that the CBC ought to make some big wood and papier mâché puppets and put tape recordings inside them, put them on display, to give the people what the Book Publishers' Council recently said they want — not books or book reviewers, but TV interviews with authors. To sell a book, you have to go on TV and exploit yourself. I've done it, it's destroying. It makes me so self-conscious I want to explode. And you're supposed to be home writing, not out performing.

This business of the personality of the writer was certainly much of the magic of Hemingway or Fitzgerald.

Yes, yes, and they fascinate me too.

There's a booming industry in the personalities of the time as much as their work.

Yes, and this distorts, I think, the actual fact of writing, which is quite impersonal. Nobody really cares who Homer is now, you know. The act of telling a story is quite a natural, normal one. The act of writing it down is probably a bit less normal, but it's just something that people do, and the media and all this immense curiosity about how other people live overemphasize the so-called artist, and put him in a very unenviable position. Of course, there's a little bit of showbiz ham in all of us too. I think that's cultivated at the expense of good quality.

You said you've always written, and it's a kind of tic. What kind of tic? Is it the need to tell stories, or is it a need to order something in your mind, to describe it or to turn it into poetry, or . . .

I think — yes, it's both a need to tell stories and a need to order. I suppose because my personality — again, this is getting into the artist-is-crazy — but I suppose all art is an ordering of experience and all craft is too, and if you find experience comes through to you in a jumbled form, you make this passionate attempt to order it, and so I would think that the person who writes often has the receiving equipment in a little different order than the ordinary person who doesn't feel this need.

Perhaps where the difference might be is whether or not you accept the conventional order of events. There are all kinds of ways of explaining things, and the writer has to find his or her own way . . .

And sorting out the versions and versions and versions of reality that we get.

Right. You talked about sociology earlier or psychology in the interpretation of personality in individuals. Obviously it doesn't satisfy you, or you would have been a sociologist yourself . . .

Well, I don't know. You know, I often look back now and think I was a fool to want to be a writer quite so much because it kept me from looking at things in an ordinary way, and I met a sociologist-anthropologist in Cyprus who was living the life that I should have led when I was there and I wish I had. She had taken a house in a village and lived among the people. I found what she knew was fascinating, but it wasn't the sort of thing I could have settled down and done at all. I couldn't have approached experience in that cold, orderly way.

Here's a nuts-and-bolts question: how you work. Do you write every day, or do you try to write every day?

I try to write every day.

At any particular time, or do you just have to grab the time when you. . . .

Well, you know the domestic timetable. I've been trying to write in the morning. At the moment the kids are at day nursery, so I work about 10:30 to 2:30. When they come home from public school for lunch, it will be harder. Once the garden gets going, though, it seems silly to be inside. I work a lot at night too — if the kids go to bed, if we're not going out.

How many words would you write on a good day, say, when you're into the routine?

I tend to write in great volume, throw out, then rewrite. I can get twenty to twenty-five pages done on a really great day, out of which maybe half a page — or, if I'm lucky, five pages — will emerge. I try to get the whole of the thing down, because other-wise I'd just get irritable trying to keep it in my head while people are asking me for clean socks. But often I'm off the track.

Do you find it hard to begin to write each day?

I would find it hard to begin if there were no alternatives, but the family is beginning to get very demanding and the phone rings a lot, and increasingly writing is a refuge rather than an obligation; if you have all your time for writing, you have to face a kind of existential despair. Now I wrap my arms around my typewriter, as if it's going to save me from sordid domesticity.

Do you like writing?

When it's going well, it's like very good sex. When it isn't, I hate it. I haven't the patience for all that thinking.

Fair enough. What kind of writers do you like to read?

Good writers. Every once in a while I start running out of writers, then I remember I haven't scratched the surface of Conrad. I find myself reading the really good people more and more. I took a couple of days off and read *Pendennis* last winter. I went on a Dickens kick when I was reviewing too much — being forced to read second-rate people. Recently I've been reading Cortázar, the South American, and Michel Fornier.

Do you like reading modern novels or do you do it as a job, really?

As a job, mostly. Because when I'm writing, really writing, I try not to read anybody in that line at all except maybe Borges. Style is catching. I can read French, I can read the encyclopedia, anything cold and impersonal is fine. But I couldn't sit down, for instance, and read Lawrence Durrell or Hemingway or Burroughs or any writer who is very well known either for his personality or his style.

Because in fact you find echoes of it in your. . . .

Yeah.

What about the whole business of influences? A kind of specious question anyway. Do you think that any writers have been influences on you?

Oh, I think almost any writer I've ever read. I just get battered by other people's personalities. This is why novelists have such a hard time as reviewers, the battering makes them unstable. Influences.

Influences. Perhaps a critic could find more. *The Waste Land*, certainly — all of us are the Waste Land generation. And a lot of *New Yorker* people — that unrecognized Canadian, Mavis Gallant, for instance. And Gide and Camus — though I've never gone far into the Camus "thing" — but French writers have meant a lot. Technically, they do interesting things we don't manage to pull off in English very often. And Virginia Woolf: the fact that she existed, and wrote her diaries, more than her style and her books, because we are not at all alike. George Eliot. "Maggie hated blame."

Are there any kinds other than bad writing — other kinds of books, other kinds of writers — that you don't like?

I don't know. I'm a pretty much jump-into-experience kind of person. I remember when everybody was talking about "isms," I used to say I was an omnist, I liked everything; that isn't true, I'm a snob, in fact, but I want to like everything — multiplicity. But the fact is, I can't stand literary bandwagons, and nasty popular literature, like novels by Irving Wallace and Rona Jaffe, which I went through — the Rona Jaffe, anyway — for the *New York Times* because I was on their women's book list, but not their first-rate one — and blew a gasket on. And I was out of reviewing for a long time after that. I guess I was unfair. And then I get angry, too, when bad Canadian writers are published, because I know who's queued up outside the publishers' door, dying to get in, and there's so little money, it seems a shame to publish bad books here, but it does happen.

Do you find yourself competitive as a writer?

Yes, I'm an intensely competitive person, but I try to suppress it. I could sit and compete, mentally, all day if I wanted to. Other Canadian writers make me nervous, and I feel badly when other people make money and I don't. But I do live more in the centre of the literary world in Toronto than I should, because my husband does book programs for the radio, and that isn't a help, one hears too much gossip. It would be nice to retire and shrug and just work alone, and say, "Oh, well, it's a great big world, who's going to miss me?"

How important is it to you to make money or even sell well?

It's nice to be read. I think any writer who doesn't admit he wants to be read is a fool unless he's a mad genius. It's nice to be read, and by your peers — and one indication that one is read is a cheque from one's publisher. And to me money is important because I'm bad at handling it, and I have a great, guilty feeling that if I wasn't a writer, I'd be doing something that would bring a vastly more satisfying return to the family. I splash around being temperamental, I rush out and spend money on impulse and make long-distance phone calls, heavens knows what I cost them in typewriter ribbon. And funny little pretensions, and I feel I ought to put that money back in the family kitty. I need five hundred pounds and a room of my own.

You feel, then, the need to pay for your time as a writer?

Oh, you could never pay for your time, but you could make some return on the distortion of the life. There are not many women with non-paying careers. I send my kids to a day nursery and I sit around thinking how can all those other people afford it, until I realize they have a pay packet at the end of the week and that pays the nursery school.

Another question which may mean nothing at all but might be interesting: what sustains you as a novelist? There must be long periods of time when — you say you like it when it's going well and you hate it when it isn't going well, and there must be long periods when it isn't going well. What sustains you through all this?

I think, horrifyingly enough, having been brought up in the work ethic. I've had to sustain my own ego for many, many years, and I find this difficult — just to keep going along, to say I'm a person of value and what I do is all right to go on doing. Now I can say to myself it's all right to go on doing it because when you're not doing it, you're a less livable-with person, but the other thing is just telling myself, well, that's what you do and you go on doing it, and if you go on doing it for long enough, you'll get better at it. And for years I was sustained by my agent in New York, who fielded all the rejection slips and said: All right, write another one. And that, I think, is the best kind of maintenance. And of course my husband, who has this queer faith that it's all right to have a crazy wife.

You have two good books out and they must sustain you now. As you said, you have a special relationship with these two, because they're the two that were published. But that must be an incredibly supportive thing too.

It helped. It convinces you that it's all right to go on. The sensible thing to do is quit, of course.

How many novels have you written that have come close to a finished form, do you think?

I generally finish things, Graeme. I was taught to finish things as a child. My very first novel I wrote in collaboration with a friend when we were teaching at Montana. I was complaining that I wanted to be a writer and couldn't write and he said: It's simple, I will come in every morning and give you the plot and you will write ten pages and at the end of the month we will have a novel, and by golly we did, and we sent this off to this agent in New York, who wrote back and said: I couldn't consider marketing anything with a plot like this — but it's extremely well written and we would be pleased to hear from you again. That can't be counted as a serious work, but it got the ball rolling, and when I was in Europe I wrote a big scrappy novel with time and everything out of perspective, that was a real learning book, the other one was just a book on which the form was copied. That next one had some lovely things in it, some lovely pieces of writing, but it didn't hang together or know enough of time and space. And then the two that were published, and then there was one I did, a detective novel in Cyprus when I was there, just in order to — I'm not good at keeping diaries, so I wrote it in order to get down a lot of information, a lot of sensations I wanted to keep. And it was another restless time, so my husband made up the plot and I wrote. But I had been living abroad then for so very long that my agent wrote back and said: I don't know if you realize how little of this is real English. So that's three and two is five, and the one I wrote last year and the one I'm working on. But it's not a body of work yet and I'm glad they're not all in print. I don't think anybody's apprentice work should go into print.

Where do you think your centre is, imaginatively? In both your books the Latin Mediterranean image is very strong, a strong force set against southwestern Ontario. With the travelling around, do you consider yourself very Canadian, do you find your. . . .

Oh, I'm getting more and more Canadian every year — I've been back eight years now, and it's beginning to drive me crazy. Canadian in the pejorative sense of being moralistic and limited. I notice myself beginning to be judgmental the same way the rest of my family is, it's driving me crazy, but I have a comforting theory which would be nice if it worked out, but it probably won't. It is a completely phony theory, because the Mediterranean is a beautiful heartland and the reason I love it isn't that I feel I have anything in common with it — it's just because everybody loves it, it is a lovable body of water with many beautiful countries on its shores. But my theory is that the Great Lakes is the same kind of heartland. I suppose because I'm really happiest on water, on the Great Lakes or on the Mediterranean, but that's really being artistic and choosy, because of course you have to live where you have to live, so maybe nothing will come out of the Great Lakes after all.

The whole business of Western Ontario as a kind of culture — it looks as if it might be possible to make it into a mythological country somehow.

It seems to me that way, Graeme, more and more. I have a little bit of a hang-up because we happen to live in Toronto, and I think there's no way I could ever get my husband to live in Western Ontario. I think he knows Western Ontario for exactly what it is. He has to live in the actual present and I can live in never-never land if I want, but I can see it as something I'd like to see, you know with a thousand years of some more seemly civilization going on, and I'd like to spend more time there. I'm really not talking about Dow and Polymer — I'm talking about a thousand years of people making things.

This brings me to a very strong feeling in your writing, and it's in mine, and I think it's a Western Ontario thing, which is Puritan, strongly Puritan. You talked about the work ethic as one of the things that supports you as a writer. You've got to finish the bloody thing, you know.

Finish and do as good a job as I can, and I rewrite and I rewrite and I rewrite, and I sure don't think that's bad, we were brought up that way, and I'm beginning to thunder about things like that to my children, and I know it's making Victorians of them, but you know, it's nice to see a piece of decent work done. Western Ontario certainly taught us that, and I think what it also taught us was to use our imagination, because it was such a bleak environment. But now for one of my other theories: Places like Scarborough, for instance, are great sources of what we used to call juvenile delinquency, simply because they're so bleak. And actually there's no way of using your imagination to make a paved-over plaza more tolerable. But we had the countryside. We had those big flat fields, you know. I guess the tendency is to people them in your head.

That, then, is the advantage of Puritanism, the finishing of things, the need to do things, by their works ye shall know them, and that's certainly the only way one can become a writer, by writing, and the only way you can judge a writer is by what the writer has written. But Honeyman was particularly attractive to Minn because he wasn't a Puritan, and there's a quotation from Honeyman Festival: *Honeyman "made it look easy to live as if living were some road you strode along and not the Puritan hurdle course you had been taught to believe in." And there is the strong sense of a bad world somehow in both of your books, that no matter what ostensible problems may face Minn, nobody is better off than she is, in fact in many cases they seem to be worse off than she is, harassed and harried as she is, and it is the glittery tinsel people who come, not from a Scarborough but really from parking lots to that party. . . . They are no better off than she is, do you think, or am I . . .*

I'd agree with you there. I suppose my world view is pessimistic, which surprises me, because I had a happy childhood; whereas my songwriter friend had a sordid childhood in a big, poor family, always poor and miserable, and he bounces around singing while I sit in pools of gloom about civilization. I suppose there are some babies who were born afraid someone would drop them.

But has it anything to do with the hurdle course? I mean, Honeyman didn't seem to have it, did he? Honeyman was somehow free of Puritanism, even though he was not a Latin.

Yes. There are people who are not Puritans, and I notice this particularly in Americans. Have you ever noticed how Americans go straight to things without all these little moral hoverings and waverings? It's very Canadian to be hung up on morals. I can remember getting to university and being amazed when they told me that every choice was not a moral choice. They told me this in philosophy, but it was pretty hard if you'd been taught that every choice *was* a moral choice. More in Sunday school than at home, I think, and this tremendously church-oriented environment that I grew up in, and little girls do reinforce these kinds of things in each other, and I'm watching what is happening to my daughter now; but where every choice is a moral choice, life becomes almost intolerably complicated. Honeyman didn't have this, and I notice that a lot of Americans don't have it, or that a certain generation of Americans didn't have it, the Jazz Age people. The psychological generation are just as hung up, but for different reasons; and every choice is a psychological choice instead of a moral one.

Was the world bad or gloomy? It isn't for Honeyman, but it is for Minn, let's put it that way. The world is a wasteland, the Wasteland Generation as you said earlier, and Honeyman was not a product of the Wasteland Generation. Does that have to do with the Puritan hurdle course again? These culturally imposed things, are we crippled by them, by the Puritan tradition? Or are your characters crippled by that?

I think to a certain extent Minn is. I don't see her as being quite as gloomy as probably you do, because I think there is a tremendous amount of joy in that book.

Oh, I think there is too.

But — you mean the gloomy world she comes from?

Really what struck me about The Honeyman Festival *is that Minn is obviously the best person who actually appears in the present tense. All these people who pour into her house, I mean, this is the world coming in, and that's the gloomy world. It's the world, if you like, of the shopping plaza.*

Yes, that's the outside world. And she's also been in with kids for so long that she's afraid of the outside world. She's painting it in gloomier colours in order to make herself look better to herself, too. Fat people always look at thin people and say: Oh, you're going to die soon. . . .

Right. There's a kind of interesting tension in Minn . . . the kind of banality that her life has been reduced to. She says: "Life was comically reduced; sin a chocolate bar at a bus stop, adventure a forbidden bath," and it's banal on that level. At the same time she also says she knows that "Women abandoned with infants are dangerous animals." Is it the banality that makes her a potentially dangerous animal?

Oh, I think so, yes.

Or is it frustration?

It's interesting, because just after the book came out, somebody was interviewing me on one of the media, and we had a fairly good interview on camera, but the conversation before that had been very tense: she kept repeating her questions about the state of captivity as opposed to life in the "outside" world, about how Minn had felt that the more captive she was, the more glamorous and at the same time more threatening the outside world was, and how there was a frustration that expressed itself in different ways and could be violent, especially here, where one woman is locked up in one house with one child all winter. She kept harping on this, taking me back over it, and I couldn't figure out why. Then I twigged and asked her how old her kids were, and I realized that she was in Minn's bag and I was out of it, my kids had grown older; so there was a point where we didn't communicate. And I thought, I'm not in the cage anymore and the book sounds awful. What will my kids feel when they read it? That I hated them? Then I thought of the long winter days when you couldn't go out, but you felt you'd burst if you had to stay in anymore, and I thought, they'll understand.

And there is the whole — on the one hand, the great surge when she talks about premature labour pains, she talks about the really magical thing, the seismic thing that happens to her, there is that element of joy, and this great power that is there. But there are frequent images of the physical humiliation that one goes through at the hands of not just men — there's a nurse or a midwife or something who is equally impersonal, I mean to the girl she sees in the labour room, and Minn decides the girl's being punished because there is no son-in-law; but there is this whole dimension of the kind of humiliation that one has is not having one's baby leaning with one's back against the wall, as Minn considers doing at one point.

Yes.

So that the real world is not just apparently threatening — it really, it genuinely is threatening. I mean, for a woman under these circumstances, it's a tough thing — quite apart from being trapped.

Oh yes, also because of the very things which are really a part of the Puritan ethic still on this continent, because of the fact that there's a view of the human body as corrupt and a view of women as fairly corrupt, because of the Puritan attitude towards the reproductive facilities, with a certain amount of original sin coming in there. We had to develop a very disciplined, sanitary attitude towards doctoring, which is breaking down now, but which I found interesting: when I was in the hospital, I did find that the male doctors were much more sympathetic than the female doctors, because they could at least make dirty jokes, but the women couldn't do this, so really part of the humiliating nature of this was that nobody knew how to take any sane kind of humanistic attitude to childbirth, and you really wanted to be a Native squatting in a bush. At the same time, you knew on any realistic level it is better to be in a hospital bed than squatting in a bush, but that people didn't have their heads straight at all.

Minn says at one point that it passed through her mind to have it in the house, but the floor is too dirty.

Yes. Yes. We're not like that anymore.

There's a question which has been raised and pushed around, particularly with Honeyman Festival *but also with* No Clouds of Glory. *To what extent do you think . . . I mean, people talk about them as women's books. Does that make any sense to you at all?*

Sure, they're women's books, because they're about women and written by a woman. I don't like them referred to in the same tone as "women's magazines," though, because I'm terribly snobbish about women's things on that low, slick level. Because so many girls at university refused to use their heads and came down on me for using mine. Remember in our graduating year there were yearbooks and we went to be photographed in black gowns with bunny fur on them, and under your grad picture was what they called an "obit," a kind of slogan? I remember one girl who

stormed at me until I tutored her in English during exam week
when I ought to have been doing my own work. Under her picture, her obit read: "Be good, sweet maid, and let who will be
clever." If I meet her kid, I'll trip him into the swimming pool.
I don't approve of that kind of woman, I don't write for her, and
I bet when I have to go on television she's the one who watches.
Fortunately, there are other kinds. Remember that glorious song
from *The Music Man*, "The Sadder but Wiser Girl for Me"? That's
what I call a woman — and when I get letters and phone calls
from intelligent women, I don't think the term "woman's writer"
is pejorative, not at all. Who's afraid of women's books?

*Oh yeah, who indeed who indeed? . . . Are there some things you'd like
to talk about, is there any kind of area of your books or your writing or
anything which. . . .*

No . . . I always prefer being plunked into situations and having to
flounder out of them, rather than working out a theory. I have a
talismanic fear of theorizing as far as my own fiction goes: if you
know what you're doing, you're not giving the big unknown a
chance to creep in while your back's turned. I want to emphasize
that I'm not being mystical about this. It's just that making fictions
is an opportunity to add two and two and make five. If you're too
careful, if you work it all out too neatly, you'll only get four. I'm
willing to try to be intellectual about other people's work, but not
about my own — that's someone else's job. Or am I just opting out
and letting who will be clever?

TIMOTHY FINDLEY

TIMOTHY FINDLEY was born in Toronto in 1930.

Let's start with this. Why the novel? You have films, you have TV scripts, you've had your work in the theatre as an actor. Have you written any plays?

Yes, I have. Plays are something that haven't come as easily and as perfectly as I might hope. I was an actor for fifteen years, Graeme, and it's something I very badly want to get to, but haven't felt happy yet that I have established myself as a playwright. Not even in my own eyes.

Well, if it's difficult for a Canadian novelist to feel that he's part of the tradition, it must be almost impossible for a Canadian dramatist.

Oh, very true. But the tradition, you know, let's get right into that right off the bat, what do we mean by tradition? And then surely the only tradition you have to worry about is the tradition of the novel and the tradition of the theatre, and not the tradition of the Canadian novel or the Canadian theatre. I think you really have to put yourself constantly in that wider picture. I'm engaged in the art of literature. I'm engaged in the art of playwriting. That is all that matters.

Do you think that Canadian writers, novelists, are inhibited by the lack of a tradition or by their sense that they need one, a local tradition?

A little bit of both. The lack of tradition I put down to being a lack of traditional *respect*, not so much a lack of tradition in the sense of where our writing extends back to. Let me explain. Canadian novelists have not, traditionally, been accorded respect. I think our writing extends through any number of people who haven't properly been explored. I think the quality is unquestionably there in most of us, but I think we're afraid we have no quality because we haven't the tradition of being respected.

Let's go back to what the initial question wanted to be, and that is: given your experience with the other forms of literature, what is it specifically about the novel that attracts you?

Scope . . . that's Point A. And scope itself breaks down into so many different territories: the territory of colour, the territory of space, the whole territory of character. You can do any number of things in a novel that you can't do in other media. But the main thing is that films and television are not literary media. But plays — theatre plays are. They're a literary form in their own right — a play *lasts*. I mean, Chekhov will always be there no matter what stupid directors do to him. A director, I always think, in the theatre is like, excuse me digressing, but is like a reader; you know, it's up to the reader to get what he can out of the book. But in the medium of film and in the medium of television, you are not your own man. So scope . . . and I want to be my own man, and I love film and love pictures, and I love the possibilities that extend out of theatrical film into television. But there is no question, it has been reduced to a mere means of making a living, and if you have a facility for it, which unfortunately I have, then you can make some kind of living doing it, but it is a very destructive, particularly destructive to the necessary ego of the novelist — creative artist, goddamnit, let's always use that word. We are artists, and I'm absolutely adamant about that; none of these damn cheap tricks about writing, you know. We are very special people, you and me and a number of other people in this country who happen to write novels.

Special in what way?

We're very special people because we have the gift of insight that is not — I don't know quite how to put this, but between insight and accomplishment, there aren't blocks. Now we all know there are writer's blocks and various psychological hang-ups that you get into, but what I really mean is that many people have insight, but no ability to go from insight to paper or from insight to dissemination, and that's one thing that we have that is special. The other thing, of course, is a point of view which in each case is special but also as a group is special, and very precious. To our great shame, as Canadians, we have the knife of McLuhan in our backs. (*laughter*) I always feel that. We share the same dentist and we often meet in the office, and I look very coldly at him and he looks very surprisedly at me looking coldly at him. (*laughter*) He may never know why. I won't speak to him.

What I'd like to know is what difference film makes to the novelist. Does it free him in any way, or can you learn from film? I'm not talking about tricks necessarily; demands perhaps?

I think one thing, really the only thing, you do learn from film and from television is what writers used to learn being newspaper journalists: what Hemingway extracted from the *Toronto Star* experience and the *St. Louis Post* or whatever the paper was he worked for down there, and we now can extract that from writing for television. You learn a certain discipline and a certain thing about economy. It's that simple.

Okay. Another kind of question. What do you like best about your work?

Sleeping in in the mornings. (*laughter*) That's crazy. What do I like best?

In your novels, what do you like best? What do you think you have succeeded at best?

I have a twisted view of life which is mostly a way I see and a way I hear, which I think has great value, certainly has value to me, and once in a while it reaches out to other people, and that is tremendously important. People are always saying why do you write, if you have all these disclaimers about ego and so on? What nonsense it would be to sit down and write and not publish. Of course you want that. The stronger the thing inside you is, the more people it has to reach, and nothing happens if it doesn't work this way. That's what you're doing, you are either screaming at someone or you're screaming on someone else's behalf even if it's a totally fictional character. I feel sort of silly sitting here saying all this to you, you know this, but what pleases me most about my work as a novelist is my own awareness of having that special twisted view, which is a dependence on the insane people to do sane things. The ultimate sanity comes from the insane, I believe. Now — be careful! What I mean is — we call the *sane* "insane." In fiction you have to heighten this, treat it symbolically.

Uh-huh, uh-huh. What do you like least about your work?

My total inability to relate . . . sexually, oddly enough, to areas of sex which either don't interest me or in which I'm not personally engaged. I suppose I mightn't have felt this if I'd been a writer fifty years ago, when the whole question of sex in literature didn't exist. I'm not saying I can't cope with this. I can, but again it is always from that slightly twisted, sort of "off to one side," kooky — not really kooky — it isn't kooky to me, I love it, but (*laughter*) I hope you're getting something from this. For instance, I have often sat down and tried to write a love scene between a completely normal man and a completely normal woman, and there is no way I'm ever going to do that without it turning out to be the biggest laugh of all time. It always becomes terribly, terribly funny. Whereas with someone like you, and other writers, I often feel: Oh, why can't I do that, the way they accomplish that sexual charge in one sentence is — but I try, I put down, you know, he reached for the something-or-other and it's all just hysterical. (*laughter*) It's all very, very funny. And I don't know whether it is because my own sense of sexual timing or whatever is out of "whack" with everybody else's. (*laughter*) . . . Terry Southern would love that, wouldn't he? But you know what I mean, and that is an area I feel I have no talent in whatsoever, and I want to have talent in that area. And another thing — I know there is total liaison between all the genes in me and all the genes in all the other people in the world. But I very often feel disappointed and sorry and I work so hard sometimes to achieve a thoughtful connection in there with ordinary life, but I can't. As a writer, I mean.

This is obviously a by-product of what you like best about your writing.

The strangeness, right. It probably shouldn't bother me, but it does.

In what way is writing important to you?

I'm going to say the corniest thing in the world, but it is true. I write because I must, one simply must do it. I don't know why. I think it is very dangerous to find out why.

So in some sense there is nothing else that you really want to do?

No. It's my genius, and I mean that with all the abeyance to the gods that is proper. I think it was Cocteau who said this: he said: Genius is really only a form of memory. And I often feel that that's what it is, you're putting down all kinds of insights that stem from some kind of unbroken atavistic memory of what is in you because you're a human being.

Not merely personal memory then?

No, no, no. It is totally atavistic memory. You go right back to the beginning of time in so many things inside of you that — I'm very Jung-oriented. I hate Freud, but I love the old man sitting on his mountain. I love all that, and his mythology, and I believe all that too.

How did you start writing?

I started writing first of all when I was sick and wanted to entertain myself, occupy myself, not entertain myself, occupy myself in some way. I had pretty nearly a year in bed with one of those blood diseases. And this was in that crucial adolescent period, and I just wrote long novels which unfortunately got destroyed in a fire and I really am sorry they did. I would hope that no one else would ever see them, but I would like to see them again myself. They were great fun. Romantic. Then it all got put inside when I got into the theatre and thought that that was going to be my outlet, and it turned out to be partly my outlet, but only another way of getting to the writing, and then about five or six years into my professional life as an actor I got into a very long run of something and had met this fascinating actress, Ruth Gordon, who was in the play, the long-running play, and I wrote something for her, and that started it going. That was what I did all day, I sat at a table and I wrote.

Do you have any special sense that your childhood or any other time in your life is especially useful or important to you as a writer?

Oh, puberty, I guess, basically, because that is when it all comes together, and — no, I think all periods of life are equally important as you progress beyond them. It's very hard to find your way through the period you're in at that moment, or to see it as having any particular merit or value. I don't know about you, but I certainly couldn't write anything about what's happening right now, while it's happening to me. I couldn't get near it, except the basic things that stem out of the past, which is the growing sense of panic, the growing — those things you can use, but not what happened yesterday.

The growing sense of panic; do you find that? You used that as an example. . . .

It's my prime example; that's partly what I'm beginning to be about. I wrote a poem for Phyllis Webb — who, by the way, should be part of the great literary mythology of this country and one day will be, in which — I do most of my thinking sitting on the john, it is one of the places I do a lot of thinking. I can't go to sleep until I've wound down, and the obvious place to wind down quietly, away from the other people in the house, is in there. And the tiles in our shower are red, and Phyllis's poems, and Phyllis's life, dwell much on the art of death in many guises, and this poem came to me which I'm not going to be able to quote, but I did have this vision of myself in that red corner bleeding, and I extended that thought to her humorously; but every once in a while I get an awful sense that it may happen, and I don't mean that dramatically, I mean that's the awful part of being what we are, is the weight of the vision of what is beyond all those doors that keep opening, and panic, coming right back to where we began, is the terrible panic that they're taking — and Jesus, don't ever tell me that "they" don't exist — they are taking our lives and our world away from us, by building roads, and killing animals and saying no to life. And that's my panic. I just become a total maniac in the car on the way into the city, for instance. I go crazy. I can't stand it, and one day I may not be able to stand it at all — although the marvellous thing, Graeme, is that really, something about work brings you out of that, right?

Right.

Maybe it is the work that saves us.

Yeah, I have the sense, you know, if I was to try to say what one of the most important things for me about writing is — I'm not sure whether it's the imposition of, or discovery of, order.

Even if the thing is something you force on it by being determined that there has to be reason and order; you can create it out of any kind of chaos, even if you have to open the door in the morning and go out and see that that order that you've imposed doesn't really exist. You have made it exist for a moment, and the moment can come back.

Do you enjoy writing?

Love it . . . I love it as itself. I hate all the other stuff that goes with it.

What other stuff?

Loneliness. If you read *Death in Venice*, there is a little passage, about three paragraphs, maybe it's one long paragraph, where Thomas Mann describes Aschenbach or whatever his name is, and shows how loneliness has its various sort of positive things, but that it also perverts. Loneliness perverts, and it is, oh god, a beautiful passage, and I wouldn't attempt to say anything more than loneliness perverts, and this is very disturbing, very upsetting, and you have to go through that to be a writer.

Right. Have you been lonely as a writer, not lonely like writers are lonely, but lonely in a way that you think could have been avoided?

So much of that has to do with private life, Graeme, which I am quite happy to go into, but I think it extends into that world, no question. I feel that the way you live very often cuts you off from people that you shouldn't be cut off from, and I'm speaking of people doing what you do yourself: other artists. You're intellectually lonely: no one — hardly anyone "understands" you, because your whole life — maybe I should say your whole *existence* is an intensified searching — not for your own identity — but for your *work's* identity. And this intellectual loneliness leads to your being emotionally cut off. It isn't merely eccentricity of spirit, you know, that makes so many of us seek the "red corners" of our lives — or that so many of us drink. I just throw that out — uhm. But we have an obligation not to be weak. This goes back to the other thing. Take me, for instance: who wants to spend their life alone with a lot of maniacs screaming, "Let me out of your mind!"?

What about being a Canadian? Do you consider yourself a "Canadian" writer?

Yes. I do. Very much so. I mean — I *am*, so that's all I have to say. I think you "are" the — what? — the Nationality of wherever you happen to achieve your sense of value. For me, that was Canada. I was born and raised in Toronto.

Why did you write about Hollywood? This obviously has caused some problem.

I've been there. And aside from that, it perfectly suited everything I wanted to do with that book, and it perfectly suited everything that happened to be going on in my head at that time, which is how all books are achieved. You don't sit down and say, I think I'd like to write a book about Hollywood. I didn't do that. But at the same time, I would like to remind people that I've never heard anybody complain that Graham Greene writes so much about Africa, or that Margaret Laurence wrote about Africa or that Joseph Conrad's greatest novel was set in Africa. Or that D. H. Lawrence wrote about Mexico.

Or David Godfrey writing about. . . .

Or David Godfrey writing about Africa. So why is that peculiar to Canada, that whole thing? What do you mean, he didn't write about his own backyard this time out — Jesus! It's infuriating.

But there is the fact — and you mentioned Margaret Laurence, and we mentioned David Godfrey — they have not been ignored or have not been chastised because they write about situations outside Canada, where you apparently have been.

But I think it happened to me because of the moment, you see. *Myra Breckinridge* came out that month — another — more spectacular — book about Hollywood — which claimed, I think you'll remember, a good deal of attention. Also, my Canadian publishers weren't behind me. Do you know they didn't even *know* I was a Canadian?

Do you think that one of the reasons that you have a problem is that you're writing about the States and Canada's particular paranoia at this point is the States, whereas we are not really worried about Canadians writing about Africa, we don't feel threatened about that?

Well, yes, it could be, except that the world I reach for, in whatever piece of writing it happens to be, is always a symbolic world anyway. So if I give it a name, then that name should be classed as a symbolic name. It isn't a real Hollywood, as a matter of fact it's a symbolic Hollywood.

Well, it's perfectly obvious if one reads the book carefully why it is that you took Hollywood, even if it isn't that Hollywood, why you took Hollywood as a perfect place for what's going on, because there isn't a better place.

There isn't a better place. There isn't a better place for the people that I created to meet and all come together.

Okay. Do you think there are any obvious advantages or disadvantages in being a writer in Canada right now?

I think there are tremendous advantages. I'm grateful that I came along at this moment in "Canadian literature." I think this is the moment when it is going to happen, when identity will blossom for individuals, and people will suddenly realize, My god, we have writers; we don't need "Canadian" writers, we have writers. I think that's the great advantage in the moment that you and I have come along. I think the disadvantage is implicit in what I said earlier about what I have to do in order to make a living, that if you have to go outside of your true profession, then that's very dangerous and very upsetting and it has all kinds of other disadvantages too.

What is the novelist's role? Does he have any responsibility to society?

Yes, he has the responsibility not to be irresponsible: of recognizing that what he wants must be of major importance, first *only* to him, and then out there. He must be very careful how he assembles the emotional impact of what he wants to say so it doesn't lash back in some peculiar way. It's all an attempt not to say what you don't want to say. You've achieved art when you cannot be misconstrued, and I think that's your responsibility. Your responsibility to society is — it isn't that I don't know the answer to this question, it's that I'm trying to do what I just said we should do. I would draw it up as a list of negatives — don't ever pontificate, don't insist that you and you alone are right — but there is no question that if you are in this affair, and I'm carefully avoiding the word *business*, but if you are in this affair, properly, then you are a prophet in some way. The mystery enters at this point, knocks on the door, and washes away anything further I can say.

Does it have to do with the atavistic memory?

Partly, but why do we need — why did they need Homer? Why did they need him? Why was he encouraged to exist? The encouraging of that existence came out of need. They need us.

Have you any idea of why they need us?

Because the certainties are so frail — frail and far between. The majority of human beings don't know who they are, or why they are. Many don't know where they are. This is the great sadness, is not knowing. But they do want to know that they *should* exist. Comfort. We provide a kind of comfort. We provide a kick in the ass. We provide all kinds of things that we all need. We need our floodgates to be opened. Novelists do this for us. I'm not saying this at all well, because it's too mysterious and too — Go right back to your question and let me just say yes. (*laughter*) You can't intellectualize about it. I'm sure other people can, I can't.

I mean the obvious kinds of things when you talked about Jung and about a sense of magic and a sense of the great importance it has for you. I mean, it's obviously a part of the way you see our role. I remember a farm broadcast talking about old buildings in Ontario, and the guy said: If we tear them all down, if we tear down all the relics of our past, we will be lost in the present. And in some sense I think perhaps one of the things the writers do is to help us stop being lost in the present. Anyway. Anyway. Does being a novelist, an artist, demand a particular selfishness?

Yes.

What kind of selfishness? Or do you want to elaborate on that?

I think there's an obligation to elaborate on that slightly. I started out with the wrong concept. I started out with the concept of gentle Jesus, meek and mild. But that is not what we are obliged to adhere to. Gentle Jesus, meek and mild, in fact went into the temple and destroyed everything in sight. That is what *we* are about, and that is selfish. It is self-centred in the sense that it is our vision of the temple as a clean place that makes us clear it out. Which is what Jesus did, and therefore meek and mild you cannot be, and therefore all things that contribute to anything that isn't meek and mild are self-centred, because you have to drive through other people's concepts, other people's needs towards that thing that you need more than anybody else needs what they need. And it is bigger than what they need. And I'm sorry to say it, because it probably is more important because down in there in the temple, they're farting about with the temporal, and all art is about anything but the temporal. It's a preservation of the future.

Good. What about selfishness in the day-to-day need to do it? Presumably you do a lot to protect yourself.

You're rude as hell to everybody that comes in the door and you're terribly rude to anybody who phones, and you have to be mean in the proper sense of that, you have to be mean with your time, have to be mean with your spirit. It's a very ugly business in many ways, and very like the theatre — with its self-centred disciplines — which I went through too — very ugly in that sense. You've almost got to be sadistic in some ways, in some areas of your own life. But never forget: artists are harder on themselves than they are on anybody else.

For you, is it the importance of the book that justifies the meanness, the selfishness?

No, it's the panic, again I come right back again to panic. You've got to get it done. I mean, it's like saying: Excuse me, I've got to go to the bathroom, and if everybody started to prevent you from going to the bathroom, there would be disaster. Or I'm going to have a baby or any of these things, and if people tried to stop that from happening, there's disaster, which is sore news for everyone, not just you. The creation of a book is exactly the same way.

So writing for you is a kind of birth, or at least, not a birth, a. . . .

Yes. Well, I mean. . . .

It's a force that must come out of you.

It's got to come out of there because it is in there and it's a physical weight, it's a — I can't speak for you, but I certainly can speak for several writers I know, and I dare say I'm speaking for you indeed. You'd go crazy if you didn't get it out. Well, it's not worth anybody having one more crazy person around, is it? Unless the craziness happens to be sane. (*laughter*)

Let's talk specifically about the books, and we'll begin with the Winslow family in The Last of the Crazy People. *They are clearly at a dead end for a lot of reasons. Could you elaborate on the reasons for what's more than an impasse even — it's a decadence, isn't it?*

It is a form of decadence; it is a — I'm not a symbolist in an overly conscious sense. I enjoy them, but I think sometimes symbolic meanings of things don't come to you until the work is either through or nearly through, and then I think sometimes you go back to heighten the use of a given symbol. But the Winslow family became symbolic to me after the whole thing was finished. First I was writing about specific things inside of myself, organized things that wanted to get out, you know. But ultimately I realized that one of the things that I had said in that book had something to do with this impasse, and that the Winslow family, as individuals and collectively, represented a lot of values and things that must go. And it was a child who, you know, in the Biblical way of putting it, delivered them from their torment, and that has its obvious symbolic overtones too.

The values of tradition that you see having to be destroyed or dismissed or gone beyond, do you see them as social values, do you see them as a sort of Canadian experience?

Yes. Definitely. In fact the particular situation in that book is peculiar to Canada. It doesn't exist anywhere else in the world, that kind of family. It has to do with some of our social history not worth going into except in the very broadest sense, and that broad sense covers the fact that Canada, being the age it is, had a rise towards a power structure, a rise towards a kind of aristocracy at the turn of the century. Even in a country as young as the States, given its extra one hundred years of establishment, there is an aristocracy; which, as all aristocracies are — was founded on money first, but its cumulative extension becomes intellectual, political, and cultural. We've never had a chance to have that happen in this country, because the rise came at a moment of cataclysmic change: the turn of the century. War brought it down; we then became, after the First World War, a cultural eunuch; we were neither male nor female, but we had the propensity of feeling one thing and of being another. A very bold way of putting that is to look at all the knighthoods that were created, all the fortunes that were created, all the businesses, all the power that was accumulated by various people in *one generation*. And it so happens that my grandfather was one of those people who accumulated power. He was a fine and valuable man, but by 1921 he was dead; by 1921 the whole structure of this country from coast to coast, in every possible area, was altered, changed forever. In my grandfather's case — the thing that he had started was left nowhere. The whole era left a residue of these people, it left a residue of Winslows, of lost people with nowhere to go and no essential background, except two generations before that they were farmers. Now there's nothing wrong with being farmers and there's nothing wrong finding yourself in some kind of limbo; but there's a great deal wrong if you cling to the limbo as a haven and deny the farmer's values of practical survival, and this is what the Winslows did.

In reading the book, the resemblance, the cultural resemblance I guess, to Five Legs *was very obvious to me.*

Well I felt that too, very strongly. They're out of the same world, no question.

It's a different, for want of a better word, class of people. Where mine are solidly middle class, yours are upper middle class, potentially upper class if we had one. But they were crippled animals like my people.

Yes.

The role of death. In both books, but in this one particularly, you talk about being, what is the Biblical phrase, delivered from one's travails? And it's the "Frankie and Johnny," the killing for love — could you elaborate on that at all? It's the only thing he could do.

I must say, that came out of an experience in my past, where this had happened to a family that I was aware of, and knowing the story, as well as the future extension of it, I was able to put those two things together. In the true story, there was a child who killed one of his parents and one sister and one other person who happened to be in the house, and made an attempt on the other lives in the house, but failed. Then he went, as Hooker does, into the hospital and suffered; but ultimately, in real life, he emerged. And I was thunderstruck by what I considered the beauty, in the sense of the simplicity, of his statement when someone then, at that much later date in his life, said to him: Can you tell me why you did it? He said: Because I loved them so. And for me, that's all he needed to say. It's a terrible, terrible thing, and all that was implicit, but that was reason enough to give me the sense of the killing in that book, *The Last of the Crazy People*; though this did not come until I was halfway through.

So it was a discovery?

A discovery all the way through.

A bit of an aside here. How much of your writing is discovery and how much of it is imposition? If that's the word.

I'll steal back something here. There was an interview which I read the other day that Tennessee Williams gave to somebody in the States. I was staggered because he said something that I had both said and known for a long time. What happens when I write? The first thing I see is the person, and the person will come and you'll hear this in your mind. (*knocking sound*) And you go to the door and you open the door and standing there is Hooker Winslow with a cat in his arms. And he says: I'm in trouble, babble, babble, babble, and a scene evolves, but it's all around the arrival of this person. It's the arrival of a person that comes first, then the milieu: where do you belong, who are your people? Then the story comes. So it all comes in that order. And I don't think you know much more except that I'm now learning that it's very important to build what I call a brick wall first. Then everybody has to get in the cars and drive towards the brick wall. They're all driving towards that brick wall, and you have to have in the structure of your writing the brick wall: they must all either pass through or crash against the brick wall — and the brick wall can be any given event.

Again coming back to the use of "Frankie and Johnny," how much of Hooker's response is love for his family and how much is a sense of betrayal?

I think the betrayal aspect was something that was so personal that I try to turn away from it even now as you ask me that question. We all face this. You can do things on paper that you can't make your mind do. I was betrayed and I have betrayed and I will never go into that. But there certainly is a great deal of betrayal there in the book. The love thing — I think as a result of my awareness of betrayal on both sides, the love thing was forced into a position that luckily in that book works; it might not have assumed that position if I had been able to be more honest about betrayal. Sometimes artists, especially writers, must be harder on themselves than is bearable.

One thing that you have done, it seems to me, you have a child, a very open child, and a child with great needs, none of which are being satisfied — I mean his mother at one time says: "God Damn it Hook, will you get out of here," and he's got his older brother who in one sense he really worships, but the only thing open there really is the possibility of croquet. (laughter) You know, because the older brother is totally, psychically emasculated by his experience, and so the betrayal of Hooker is really a cultural betrayal, isn't it? The personal one, you couldn't put your finger on any member of the family and say: You should have done differently. Because in fact they are all totally trapped in their own sense of having been betrayed or used.

Used by time and used by history too, as much as anything else, as much as by other people. And the one thing that comes absolutely out of real life in that book is, again back on this loneliness thing, that was my childhood. I spent my whole childhood with maids, sitting in kitchens, and that was why, when I went to the theatre and saw *Member of the Wedding*, it formed a great crisis in my life to go and see that little girl sitting in that room with that maid. I've never gotten over the fact that that woman, Carson McCullers, had put me on that stage, and that that was what writing could do. There's an answer to something earlier: it's the power it may have on you that makes you feel writing is important. More important than anything.

I recall when The Last of the Crazy People *came out, a number of people remarked on the influence, they said, of Southern writing, American writing. . . .*

Southern Gothic. Well, it's true, it's there. I went through a McCullers/Tennessee Williams "period." But not the others — unless you call Styron a "Southern writer." Certainly my writing draws some of its character from Carson McCullers — because she wrote so well about *my* life. My sense of scene structure comes very much from my early theatre experience, which came about at that moment when Tennessee Williams evolved as a master. That was how I first had my visions, out of that mould. I don't think one has to apologize for that.

You're not being accused.

I'm not being accused, no, but I did — I must say, here he got all defensive — (*laughter*) I did get very upset when people failed to recognize that, I think as Nathan Cohen pointed out, sure it's Southern Gothic: Southern *Ontario* Gothic. And *that* exists.

And the sense of decadence. I think perhaps because we are so monolith-ically middle class as a country, a lot of reviewers, not even critics, are totally aware of the nature of the dead end of the Family Compact or the dead end of the thwarted robber barons or whoever you described.

You've hit it right on the head, and that is it, the dead end of the Family Compact. It couldn't be better said, and those were the people I grew up with. And all the pretensions that have come out of that, which are tragic pretensions, and of course comical — because it's tragic, it's equally comical. In fact, I would love to explore it again.

Right. I move from the first book, an Ontario book, a family book, there's a big leap, a big apparent leap, to Hollywood, to a much more public world. What sort of things led to that leap?

Ambition. Also the larger picture of wanting very much to get involved in larger ideas. Some parts of *The Butterfly Plague* — Don't make the mistake, Graeme, of thinking that because it became larger, it didn't home in on families too, because to me the Damarosch family is again a family that has great significance as a family of people. They're very like the Winslows in their way. Only instead of having an Iris who is to sit in the kitchen, you've got a Naomi — a mother who sits in a darkened bedroom. They really are one woman. And the figure of that woman haunts me and will probably be in all of my books. The Iris-Naomi figure is of the brooding woman of non-intellectual sensibility. Many women resent this representation of themselves. Right or wrong, I maintain these women exist. I've known them and they are inevitably fine people. They cope. Ever heard of that?

Could you elaborate on what Naomi and Iris have in common?

The embrace, the non-sexual embrace of the mother. By that I mean no-sexual, in the sense of man-woman fucking, you know. They can give without having to channel their giving through sex.

They have that, but they also both of them have a much simpler view of the world than any of your other characters.

Yes, but on the other hand. . . .

When I say simpler, I mean more immediate.

Right. Intellectually, I think they're probably smarter than anybody else, because everybody else has fallen into some kind of intellectual trap where their point of view is twisted away from reality by the brain — whereas the Iris-Naomi point of view is hyper-realistic — it's always based on undiluted reality. There was one moment I was very pleased to get onto the paper in *The Butterfly Plague*, which is the moment when Ruth, the daughter, appears in Naomi's bedroom, and they go through a thing in which Ruth tries to get her mother to tell her all the answers about life.

Page 145. (laughter) I just wanted to ask you about that. Let me read this: "Naomi said: 'Now you listen to me, you just listen. There is a flaw, you will accept your blood and let that be the flaw I speak of.' She paused and went on. 'Each man is race, potentially a whole race but each man is flawed. Great intellects are held prisoner in the bodies of impotents. Physical beauty is trapped in the bodies of Lesbians and homosexuals. Poetry is consumptive, artistry is bound in by insanity,'" and so on and so on. And she sums up by saying: "'And we, like royalty, are over-bred'" — which again is the Winslows, isn't it. "'But the greatest flaw of all, the very worst, the most destructive, and as I said before the seat of all our woes and pain is this dream, this impossible quest for perfection.'" Is that the passage you referred to?

The whole of that passage is what I was leading up to. I was leading up to say at one point, and I can't remember what the question was, but Ruth asked her something and Naomi had no answer, which is the first time that had ever happened to a character for me, and I just let her have no answer. Why strain? If she had no answer, then neither had I, in the sense of creating that character. But as far as that's concerned, I'm glad you chose that, because that's one of the other — god, we all suffer so in this world of ours, don't we, Graeme? — the other things about panic and torment that I was talking about which I think are important to us, and that is that sense that I was brought up with, which was, you can never suc-ceed, you will never, never, never make it. You haven't got it. No one has it. But there are these gods — and that is to me the great tragedy, that our mythology is involved in the impossibility of per-fection. We're taught to look up — to be *humbled* by impossibility.

I came across a quote by Shaw yesterday, browsing, and it said: "Beware the man whose God is in the skies." (laughter) Is that the kind of thing? I mean, there's no question in both books that there is a kind of need for perfection, and that if one can't achieve it, one will have nothing.

One would have nothing, but also the whole thing is bound up in that sense of longing, it's the longing for the one perfect — as with Ruth it was the perfect child, which extends to the whole racial thing which is in that book. But even perfection is flawed.

Ruth's search for perfection, or need, in the most fundamental sense her need — well, there is the clear parallel with Nazism, and racial perfection, that kind of perfection, and the evil that results from it.

The evil that results from it, but also the thing which again I think is fascinating both from a literary standpoint and from a standpoint of real life, which is that terrible thing that we all have, that I'm convinced we all have inside, our need for perfection which tells us that they had some of the right ideas. But our abhorrence of Fascism, Nazism, or hopefully our abhorrence of it, certainly mine, turns us so quickly from that thing that we find ourselves saying, That thought didn't happen. I didn't think that. Stop it, you know. That is the thing that fascinated me about *The Butterfly Plague* — it was that terrible flirting with — "I want perfection, Mother. Tell me how to get perfection." *You can't have perfection unless it is going to be evil.* Wow! That's strong stuff. I don't mean I've accomplished a strong thing. I just mean that's a strong thing to be confronted by.

A rather curious thing, after Ruth's union, real or imagined, with the "messenger of race," this curious lurking, ever-present figure, she sits by the brush fire and she discovers she'll never be afraid of fire again. And you say that "the smell of fire and smoke could never terrify her again . . . the smell of them was the smell of imperfection burning, being burned away forever." Now what did you mean by that?

Why do you ask such questions? (*laughter*) What did I mean by that? (*laughter*)

What did you mean by it in the context, right, a terrible question. Did you mean that the burning away of actual imperfection or the need for perfection?

In answer to your question, my instinct is to say now, which is, you know, some years after writing the book, the need.

The need for perfection, right, because the book ends on a very human, a very immediate level. After all this, the catastrophe and the unreality and the incest and the horror of what is going on and the fires and the dishonesty, personal dishonesty, it ends on a note of two young people very easily coming together, so that it's as if, because these characters have done it, because they have gone through it, somehow there is the possibility for an immediacy.

That is the great thing, there's always this possibility of the innocence, but to me, you've seen a nicer end to the book than I have.

I was asking, Tiff.

All right, fine. To me, the real ending of that book comes wherever it is where it says: "We all know that a plague lasts for seven years." So you know it's going to repeat itself. The whole damn thing is going to happen again in some other way, and of course, because it was set in the historical period it was, you begin to know, yes, you know what *did* happen — the Cold War — the McCarthy era — Korea — Vietnam —

You do leave it open whether or not the plague is going to come again for sure.

Oh yes, the thing is to define what the plague is. Somebody said that they thought it was tremendously significant that the homosexual and the black man went off together, whereas I had meant something entirely different, which is the weak depend on the

strong — it's that simple. The weak who are beautiful, that's Tennessee Williams, "All ye weak and lovely people," whatever that
thing is of his, "Don't fall behind with the brutes — go forward
with the poets." The symbol there to me is that that kid went off
with the one person who is going to survive come hell or high
water because that was the black man's tradition — he must.
Whereas the kid mustn't. I mean, he doesn't feel he must.

And hasn't got the —

Hasn't got the ability, no. He's queer. His genes won't survive.

*It isn't just perfection. One of the demands of perfection, which is true
in* The Last of the Crazy People *too — I mean the only reason that
Hooker can kill for love is because he has a perfect image of love, which
is the ballad image of love in a way . . . It is not just imperfection, then,
it is reality.*

That's it, Graeme.

*Your people are separated from it, or it becomes quite explicit that they
can't accept reality. Ruth in* The Butterfly Plague *says: "Everything
isn't a dream or a nightmare. Some things* happen." *Now that is a desperate assertion on her part, because she's in bad shape at that point.
And she also says: "We are the living dead, walking around dead until
we are forced by circumstances to live." Now this is true of the Winslow
family. She could be describing them, couldn't she?*

Yes. But I equally believe that of you and me.

*How does one break out of the dream or the nightmare? I mean, forced by
circumstance to live, or is there something an individual can do?*

I think there is something an individual can do. I think that is
implicit, too, in both those books and in everything else I have

written, including all the private things. For me the doing is my writing books, the —

For Hooker is it the killing?

For Hooker it is the killing, because that is the blessed relief of action. It's almost like orgasm in a funny way. It's a terrible striving for a necessary climax without which we do go insane. If I did not have the writing of books — I'd be an impotent human being — without climax.

What about the morality of climax, or is that less important than climax itself? For example with Hooker killing the family. Given the logic of the book, there is absolutely nothing else he can do, you know. He is totally. . . .

Right. That's it, that's it. The whole filament of tragedy, of course, too. It's to do the thing he must do, and that's what I mean by "orgasm" — it's to do that thing that simply must be done and, if you avoid that thing that must be done, then . . . wham! Ruth did it too, by imagining that reality happened to her. This was her particular kind of madness. With the exception of her mother, Naomi, everyone else is succeeding at getting *unreality* to work for them. Right? Therefore, Ruth reasons, if I believe in a different reality, I must assume it too can be *applied* to life. She forces her reality to work. She believes she is having that baby. Of course, she isn't. But, she believes she is — and she has discovered, by watching the other people in the book, that *believing* is all that matters. According to the way she perceives everyone *else* is making it through life, Ruth has entered the "real world." I'm very sorry, now, that I didn't *say* that in *The Butterfly Plague*, I mean, say it boldly in black and white. This is where you make mistakes you wish you hadn't. I thought that if I laid too much explanation into the book, I would destroy the character of the book, which is dream-like, nightmare-like. Also, another error or omission: all those events leading up to Ruth's "rape" of the Blond Man are historically tied in to what was actually happening back in Germany at that time — (events which Ruth must've read in the newspapers and translated into her own reality) — such historic events as the Kristallnacht, the burning of the synagogues, the Reichstag fire, the shooting of the German consul in Paris: all of these things really did happen . . . and their dates parallel the dates in the book when Ruth's "events" take place. What I was trying to express was that Ruth translated them into this "thing" . . . not even a human being, but a "thing" . . . almost only an *idea*, that went around murdering people and lighting fires and doing all these things. Now — in fact — her translation of reality was correct. An "idea" *was* going around killing things. The idea of Fascism. And she was also right, incidentally, about Alvarez Canyon too. The goddamn Plastic World was on fire and they tried to save it . . . everyone wanted to save the Plastic World of Alvarez and *they wanted to let all the real things die* up against that fence. And, too, of course, I'm saying in the book — this is all being repeated right now. This is a book called Hollywood, 1938 . . . about America . . . North America, *now.* I am appalled that no one saw that. But, this is part of the terrible frustration; when you realize afterwards, after the fact, that you haven't made it clear. Still, if you have chosen to be — perhaps with my work "satiric" isn't quite the right word, but let us say "satiric" . . . if you have chosen to be satiric, then you also have to accept the consequences of not being understood. But, it still doesn't kill the frustration. "Do I say this? Do I say that? What do I say?" People are affronted if you explain . . . and mystified if you don't.

How much do I get away with?

Yes.

What with Naomi talking about doing what must be done, living out what must be lived out, how did she do it, because she obviously in some sense is — the word isn't wise *in the sense of wisdom, but she is searching. She is real, let's put it that way.*

She is a realist in every sense; if you follow her story through very, very carefully, she does all the natural things. She doesn't just let them happen, she strives, and where she meets a wall and realizes it's too big for her to climb, she doesn't bother to try to climb over it. When she comes to the age when she can no longer be a film star of the kind that she was, she very gracefully withdraws. That is over. She takes her hemophilic child to all the doctors, she does all the right things for him. When they say there is nothing you can do, Mrs. Damarosch, she says: "We must live with this." She's dying of cancer, it's the same thing, the whole thing, she accepts the reality: that is her whole procedure through life, and I think that I ain't got it, but I see that that is what we must learn to do as a race, to live within the bounds of that large reality, which you define in books symbolically.

Dollie says in The Butterfly Plague, *it's really a kind of central thing, at least I see it as a central thing in your writing: "You die when you can't be real . . . when you can't see who you are, and when you cannot see what is." And that underlies the death of the Winslow family. Because they have no role, they have no sense of who they are.*

Right. It doesn't matter what that concept of reality is, either. It's when you lost touch with it, you know, when we are not we, we die. That's basically what *The Butterfly Plague* is about.

Okay. Let me ask a final question. Are you working on a novel now, or what is happening to you? You're involved with Jalna *and —*

Involved with *The National Dream* and with *Jalna*.

Both television.

Both of these are television series. They will engage my time and my energies for the next while. What I'm going through now is the end of a period where I wrote a novel which, as a consequence of many things, partly too much work in the other area, did not work. That was a great shock to me. It was an extremely pertinent novel, but it was a static novel, and I have to face the fact that that is so. It's a static novel, nothing happens. Comic things happen, but there is no central event — there is no brick wall as I said before. So I'm now at the place where — I hope this isn't going to happen for the rest of my life, but just now I am sort of confronted with a lot more of the closed doors that now I've got to get busy opening. Beyond these doors are feelings about novels too which I know I'm going to write, and I am determined I am going to explore the play, so I'm into a couple of plays as well. All that matters is that you go on writing.

Do you think that your experience, say, with film, you know, earning a goddamn living, and money — money for writers is necessary primarily to buy time — do you think that that has hurt you as a writer, as a novelist or as a dramatist or . . .

In the long run, no, nothing hurts you, unless you let it defeat you. That answers that part of the question. In smaller ways, I think it probably has, because it makes you impatient, for one thing, and I think impatience is a very bad mood in which to do any kind of creative work; but the biggest thing of all, Graeme, about all that world that we're talking about, the world of film and committees and television and so forth, is this thing of manipulation, that your mind is being, as somebody said — it's an expression in the current jargon that doesn't come naturally to me, but I liked it — this person said to me: "Now I don't want to play with your head."

God, what a marvellous image! Literally to me that meant taking my head off and sort of rolling it around the room and caressing it and then kicking it; and all this, all these things, that's what's been happening to me. Now I've left myself wide open, it's as much my fault as anybody's, but god, what a lesson. It's all that; they destroy the thing that you are, the very value you have is the first thing they go to, and they go to it with knives twelve feet long. But someday out of that is going to come a book or a play or a character or something. Of course it all has value. But — will I live? What I'm terrified of is, he finished writing *The National Dream* and he finished writing *Jalna* and he was killed by a car (*laughter*) and didn't get that other book written, you know, which is that thing about wasting time. Is making a living a waste of time? And that is a terrible fear, but you know that.

DAVID GODFREY

DAVE GODFREY was born in Winnipeg in 1938.

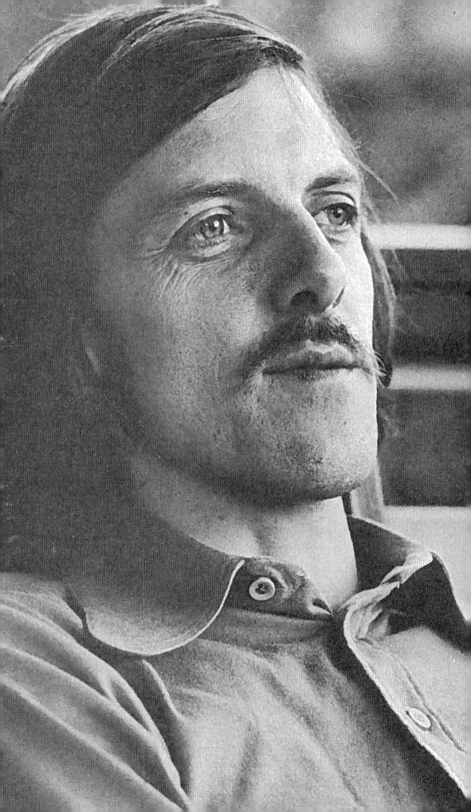

I'll begin with a general question. Do you think the novelist has a role? Does he have any responsibility to society or . . .

Well — it's a big question to start with. I found in my own writing as I've read a little more about how society is organized — the ideology behind our supposedly value-free society — that the wall between the individual as writer and member of the group disappears. There's a real tendency, especially for the novelist . . . the novel is a Protestant form as far as I'm concerned, basically, and it comes out of protest, and it comes out of a sense of the individual being very much alone. And once you get beyond that ground, it's difficult to write novels. A novel is an unhappy form in certain ways because you can't participate in it — it's a kind of art you have to do alone, and once it goes away from you, it's gone, you know, and it can't come back. If you compare it to music, where you can see your audience and feel your audience responding to you, then it's very indirect. So the role of the novelist in society is a very ambiguous one. If you are a novelist, as such, like James Joyce, it presupposes a certain relationship between you and the society. You don't relate really to the society; you relate to a bunch of other individuals, and in that case, circumstances affect your popularity. Most popular novels, in a sense, arise at the point where some group or subgroup is rising or discovering itself within the society, so that you have the origins of the novel in the rise of the lower middle class into the middle class in England, and . . . I mean there are exceptions, you know, like *Tom Jones*, which in a way is a defence of an old class or . . . one could say, a discovery by an old class of certain of its values. You have many other examples, the black novels in the States as people, the society, discovered itself. About four years or five years before the general ideological discovery, an intellectual discovery, the novelists come along and do it; and I think you'd probably say the same thing about women novelists, at least in Canada, you know. The lines really are all laid out four or five years ago by people like Margaret Laurence, and then the theoreticians come along and discover her on their ground. And probably the popularity of the women's novel will peak just like others have.

You see the novel, then, as a kind of, not prophetic in the mystical sense, but predictive.

Yes, in a sociological way.

You believe the novelist is a kind of weather vane for the way things are going, or they reveal forces in the society before anybody else?

Yes, definitely. You get those people who have a sense of social oppression, and they're a kind of weather vane and they speak for a group that's coming along but isn't quite vocal yet. A lot of African fiction comes out of the same kind of thing, and that's when the African novel was born, in the period of independence.

Okay. What does this say about the novelist, and about the novelist's relationship to his or her society? Are they more acute? Are they more perceptive or what is it?

Well, it depends. I mean, someone like Turgenev is probably more acute, more perceptive; in many cases, I think they're just more battered. Very few novelists, I think, of this type, Baldwin being one exception, are really that coherent in an intellectual way that they can try to describe fully what they are discovering. You know, it comes out in the fiction — that's the way it comes out, and it usually comes out of pain too. There's always a lot of humiliation in novelists' lives, I find. Those forces which later cause people to revolt in a social way, in them cause a revolt in a specific artistic way. One distinction that I make is that the novelist on the whole tends to register a protest against society and the way society is organized. Now there are other things you can do in terms of your relationship as an artist to society. You can praise and celebrate the society or record its histories, and write epics. You can also simply provide enjoyment for the people within the society; now certain novelists do this of course, and just accept the values and the mores of the society and tell a tale within it. It depends. I would put Arthur Hailey in this category, in these terms he's not a novelist, he's just a tale-teller, and nothing he says upsets or reveals society.

It supports it in many ways.

It supports it in many ways, yes.

While dealing with his own individual pain and perceptions, or whatever it may be, what kinds of responsibilities do you feel a novelist has, if any?

Well, it depends on the state of the culture. If the culture is *really* oppressed, then I feel probably he should be out leading a revolution. You know, you can't write under all circumstances. It gets tricky when the society is, you know, a mixed society, full of a certain amount of oppression but with a certain number of good things going for it. Then he's got to decide, well, in what way would he be most effective? But my basic premise is that everyone has a responsibility to society and the only way you can really lead a full life is in doing things with people and for people. As a young man, I was very impressed by Joyce and the whole bit of escaping the nets of religion and family and the state. But you know, that's absurd, because you're escaping life when you do that. And form for its own sake doesn't interest me as an artist.

So the novel, given it's a social form, it almost sounds as if it's a social action form or potentially a social action form for you.

Yeah, well, everything I do is. What I would like to see is people realizing that everything you do can have the same mixture of the artistic and the purposeful, and, you know, get away from these false distinctions. A novelist as "novelist" examining the most intricate portions of the novelistic form, that's a kind of Protestant specialization, you know. Why should you let the ideology of society push you in that path, and say: Look, you're a novelist — we brand you as a novelist and we'll judge you according to what you do with this form, whether you push it out another inch or not. That keeps the society functioning the way it is, in a sense, and to me the revolutionary thing is to ignore that and say: Well, that's one of the real prime dangers. Instead of being a super-revolutionary, going off to write your "great" novel, even though no one understands it in the society et cetera, et cetera, but it's "great." That's a mistake; you know, it's a dead end.

Isn't there a danger on the other side, though, that if you write within the context of some revolution or some idea of revolution or some idea of change, that you're as much trapped by that as you are by Establishment attitudes towards the novel?

Well, you have to be trapped by something. I mean, you have to accept compromises. No one is going to find the perfect way of life out of his own being. I'm far from an Emersonian. I don't think you can plug into any individual-discovered set of values, set of ideas. You know, they're all around you. Your society may have great lacks, and it's up to you to try and discover those and analyze them, and to bring as many ideas as possible into your own thinking. But you're going to be trapped by something or some set of ideas which you incorporate in your writing, your responsibility to yourself as a writer. In that sense you have to make sure that the set of ideas is as rich as possible.

A different kind of question. In what way is writing important to you?

Well, I'm sort of in a quiet spell now, the first one I've ever been into. I haven't had time to analyze this. Obviously, writing is very important as a way of proving myself, proving my existence and proving my quality — fame, you know, the search for — Freud is absolutely right, you do it for fame. You have a certain amount of respect from your peers for doing that, and I think that's a good motive, you know, you open up a lot more possibilities. First you drive yourself for that fame reason. I mean, you've got to get that first book out, those first two books, you've got to do them and they've got to be good. It's your whole identity. Once you've done that, you sort of stop and take a look and say, that's a crazy way to spend six years of your life, you know, putting all those words down on paper, because they don't — I mean, people say they're fantastic, but they don't really capture more than about three percent of your life, and it seems it would be better to go out and live some life and enjoy your children and make some money. You really wonder why you write. Certainly in Canada, you don't get any continuing support for being a writer. So in a way, it's important to me because it is, well, for two reasons. You look back and you read something that you've written, and maybe it doesn't have to be published, but in your notebook or somewhere, and you can't recall the situation, except that it's down there, you can go back into your own life and. . . .

You partake again?

Yes, *through* it, and that's really like living again. Yeah, then you have the choice, so I can spend two months capturing this day or this hour in my life or people around me's life, or in that two months I can go out and live X experiences, and you start balancing one against the other.

Two things there. One, you talked about writing as a way of proving yourself or establishing yourself with your peers. Do you have any idea why you chose writing to do that rather than another form or another way of doing it?

Well actually, I started out to be three things: a musician, an engineer and a writer. That was sort of the progress. I really wanted to be a musician, and then I decided, you know, in terms of social respectability, I'd be better off as an engineer, but I was writing — this was when I was fifteen, sixteen, seventeen, and most of what I wrote then was love poems to beautiful fifteen- and sixteen-year-old girls, terrible stuff, *(laughter)* but direct emotion going down on the page. I guess why I became a writer was I was better at it at that age than I was at being a musician. I couldn't hack the discipline of being a musician and, you know, writing allowed all the turbulent forces in me a means of expression.

A couple of times you've come back to "expression" or "putting it down" or "isolating" it; do you find that that is one of the central attractions or appeals of writing, being able to say it?

Yeah, yeah. Now right at that moment I'm not sure that I've got that much to say. I'm looking for a kind of big — big task. You get to a point where you've got a certain amount of turbulence in yourself, which is your psyche, and you've got to get it out, and you've got certain humiliations that you've got to get out, and once you've got them out, that particular drive dies down.

That's a kind of exorcism, is it?

Well, in a way it's involuntary. It's inside you and it's, you know, it's going to come out one way or another. You've got to get it down. That force dies, then you start thinking, what am I trying to do? Am I trying to make something great that society will treasure, or am I trying to reveal the society to itself? You know, you move out from what Joyce would call the lyric towards the dramatic or the epic in that sense. You know you have to pull in other people, pull in other people's lives.

How did you start writing?

Well, I went to — being a Nova Scotian, I went to Harvard after high school in Ontario — I mean, the Nova Scotian elite always goes to New England schools — and I took a course in contemporary American literature, and also a writing course with Geoffrey Bush's son, and I had a lot of competition with, you know, good young American writers in that time, and I wrote some good stories and enjoyed doing it. Then I came back and went to school at Trinity, and that was somewhat disastrous. That was the old Trinity, and I found myself in a lot of social conflict with kids from private schools whose lifestyle and life expectations were in complete conflict with mine. And I wrote as a kind of escape out of that, and also to compete with them.

What do you like best about your work so far?

Well, looking back on it, *New Ancestors* is coming out in paperback, so I've been proofreading the galleys once again, and I think the best thing I do is get outside myself, or at least split off some segment of myself that's close to someone else, and expand it into their life and, you know, write about them, write about other people. In *The New Ancestors*, that kind of big structure forced me to do that.

With New Ancestors, *as a first novel, one of the clearest things about it is the ambitious nature of the structure, you know, because you really are dealing with others, aren't you? Not only with others "personally" but others "culturally." To what extent did you set yourself that challenge, and to what extent was it unavoidable?*

Well, I started by working the Michael Burdener character, and in many ways Michael Burdener is simply an English me, you know, and I think what happened was that writing him out enabled me to get a certain distance on myself. I changed him a little, but I really got some things, some nasty things, out of myself, and the carry-over from that pushed me out into these other people. I set them up as his wife and whatnot, and then there were certain intellectual things I wanted to do. I wanted to really show what an African society revolution was like. But I think it might have bogged down in dialectics if I hadn't come back to the people who were in it, so once I had done Michael, then I had this structure as an analysis, which eventually just disappeared and the people whom I had put in took over.

What do you like least about it?

Well, I guess there are two problems. In a way, it's not really me, or really my society, any of it. It's not really me in the sense that — there's a certain amount of anguish and existentialism and a kind of intellectual overlay, which determines the patterns of the people, which has nothing to do with the patterns of my life: you know, I lead a very happy, exciting life, and I don't know how you get that into fiction. I'm not sure that you should *try* to get it into fiction, but I would certainly like to get it in some art form. The other thing is, you know, *Death Goes Better with Coca-Cola* is about a certain reticence in Canadian society, but it's all very symbolic, the people are real enough but it's a kind of shorthand book, and *New Ancestors* is about Africa, and there's great chunks of Canadian society which I would like to think about getting into.

Do you see the possibility of writing a comparable book about the Canadian situation, the Canadian experience at the moment, as in New Ancestors, *that kind of depth, that kind of richness, that kind of attempt to deal with all the things that are happening?*

Well, one of the problems is that I work a lot backwards from language, you know; that is, just almost visually I work with words, and musically I work with words. They do certain things, and I put them together and in a way the content is secondary sometimes — to deny the critics. (*laughter*) It's not that I have ideas or have a certain person and then words magically come up to describe them. I start with the words, put the words together, and the content of the people grows out of the words. I mean, this is my sort of infatuation with Joyce; in a sense you're trying to say things in a different way. You're really trying to open up the language and then you move back to the form part of it. Now in Africa, that was very easy to do. I mean, you have different dialects, different languages, you have strange kinds of English, you have a lot of new writers writing in different ways. You have a real richness in the people's vocabulary, in the conflicting vocabularies of a different culture and whatnot. Once you start writing about Canada, you get into the problem which I ran into in *Death Goes Better with Coca-Cola*, and that is, reticence is the natural form, you know, and you write these kind of tight-lipped stories. You can see it in the best Canadian fiction too, in a way. *The Stone Angel* doesn't have, if you look at it closely, more than I would say four percent open speeches, and *The Double Hook*. The speeches aren't real Canadianism. Purdy I think is great at getting it, getting it out, and Kroetsch is good too. The first piece of fiction I wrote was a novel about a Finnish lumber camp I worked in when I quit university, before I quit university, and there we had verbal richness, I just wasn't smart enough or trained enough to. . . .

We don't assume it's there.

Yes, you're just not — at that time, I was twenty years old, and you — it's terrible, but you just turn off the language. This was a lumber camp full of Finns and Swedes and French Canadians and Hungarians, you know, it was perfect, and so I went in there as a Frontier College instructor at night, teaching them how to speak Canadian English properly, and I shouldn't have been doing it. I should have been out listening and writing it down, which is what I did in Africa, and getting it all down so that you have pages and pages of notes and then, when you need a particular phrase, you go to one.

What is it about the novel as a form that appeals to you?

I sort of told you what frightens me about it, which is this individualism. I suppose what draws me to it is that there is a certain amount of tragedy in Western European Protestantism, and, you know, the novel is the form for revealing that, and that's where its power comes from. You know, Dostoyevsky and Turgenev, those to me are the models more than Joyce. You take the isolated individual or the decaying society, and you reveal it that way. I think I'll come back to your other question about Canadian society. My answer to that would be it's very difficult to get it all down in one particular novel. You'd have to work out a chain of novels, because it's a very, very disparate society, and you'd have to go at it historically too. I guess what I'm saying is, you'd have to push it towards the epic. You'd have to use your novels as portions of an epic.

Is that because we don't have enough novels, we don't have a tradition of people doing it for us?

Yes, partly. But you've got to go back over the last four centuries, is what I'm saying. I mean, I think it's very difficult to write a tragic novel about Western European society now because, mainly, there's no tragedy, there's just gross stupidity. You know, if I were an American, I don't think I'd write novels about it, because there's no cause, there's no force oppressing anyone except their own stupidity. I mean, Nixon is stupid and the people who are opposing him are stupid. You really get the feeling that — I mean, if you're Turgenev and you're fighting the Czar and whatnot, kind of a real evil, and the people are poor and they're serfs and the whole thing — but you know, when you have a population like Canada with all kinds of food for everyone and all kinds of libraries and universities and high school teachers and the whole thing, and good salaries, the fact that we would permit the Liberal government to sell the country out or permit the Liberal government to let the people on the investigation committees in Vietnam lie on behalf of the Americans, it's not evil, it's not tragic, you know, it's just stupid. And you really feel that you should be doing something about it, rather than writing about it.

Okay. Whom do you write for?

Ah — Margaret Laurence. (*laughter*) No, this is one of the problems. I used to be able to say, well, no one in Canadian society really *knows*: like Richler in a sense, I felt very alienated in society. No one in Canada really knows what is going on, and no one really knows how to write well, and this is the early sixties, and therefore I haven't got an audience. I mean, obviously nobody in my graduating class in Trinity College is going to read what I write, let alone understand it. Therefore, I write for someone who I feel understands, and I guess I still do that. I know I write for an ideal reader, someone who knows what I know, and I'd hope that the ideal reader would be happy with what I'd written. But in a way, one of the things I'm thinking about is that now that I am a musician again, well, it's interesting. Who *is* your audience? Why not satisfy them, take feedback from them? I play in this band now, Oketeke, which is all Africans. What we play best is music that we've written ourselves, and which uses a lot of traditional African rhythms, you know, in a new way. We also play all the standard rock and we play a lot of West Indian stuff because we play for West Indian audiences, and a lot of the popular African stuff, highlifes. And there the artist's role in society becomes very clear, because you're playing for — you know, most West Indians don't really understand African rhythm, and when you play them, it just sort of goes dead. And then you play their rhythm and they're happy, you know, with reggae and calypso, and they're contented, but it's not artistic for you to do that for them. Despite all I've said. It has a good social function, but it's not taking anything out of you. You are playing something which is known and fixed and given. Then you go and play for the dentists or whatever, and you play them North American rock and they're getting off on it and expressing their frustration and alienation, but again it's not artistic for you. And it's really only the stuff that you're creating and that's new that you can accept as an artist. It's all very well to say that you should have a social function and that you should be giving the people what they want, you know, but if what they want is too simple and old, then you just don't do it all the time.

What is the great attraction of Africa, what is the great attraction of the black, in your music and your novel?

Well, it's interesting, because what it was, obviously, was a sense of freedom as an individual to play music and directly express your emotion, as opposed to the, you know, the Protestant tradition in which you didn't express any of them, and the dead rituals of the United Church of Canada and the Anglican Church of Canada. That's what it was initially, I could express myself as an individual. Then you find the thing that really fuels that expression, in many ways, is a living social group, you know, in the sense of the responsibility of the individual to the group. And the dead thing in Western culture at the moment isn't the imposition of the society on the individual, really. It's the lack of feedback back and forth between the individual and the institution, the institution and the individual.

The lack of partaking, in a way.

The lack of, yeah, the lack of communion. (*laughter*)

In some ways one of the major concerns of most of the writers, say, in the age group that we would consider ourselves, making that a very flexible age group, has been to come to terms with, in many cases very angrily or in an injured way, with what you just called the United Church, Puritan or whatever it was, the lack of ability to express, the lack of ability to feel, the imposition of rigidity, but you haven't, except in passing, really, it seems to me, felt it necessary to deal with that head-on. You've been able to go off and look for the vitality which you found, say, in The New Ancestors, *in the new experience in Africa. Do you feel a need, or. . . .*

It's my Welsh ancestry partly. I think it affected me very strongly, maybe even more strongly than some other people who have been able to deal with it head-on, and I very desperately sought a counter-vitality. You see me now kind of charged up by having found the vitality; it may not be clear, but when I was twenty, twenty-two, twenty-three, I was very, very suicidal, you know, because of all that — that death force you and Symons write about so well, which I couldn't even dare to face.

Right, and then the thing is, do you think you'll ever need to, or want to, at some point, deal with that force?

Yes.

You see, my concern as a writer, obviously with Five Legs *and Communion, is a grim, even neurotic concern with what is destructive in all of that. And you haven't done that at all. There are a couple of relatives in* Death Goes Better, *but you meet them after the decay is almost terminal. (laughter) I mean old uncles, you sit there in the front and they don't even recognize you. They sit there with their cups stuck in the egg on their plate, you know, and it's obviously there, but it's a total given for you. They don't recognize the protagonist — and the protagonist, the observer, the analyst, just sort of throws his hands up in a mixture of despair on the one hand, but a "Well Jesus, that's it" on the other. And you go from that straight into the vitality, or at least the possibility for vitality and life, in Africa. I guess what I'm asking is, are there things you want to go back to?*

I did write one novel, which I never published and I probably never will, which in a way was an attempt — My family is very archetypal Canadian, it's all there. My mother's ancestry was part New England refugees, United Empire Loyalists. You know, forty thousand acres divided amongst the sons and divided and divided and divided and divided. That was the maternal side. The paternal side were Scot fishermen, who settled in Nova Scotia before the Revolution, the early Canadians, and, you know, fished and drowned in the Straits of Canso. My father's parents were Welsh evangelical Anglicans, at least his mother was, and they settled in Saskatchewan and homesteaded, and when I think of this chain and all, what I'd really like to do is circle around it historically and try and see them as individuals. There's a lot of vitality in them, especially in their early thing. If you go back, if you look at the way they kind of destroyed you, bang! you can only be negative about it. But if you circle back and look at the forces that *they* were fighting against and the humiliations *they* were fighting, it's incredible.

One of the problems a Canadian writer has is that you have to do it all. You know, the people who preceded us have done — I mean, some of them really remarkably, very beautifully, I think of Sinclair Ross or Ernest Buckler and so forth, remarkable things — but in fact it is still a territory without maps, isn't it? If you were an American in your position, someone would have written about that, some of that would have been done for us.

Well, I don't know. In a way, I think we're better off than Americans. I think one of the real failures of American literature is it doesn't explain American society at all, you know. American literature all comes out of Locke and individualism and the Revolution. There is just nobody who is . . . who has examined the premises on which they all write. Faulkner gets the closest.

Faulkner, Hawthorne, Melville, and . . . I mean, they're the guys that explain Vietnam, and Mailer in *Why We Are in Vietnam* is getting close to it in a psychic way.

Okay. Let me ask you more specifically something we're moving into. What about being a Canadian writer? You obviously consider yourself a Canadian writer.

Yes. Well, there is this problem of the lack of vocabulary which for me explains the way I write; it is a real problem in getting wound up, but you know, I think that's solvable. I think I'm a writer and I was born a Canadian; you can only — well, after *New Ancestors* I can't say you can't write about another culture. (*laughter*) I'd like eventually to go to India and maybe do a, you know, an Indian novel, there's enough big things there in Canada's past if you could get at them.

I'm asking the same question again, I guess, but you write New Ancestors *and you want to write an Indian novel — what is it about Africa and India as opposed to the Canadian experience, why do you feel that you have to do other things before you write. . . .*

Oh, I didn't think before — I think, as a writer, you have to look for the most understanding, in the world, that you can get before you die; and there's really no sense in explaining something that someone else has explained. I think there's a lot of work to be done about the Canadian past, and as it affects — you know, a sort of intellectual *Jalna*, or a true *Jalna* or whatever. But I like to stretch my mind, and that's why I think of India.

The obvious question of advantages and disadvantages of growing up as a writer or potential writer in Canada. . . .

Well, it's hard to think of the advantages. It really makes you rely on yourself, I think, and a sort of "survival of the fittest" is the only real advantage. Well, there are certain other advantages. You've got the Bible, so many lines every Sunday, dead-on; well, that's good literature, that's really imprinted on you early. You've got a real sense of dislocation in that people don't understand — you grow up in a society that doesn't ever *think* about itself, which is a strain; and you have this impact, this huge impact of the American society coming down on you. It's like a chamber of horrors, horrors and beauties. On the other hand, you talk about Protestant reticence and neuroticism, et cetera, but in a way, I mean, this is one thing you have to get out if you're going to write about Canada. The people are better in some ways, I mean they're more pleasant. The people, as a whole almost, have made certain adjustments — this is one thing the writers haven't brought out. *As For Me and My House* is not quite accurate in the sense that — I don't know how it was during the Depression, but the people do self-benefiting and mutual-benefiting actions, to overcome some of that. They, in a way, know that they are sick. They know the society is sick and they do things to cover up. They also do things like attack the minister's wife, you know, and humiliate her and are constantly malicious, but there are counterforces at work too. An instinctive search for health that only *The Double Hook* ever begins to make clear, and Reaney.

Right. What about nationalism, do you think that it is beneficial for writing as a craft, writing as an art? Do you think it will make any difference?

Oh yes. Yeah, I think — well, if the world gives in to Americanization, that's going to be very bad for the writers, because the best American writing is very negative writing; it's sort of, you know, how good can you be at attacking your society? And if you operate on cancer daily, it begins to affect your life, so I see nationalism in the current world as a defence mechanism — the whole thing is biological — it's a defence mechanism against Americanization. People know instinctively there's something wrong with Americanization or Russian, or any great congregates of power. On the other hand, if there was no America, I'd like to see five to ten societies in Canada. Then I think they would all grow and develop and be better. I think, for the survival of man as a species, you need the survival of different cultures; so I'm against liberalism and individualism. An individual is not the same as all other individuals and he is not the great carrier of survival. The culture is. The culture has to take care of the sick and the mad and the distorted within the culture.

And the tradition too?

And the tradition. The individual just can't do all that. But there are lots of ways in which different groups of individuals can work out their social relationships. So we need lots of possibilities going on. Nationalism seems to be a good way of defending that against the overpowering unity. One world and one society doesn't appeal to me at all.

Does being a novelist demand a particular kind of selfishness?

Ah — yes, I think so. I mean, a certain amount of egotism, in other words, why would you do it? Yes, you sort of get hooked in early because these famous writers, Shelley and Keats and Wordsworth, they're well known and they're famous because they were writers — you know you want to be selfish that way. There is a tougher kind of selfishness that comes in, at least in Canada, if you're going to keep on being a writer, you've got to be selfish in that sense.

Is it because of the lack of continuing interest?

Yes, yes, but that's a different kind of selfishness — it's not the selfishness of a major capitalist. It's egotism more than selfishness. You're not getting anything out of it.

Do writers know something special about the world, or whatever, in the way, say, that physicists or anthropologists or sociologists do?

Yes, yes, I think a good novelist stays close to the people. Now, I think — I mean, *New Ancestors* is full of borrowings from anthropologists, borrowings from all those people, especially physicists, which no one has pointed out. I don't think you can cut yourself off from what other human beings are thinking, but at the same time, an anthropologist or a physicist couldn't have written *New Ancestors*, so you kind of steal all their ideas and then you go out and steal the people's emotions and then you make a mixture. (*laughter*) That's how you write a novel.

Is the writer's talent to bring things together or does he see things in a different way?

Well, you have to modify, you have to see what the anthropologist says and then you have to see through it, and partly you can do that because you see what the physicist said and the sociologist and the general think, but you have to see through what they're thinking too.

Right, and what is the vantage point?

I don't think many writers do this; this is one of the problems with modern novelists, they don't think. They figure they can do it all just out of their own brains or just by going to the people, and you can't, you have to do all three.

One of the things that came back to me several times in reading New Ancestors *was a kind of quality out of* Under the Volcano. *Does that make any sense to you?*

Well . . . I mean, no one has gone into this, but *New Ancestors* is in a way a playing around with other novels, and, you know, strange ones in many cases, but *Under the Volcano* was one, and *Bread and Wine* was another. There are all kinds of parodies in that. I mean, it's one of the ways you get to the richness of texture and structure — by playing.

But it wasn't only that, it was something to do with the kind of chaos that surrounded everything. There is a quality about all the possibilities and the alternatives, the incredible richness. But at the same time, a kind of doomed thing.

Well, I mean, Lowry is influenced by Melville and Dostoevsky, and I *have* read them too, but you know, I think he's really an important writer, and a really good writer can make every word count, you know, and reverberate nineteen times, and that's what I tried to do in *New Ancestors*. In a way, if you want to draw the parallel, *New Ancestors* is what's happening outside of Geoffrey's world. He never really gets outside his world. I mean, there's that Indian riding off, he's killed on a horse, bang. But what is that Indian thinking as he rode off, and where was he riding off to, and what were the people thinking? And some of Lowry's ideas are important to me. I mean, he's a master of humiliation. Faulkner and Lowry — they know what humiliation is, and that's the guts of their work. And Dostoevsky and Turgenev.

I wonder if you could elaborate more specifically on the novel as a tragic form, and the problem that presents for the individual writer who doesn't want to be merely tragic.

Well. . . .

The possibilities that writers find for celebration within their own lives, but it's difficult to find in their art.

Yes . . . the novel can do other things. It can entertain and it can chronicle and whatnot. MacLennan's fiction is good fiction, but it's chronicle and, you know, it should be examined like that and not in terms of a novel. If you're looking at the novel as novel, then when it's best, it's tragic. And it's individually tragic too — it's the death . . . the destruction of one individual psyche. Now you try and get the other thing, you can squeeze Bloomsday into the novel form and you squeeze a play into a novel. But that's not the novel. In the good novel, Melville — Captain Ahab, bang, down he goes, *The Brothers Karamazov*, down they go, you know, the Consul, down he goes, bang, they are individuals, the society doesn't mesh with them, down they go in great pain. When you try to get a sense of celebration, a sense of joy into that form, it doesn't work. You *can* get a sense of ritual manners into it, a Canadian nurse novel or something, that's artistically non-powerful. Now, say *White Figures, White Ground*, Hugh Hood was really dealing with that problem very nicely, I think, in a way. He got around it by having his characters an artist, so you have these beautiful paintings inside the novel which act to draw together the more joyous emotions. But the novel itself doesn't really do that.

Do you find that the novel being a tragic form, or a form concerned with the decay and the destruction of the individual psyche, is a depressing form to be involved in as an artist?

Well, I think that depressed people tend to write novels. I think it works that way. I can't see a sort of happy, joyful and adjusted person really writing a good novel. In a way that was one of the problems with James, that he never really felt the great pains and disbeliefs.

And the thing is with Lowry, he did feel them and that destroyed him.

Yes. But he was trying — he had already gone the other way too, in *Forest Path to the Spring*. Well, how much closer can you come to expressing joy?

A general question about "The Hard-Headed Collector," a really intriguing kind of pilgrimage in reverse which is a really humiliating betrayal of idealism, isn't it?

I wrote that story, I guess, in 1966, you know, in America, and I wrote it in one go, the day after, the night after, actually, I read the *New York Times* article about Hershorn, that's interspersed — this was before I'd read Walter Gordon or knew anything about Canadian economics, but it was what your gut knew, you know, your gut.

The real rape.

Yes, the real rape which suddenly — I guess it's in all my stories, but it suddenly became clear. I think it is too late in a way, but on the other hand, it's what's in the story. And our writers, I'd also been kind of self-defensively reading them, because I was studying for my Ph.D. in American Literature, you know, I was getting ready for my comprehensives, so I knew everything about the American writer. I knew whose wife helped write what page of what novel. I failed my comprehensive the first time because I got into a screaming debate with these people, because in attempting to answer their questions, I would bring in African writers and Canadian writers, and get very defensive because they would expect me to know the names of the seven people that sued Mark Twain, but they would not even know who James Reaney or Chinua Achebe *were*. As bad as Richler. So maybe you'd be trying to draw a point and you'd pull out from some other culture an example, and they would consider that irrelevant, and also it was slightly humiliating to them, so the next question was even . . .even nastier. So I was preparing, revving it up for the second time, and. . . .

But the intriguing thing about "The Hard-Headed Collector" is the people he loses on his pilgrimage. They are all involved in life in some way or another, in many ways a grotesque reflection of life. They get diverted and end up doing what in the process seems to be a kind of falling by the wayside, but at the end they're obviously better off than the poor sod who ends too old too late at the end of the goal.

I guess what I was talking about was the other side of *As For Me and My House*, and what the people are doing instinctively is in there. The people as saints. Each of those guys is a writer. That was one thing in my head, you know, like the guy up in Northern Ontario showing the inverted image of a farm, that's Jamie Reaney, and you can sort of make lots of other connections, so it opens up. I'll let the young scholars now play games at saying who's who. For me there is a way of having a lot of structure condensed, in there; but the other thing is that each of them chooses vitality and maybe they didn't make it as a nation, which is really what I'm saying. Maybe we're going to end up not making it as a nation, but as individuals and as sort of groups of society, we've gone a lot farther than the Americans in terms of breaking out of our Protestantism, and maybe there's hope in that process. Maybe the magical way you create the nation is by all this sort of falling by the wayside.

Okay, let's ask a kind of final question. What do you see for yourself, do you see another book coming up? Do you see more short stories? Do you see a waiting period? You've been incredibly active in social or external terms for the last few years or so. . . .

Yes . . . for the last two years, especially the last year, in a way I'm trying to reverse . . . you know, the reversed journey of "The Hard-Headed Collector," independent publishers, we try and get a group of people who are doing things, that is, providing jobs and the whole industrial bit, but with a joint cultural purpose, and try to get them working together, or increase the degree to which they work together. That's the reverse of the process.

Okay. One of the things that underlies many of the conversations I've had with novelists is a real concern that one is forsaking the fact of living in the process of writing. This is a fairly strong theme in your attitude towards your writing as well.

Yeah. I mean, when you're adolescent, life is so intense to you that you don't mind cutting it all off to write, because it's just impinging on you. But as you get older, your son is seven years old and you realize he is never going to be four again; and you have another son who is sixteen months, and you can just sort of sit and play with him for hours, knowing that it's all going. And art is all around you; you know, you're living in it. You get really greedy for life, and you want to grow crops and play music and dance and the whole thing. And it's harder to cut yourself off.

It would be interesting to know whether or not the greed for life comes out of having spent time writing novels, or whether in fact the greed for life makes one write them to begin with, and the dissatisfaction with the apparent availability of life on your own terms drives you into writing novels.

Yes. Yes, you could say that life impinges on you when you're an adolescent and you want to become a novelist, but you know, it also is usually the wrong kind of life, not your own life — restricted, and not life the way you think it should be fully led.

MARGARET LAURENCE

MARGARET LAURENCE was born in Neepawa, Manitoba, in 1926.

Okay . . . some of the questions aren't going to make any sense in your particular context, and if so, just say so. I'll begin with a question about the novel and what the attraction of the novel is for you as opposed to other forms of writing.

Well, I don't know about the attraction of the novel against other forms of writing, Graeme. I have written a lot of short stories as well, and it seems to me that it's really the material itself which decides the form. Some things seem suitable for a short story and others for a novel. I don't feel that the short story is any less difficult a form; in fact in some ways it's more difficult. I think generally speaking, with my short stories anyway, I've had one sort of main theme into which I go fairly deeply, whereas with the novel I have a whole lot of interrelated themes and dilemmas. I don't think you necessarily do more in the novel — it doesn't attract me any more than the short story — it's just that the material itself chooses the form.

Right. And then the short story material is more concise or more intense or limited in scope . . . I don't mean in meaning, but in scope?

One is tempted to say that in a novel you have more scope. I'm not so sure that's true. I think one generally tends to deal in a novel with a greater number of themes, and of course a greater number of individual dilemmas, than in a short story. I don't believe that a novel is any less a concise form than the short story. It doesn't matter how long a novel is — you still can't afford to waste any words. It can be six hundred pages, if it really needs to be six hundred pages, but it still is a very tight form in that sense. . . . You know, if you have this kind of feeling of respect for words, you really can't afford to waste any of them.

Okay, how do you find films, for example Rachel, Rachel? *Did you find any attraction in films or do you learn anything as a novelist from films or any of the. . . .*

I think that every writer, in this particular time, in our age, has learned a great deal from both films and from TV, not consciously, perhaps, but I think that these things have influenced writing. My writing has always tended to be very visual, which is just partly my natural way of doing things. But yes, I do feel that — in ways I find difficult to analyze — my own writing has been influenced by both films and TV in the sort of visual techniques that we use, although I think that the two forms are totally different. I think you can do things in film that there is no way you can do in a novel, but of course vice versa. In film it is very difficult really to get inside the head, to get to the thoughts of someone. You can't have a sort of constant voice-over. This is what they did with *Rachel, Rachel*. In my novel, *A Jest of God*, it's all written from inside Rachel's head. It's in the first person, the present tense, and it is all her viewpoint. Well, this was one difficulty, of course, they had in writing the screen script, because they couldn't have interminable voice-over; they couldn't have too many of her thoughts. They had to convey it in other ways, and this is one thing that I think

Joanne Woodward did extremely well. She conveyed a great many of Rachel's emotions simply from the appearance of her face, and the way she walked and the whole movement of her body, which was a very skilled performance.

Very efficient, yes.

I say that novels and short stories have been influenced by film, as indeed I think they have. But I do think that we have to try and consider very deeply that as far as the survival of the novel form is concerned, we have to concentrate to a very large extent on things that film cannot do, which is partly the getting inside the individual's psyche. And I've had this problem this summer trying to write the novel that I'm working on now; of course one has always known it, but it struck me very forcibly this summer how impossible it is in words to describe, for example, colours. Looking out at the maple trees turning red across the river and trying to say, how do I get that into words? And you have to say, that is something a film can do which I really can't do adequately in words, and one can't do it even with images or figures of speech. There isn't any way you can really catch colour the way the eye catches it. But on the other hand, there isn't any way that a film can catch the inner workings of the individual brain in the way that a novel can.

You said for the survival of the novel; do you think the novel is threatened as a form?

Personally, I don't think that it is. Everybody is always announcing that the novel is dead, but they have been saying this for very many years, and the novel does go on. I think that in terms of the influence of film and TV on the novel, it's obvious now that no longer do we need, for example, in novels, in prose fiction, lengthy descriptions of place that used to be very common in novels, simply because these are things which film does better. So I think many contemporary novelists are really cutting down on the amount of physical description.

So in a sense, we're potentially freed by film. . . .

In a sense, yes.

Would you have liked to have written a script for Rachel, Rachel?

No, I wouldn't have touched it with a ten-foot pole, and the reason is that it is a completely different medium; it is not a medium which I have ever learned how to operate inside. I don't think I would have been incapable of learning, but I wasn't really interested in going into it and trying to learn how to do it. And the other reason is that when I sold the film rights to *A Jest of God*, I was working on *The Fire-Dwellers*, and that is what I was interested in.

Right, and you sell it and it goes and that's. . . .

You think that you're not going to be at all interested in what kind of product comes out, and after all, you don't really have control over it. So I resigned myself. However the film turned out, I wasn't going to be at all interested. But of course I was.

Sure. What did it feel like when you saw it for the first time?

Well, it was rather spooky, in a way. I was kind of sorry they weren't able to set it in Canada, because in the novel the background is very important. But at the same time, I thought Joanne Woodward did a splendid job in portraying Rachel. But I did actually maintain my feeling that whatever the film was like, this was their work. It wasn't mine. It was just interpreting it in a different medium, and . . . so I didn't feel in any sense personally responsible. I thought they did a good job, but if they hadn't, I would have felt sorry, but it wouldn't have broken my heart.

Okay. Let me ask another kind of question. Do you think that novelists or writers know something special about the world, say in the way that — the example I give is anthropologists or sociologists or physicists — do they have a special kind of. . . .

This is something I don't know. I feel ambiguously about this, because I think in one sense we'd all like to think of ourselves as some kind of magician, and in a way, I suppose we are. I have the feeling that it isn't that novelists or writers in general know that much more or even different things about the world and about one another. What we're saying is what everybody knows or a great many people know, but hardly anybody says.

So the talent then is in the saying.

In the being able to *say*, both from the point of view of being able to say it with some kind of communicative skill, and being able to *bring* yourself to say it. This is the most difficult thing. There's not only the talent in writing well, writing effectively. The greatest problem of all is to try and tell enough of your own truth from your own viewpoint, from your own eyes, to be able to go deeply enough. To make the leap of the imagination to get inside another character, and to be able to tell as much of that truth as you can bear to tell, and this is very hard. It sounds easy just to tell the truth. There isn't anything more difficult.

Another general question. What do you think the writer's role is in a society? Does the writer have a role to begin with? Does the writer have a responsibility? Those are two questions.

Well, I'm not sure that the writer's responsibility is really any different from any other human being's responsibility in life. I don't like to think of the writer having to take on a conscious social role in this sense. I would like to be able to discover a way of writing about things that I feel passionately about, such as the rape and the killing of our planet, without writing propaganda. I think a very few writers have managed to do this. I am not one of them. I've never discovered a way of doing this in my own writing. I do think that the main responsibility of the writer, apart from the fact that one responsibility of the writer is to try not to bore the reader, is what we were talking about just a moment ago, to try and tell as much of your own truth as you can bear to tell.

All right, what again about the role part of it, say there are a certain number of writers in this country, serious writers — do you think they have a role in the country, that is . . . Let me leave it at that . . . do you think there is a role? I'm not asking do you think they are valuable, because that's . . . Perhaps I'm asking in what way you think they're valuable.

I think that human society, wherever it is, anywhere in the whole world, needs fiction and poetry in the same way that human cultures forever have needed their storytellers and their poets and their singers of songs. And I think this is partly so that we can see ourselves reflected in these various fictions. One would like to believe in various high-minded things like raising people's consciousness and so on. I'm very dubious about this, but at the same time, I would feel if a writer has any role at all, any kind of social role, this differs from writer to writer. I don't think everybody feels the same about it. Personally, apart from simply wanting to create fictions for reasons that I find mysterious, I would hope that with my own fiction, if anything came across at all under the surface, it would be something to this effect — that human beings are capable of great communication and love and very often fall very far short of this. We simply do not communicate as much or at as deep a level as we are capable, and one would hope through one's characters to point some of these things out.

So the role . . . I mean, when you're talking about the writer's responsibility to be true, and as much as possible to tell the truth as he sees it, that could very well be the role in a way, couldn't it?

Oh certainly, and of course the thing is that each person, each writer, is not going to perceive the world in the same way, not going to perceive the same things going on between human individuals, so of course this is why I feel in a profound sense that ours is a very non-competitive profession. There really is room for an unlimited number of different points of view in this way, because my eyes are not looking at things in exactly the same way as yours, very obviously. So I like to see how your eyes are seeing things.

Because whatever we do, it's always only going to be a partial truth . . . from any individual . . .

Oh certainly. People very often have said to me: Don't writers generally tend to stab one another in the back a lot? Graeme, the writers I know don't. We are really interested in what the others are doing, but I think that a lot of us feel, as I do, that we're kind of members of a tribe. We don't have to stab each other in the back; we're not in competition.

Yes, the only competition that I ever encounter I might say generally in writers is their competition with themselves.

Well, this is the thing. . . .

Yes . . . which can be pretty fierce.

Oh terrible, and the longer you are in the profession, it doesn't get any more easy. It becomes for me more difficult all the time, partly because I probably become more self-critical all the time, and partly because one discovers at some point the things that you can do and the things that you can't do. You discover your limitations. You find ways around them sometimes, and sometimes you don't. At one time, when you first begin, you don't know that there are some things that you're going to find it impossible to do in your writing, and then you discover those things. So this is a humbling thought. Each time when you begin again, it's almost as though you were starting for the first time . . . but more difficult.

When you talk about things, say, that you've discovered you can't do, are there some things in your writing that you have discovered you can't do but you really would have liked to have done?

Yes, I mentioned one just a moment ago, about some of the things, social things, that I feel very strongly about. The destruction of the planet is one of them, but by no means the only one. I feel very strongly about a great many things, and I have not yet discovered a way of dealing with those things convincingly, movingly, in fiction, without writing propaganda, which I won't write.

Or tracts, if somebody wants you to write a tract, you can write a tract . . . but don't do it as a novelist. Okay. Whom do you write for?

Well, that's a tricky one. I write primarily for myself, and in order to . . . really I suppose to better understand both myself and the world in which I'm living. Each novel is a kind of voyage of discovery, but once the first draft is done, then I write for whoever will be interested in reading me. I don't write totally for myself. The first time through, I don't think of anybody. I haven't got an audience. I'm my audience, and I don't know what I'm going to discover. But once the first draft is done, I do think of potential readers, in the sense that I feel that I want to make things as clear and as effective as possible.

Could one make the distinction, and this is probably forcing it, that your audience appears when you are really zeroing in on your craft as a writer. . . .

That's right. . . . I'm glad that my books are published in both England and America, because I think that every writer wants to be read by as many people as possible. But at the same time, I really do write mainly for my own people, who are Canadians — I care about the response here more than I care about the response in other countries.

Is that because you share things with them, do you think?

Of course. The thing is that we come from a very common background, even though this country is geographically different in different parts, and it's culturally very different too — it's not the same thing to grow up in a Newfoundland outport that it is to grow up in a prairie town, as I did. But there are certain things that we do share. Naturally one wants to be able to reach beyond one's own geographical boundaries. I like to think that my books basically deal with human dilemmas which could be understood and comprehended by somebody in Africa or New Zealand. But at the same time, there is a kind of cultural thing, which is deeply related to one's own people, one's ancestors, and therefore the response of your own people tells you something about how genuinely you have spoken.

Right. It's going to be harder to fool them than the African . . . the African may be fooled because he doesn't know?

That's right. What you can't fool anybody on is the human dilemma which is totally international and without boundaries. But there is another dimension of writing — the ancestral thing, the family background, the trueness of the idiom. This is something where only your own people can say yes, you've done it or you haven't done it. The feel of place, the tone of speech, how people say things, the concepts you grow up with, the things that have been handed to you by your parents and your grandparents and so on — I have to measure the truthfulness of what I'm saying in these areas against my own people's response.

How do you work? When you're working well, how do you come into a book?

I come into a book with incredible difficulty. I try and put if off; I postpone it. I do everything possible not to begin until it becomes absolutely impossible to evade any longer, that is, the torture of writing becomes less than the torture of not writing. I've gone through long periods, a whole year at a time for example, of being really quite unable to write anything. But once I actually get into a novel, I don't seem to suffer from very many mental blocks, and then I work, if possible, five days a week. I never work on weekends, but I have to keep inside the novel for five days a week, and of course this is one reason why the last two summers working here in my little shack on the Otonabee River has been absolutely ideal.

You write longhand?

I do usually write longhand.

And how far — I mean, when do you start typing, or does somebody else type it for you?

No, people don't type for me, partly because with the first draft I couldn't bear to have anybody but myself see it; and partly because when I put it first into a typescript, then I usually do a great deal of rewriting and cutting at that time. When I've got the first typescript, that is really a second draft, and then I begin work on rewriting that.

You said that the novel is for you a discovery . . . a voyage of discovery. How much do you know when you start out, how much of the novel do you have in your head when you start out . . . what do you start with?

I always start with the main character or, as it may be, characters. Usually there are a number of people who have been inhabiting my head for a number of years before I begin on a novel, and their dilemmas grow out of what they are, where they come from. When I begin, I do have a fairly strong hunch about some of the major events in the novel — in other words, I've got a fairly clear picture of the skeleton of the thing — but I have absolutely no idea of the detail, and of course even the main events can get changed in the doing of them. You think you know what is going to happen, and then you realize, writing it, that isn't going to happen at all; something else is going to happen.

A question which may or may not be meaningful: what do you like best about what you've written so far? I don't mean what book, I'm not asking for that kind of . . . What kinds of things please you most, say, in the body of your work? What do you think are your real strengths as a writer?

I don't know, because I think that a writer is a very poor judge of his or her own work. I would hope that the thing that comes across the most strongly is the creation of individual characters.

Okay, and the other half of that question, and if that was potentially meaningless, this one is even worse: what do you like least, what kinds of things do you think you had most trouble with, say, in the body of work? And again I'm not talking about individual books.

Well, I've had trouble with so many things that it is hard to put my finger on them. I find it hard to get a broad screen, as it were. I think that probably my scope is a little narrow. I also find it difficult to create the feeling of living in a city, because I hate cities, and sometimes the characters just have to be in a city. It can't all take place in the country. I find no problem with the country. I don't go in for very long descriptive passages, but one hopes to create a certain sharp sense of place in a relatively few words. I struggle enormously with this kind of setting in a city, and I don't think I do this at all well. It's because I am capable of walking down a city street practically blind, because I don't really see cities. I really see the country. I notice things. I don't notice cities in the same way because they frighten me and I don't like them.

Right. . . . Another kind of question. Does being a novelist demand a particular kind of selfishness?

Not only selfishness, it demands a certain kind of unscrupulousness, if you're going to write at all. You have to create a situation in which you are able to be alone for part of the time each day when you're working. And to do this you can't necessarily be available, say for your children, sometimes even when they need you, and you try and balance things. You don't always succeed.

What about a more specific kind of selfishness — have you found, for example, people or situations that you would really like to use, you know, as fiction, whatever it is that we do to it, where you think, maybe I shouldn't do that, because of. . . .

Every novelist has encountered this. I have never written anything that is directly autobiographical, except for one book of short stories, *A Bird in the House*, which was based on my own childhood, myself as a child, and my family. And yes, with that book, I had great doubts because even though those events had happened many years in the past, and although both my parents were dead, there were other members of my family, and I did think . . . good heavens, how are they going to feel? And I really hesitated about this, but all you can do in the end is hope for the best; you have got to do it. But I think every novelist has also encountered the same thing where characters are certainly not drawn from life. They appear from somewhere, and they seem to be very much themselves. They are nobody that you have ever met, but you may be drawing on real people, not even consciously. In the end all you can do is to hope that your fictional creations are genuinely fictional creations, and if some of them have been . . . if some of the things . . . events or dilemmas in the book have actually come from life . . . I'm sorry, that's too bad, I can't help it.

It also may be a measure of your telling the truth, not about individuals but about human experience.

Oh, certainly. And you have to take the risk of hurting somebody. I know I felt quite a lot of doubt in a somewhat different way when I wrote *The Stone Angel*. I had to write it, but I did worry to some extent about hurting a number of old people who might read it. But I had to take that chance.

What about being a Canadian? Do you think that Canada is a particularly difficult place to grow up in or has been a difficult place to grow up in as a writer? What are the advantages and disadvantages of being a Canadian writer?

I think at one time it was extremely difficult to be a Canadian writer. We still had for many, many years a kind of colonial mentality, a great many people felt that a book written by a Canadian couldn't possibly be good. It had to come from either New York or the other side of the Atlantic to be any good. This whole cultural climate has changed incredibly, and particularly in the last decade. My first book was published in 1960, and the change in those twelve years in the whole cultural situation in Canada has been enormous. Canadian writers are probably in a better situation now than they have ever been before. Very few Canadian writers of any seriousness or worth do not find a considerable readership in their own country.

What about growing up in a small prairie town? Was it difficult to imagine yourself as a writer? Was it difficult to believe in the possibility of being a writer?

I think that I always knew I was a writer, right from the time I was able to write, you know, but I didn't really believe until many years later that anybody else would ever think I was a writer. Various writers had a very strong influence on me at that time when I was growing up, when I was in my middle teens. That was when I first read Sinclair Ross's novel *As For Me and My House*, and I read W. O. Mitchell's *Who Has Seen the Wind*, a little later on. These two writers had a great influence on me because they were writing out of a prairie background which was very similar to mine, and I thought: it can be done.

How did you start writing? You say you were writing in your teens?

Oh, I started writing when I was about six or seven years old. I guess I started writing . . . oh, I suppose small poems, stories, and so on.

At what point did you believe or begin to believe it possible to be a writer, full-time?

I don't know, Graeme, it was a very long time. I suppose I would have been about twenty-three when I began to realize that this was really what I wanted to do with my life. But at that time, I didn't have any faith at all that anybody was ever going to publish what I was writing. And I did, of course, then start sending out short stories and so on, and for a number of years they weren't published, thank heavens. *(laughter)* When my first couple of short stories were published, and then again when my first novel was published, I began to feel that other people might really think I was a writer.

What about the whole question of being a woman, growing up as a young woman, and a writer? Do you think that women writers have a particular difficulty, say, that men writers don't have?

I haven't experienced very many of them. I think there are advantages and disadvantages. For me the great advantage throughout the years when my children were much younger was that this was a profession which I could pursue, while at the same time being at home, you know, when my children were there. I could always be there when they got home from school. But I think one disadvantage . . . well, I think a great many women have a lot of difficulty in establishing enough confidence in themselves in any kind of profession such as writing; I certainly did. One disadvantage, as well, is that some of my work, particularly my novel *The Fire-Dwellers*, received some real put-downs from a number of male reviewers. They didn't even say it was a bad novel; it was just that if anybody like Stacey existed, they just would rather not know. And the other thing is . . . this is not done so much anymore, but at one time people used to say as a compliment that a woman writer

wrote like a man. Well, this I used to find infuriating. I write like a
human being, one hopes, of course with a woman's point of view.
I am a woman. But who ever said about a male novelist, he is a
man novelist or, worse, a gentleman novelist?

*Why do you think it is more difficult for a woman to believe in herself as
a writer than a man?*

Well, I think this is probably true of women in a great many professions. I think it all has to do with what Women's Lib is saying
right now, that women for a long time in some ways have not
only been regarded by men as second-class citizens — they have
even regarded themselves in this way. I can remember the days in
which various men have said to me, not really meaning it as a put-
down, perhaps not even knowing it was — "It's strange, isn't it,
that there never have been any great women writers or painters?"
And then you think: My God, probably I can't do, you know. . .I
can't even be competent. These inherited outlooks are hard to
overcome. But ultimately you realize you can in fact overcome
them.

*All right. A fairly obvious way of starting to talk about your books is to go
with Hagar, who discovers, at the end, that what she wanted to do was
rejoice . . . but that the chains that she carried were the chains of pride.
The chains that the other characters carried, that is Stacey and Rachel,
seem to be more fear.*

I certainly think it with Rachel, it was fear.

Stacey says at one point that she is afraid of life, doesn't she?

She says: I'm scared to death by life. I think that this was true
of both of them, probably, which was basically, particularly with
Rachel, a fear of herself. Her martyrdom had been at least partly

self-chosen, although it took her a long time to see it, but she does see it at the end, as indeed probably all martyrdoms are at least partly self-chosen. The great thing at the end was not that her life was going to change totally, but that she had at least lost some of her fear; she wasn't, for example, afraid of looking like a fool anymore, which was a kind of liberation, and her role with herself and her mother had in a sense reversed. She realized she was not about to leave her mother. She was going to look after her, but she realized that she was in the mother role now.

She was going to look after her on her terms.

She was; she had to.

Yes. A couple of things — the fear seems to be particularly in Rachel, but also in . . . to a certain extent in Stacey . . . it's somehow a fear of the life that they had within them, isn't it, like the life force and the possibility for living they have within them.

Yes, I think more so with Stacey than with Rachel. What happened with Stacey was a thing that was partly outside her. She had found herself with a man whom she still very deeply cared about, and with young children as well. She did feel trapped, but at the same time, this was partly simply circumstance, partly not of her own making. Of course, her husband too was trapped in the domestic situation no less than she was. Now, whether they could ever find their way out of that, one doesn't really know. That goes beyond the book. People have sometimes said to me: What happened to her later? Unfortunately, I don't know what happened to her later.

The thing that she does bring with her, however, and it's very early in the book, and she is looking at a photograph of herself when she was a child, and she discovers that she had been pretty, that she was pretty as a child, but she didn't know it or believe it then.

Well, this again was the lack of self-confidence. I'm sure many men feel this way too. Mind you, what she also discovered about herself in the end, her real self-discovery, was that she was a survivor. She was not going to crack up. She was going to survive.

From the fear of being foolish, obviously Rachel had somehow to discover that she was, and that she was all right after having discovered it. That was the liberation.

Yes.

Now, foolish . . . is that also frailty? Is it just the human frailty that she . . . she didn't want to embody that frailty — she didn't want to look like a human being, in a sense.

Rachel's hang-up in a sense was very similar to Hagar's, although it was very, very concealed. Because anyone who is desperately afraid of having human weaknesses, although they feel very un-self-confident, as Rachel did, is in fact suffering from spiritual pride.

Right. Almost to the point of arrogance. But things have been done to them by the culture in a way. They're forced to live out things that they despise. Stacey says, I think it was Stacey, she has to perpetuate things that she hates, and she finds herself perpetuating things with her own children.

Yes, I think this is true. Individuals can to a considerable extent liberate themselves. But I don't think that they can ever wholly get away from some of the things that they have inherited, cultural things, concepts, and so on. And I don't think that real liberation comes from turning your back on your whole past or on your ancestral past. Rather it comes through coming to some kind of terms with it, knowing that there is a certain amount of mental baggage, which you would just as soon not carry, but nevertheless you're stuck with it.

Yes, the word coping *is used, I think, both by Rachel and by Stacey, or at least the idea that one of the things that you have to do is to cope with who you are.*

I'm sure this is true of both of them and of course with Hagar too. None of them get away from their particular sort of cultural heritage — I use that in the broadest sense — because nobody does. But within that, there is still a fairly substantial degree of personal freedom which is possible.

How does one . . . how do you see in the books . . .how does one go about achieving that personal freedom?

Well, this has happened in these three books in different ways. I didn't really know until I got very close to the end in what particular detailed ways these various characters were going to either come to terms with their own dilemma or not come to terms with it, how they were going to sort out things. And of course what happens, I suppose with all of them, is that it is a limited victory.

And they really tend to be helped at some point by another person, even though that person may let them down, and in some sense does let them down, like Rachel's man. Nevertheless the involvement of that other person was really fundamental.

In point of fact, he helped her a very great deal. What she wanted from him, what he realized she wanted from him, and what was impossible for him to give, because it is not possible for any human being — she really wanted him to save her, to enter her life and say: Come with me and all will be well. One individual cannot save another in that sense. We are not God, but what Nick did for Rachel was to enable her to reach out, hold and touch another human being, which was what the sexual experience meant for her. It was the reaching out to another person and making herself vulnerable, as Rachel was able to do ultimately, with Nick, which led her to be able — to some limited extent — to liberate herself.

Yes, and this is flogging the horse likely, but there only can be a limited success, because again Stacey says, "Everything starts a long time ago," she says at one point, and she also says, "The past doesn't ever seem to be over," and so that whatever success one is going to have has to be within that.

I think so. For me the past is extremely real. I can't believe that all of life is contained in today, and the past goes back a long way. I mean, it goes back not only as far as one's own parents, for example, but the grandparents and the distant ancestors, and a great deal is passed on. One does change. People change from generation to generation, but they don't change totally.

Yes, the whole role of uncles and of grandfathers is a very powerful influence on your characters even if they don't appear in the book — they've appeared in the previous books . . . and these things are assumed, aren't they?

One might think perhaps I got a strong sense of tribe in Africa. I don't think it came from there at all. I think it came from my own past, as the most important things always do. I do have a very strong sense of a kind of tribal society.

And the ancestors, the grandfathers, I mean they're so clearly cultural ancestors as well as personal ones . . . as Canadians.

I think so, very much.

*Yes. . . . One of the stories, at the end of it, she sees a ladybird . . . "a lady-
bird laboured mightily to climb a blade of grass, fell off and started all
over again, seeming to be unaware that she possessed wings, and could
have flown up." To what extent are your characters in some sense like
the ladybird?*

Very much. I must say that it was an image that just came into
the story by itself, but I was fully aware of what significance this
had in relation to the characters. Of course Vanessa herself in that
particular story was not yet fully aware of that meaning. In the
whole collection *A Bird in the House*, she herself was partly a bird in
the house who wanted to get out, and of course the image of the
trapped bird is used several times throughout those stories.

It's pretty ominous, too, isn't it?

Yes, it is. She relates, too, to her grandmother, her grandmother
Connor, who in the first story has a pet canary. The canary is
actually fairly happy in its cage, as the grandmother was. Vanessa
herself, like her father, was much more the kind of trapped bird
beating its wings against the window and wanting out.

*The canary has no memory or idea of being wild or free. Whereas Van-
essa does. . . .*

And as her father did as well. But Vanessa knows that she's going
to get out and she does.

*The idea of flight, of wings, is simply one's life and capacity for life in
them, because that's really what they assert, isn't it?*

Yes, I think it is. This type of image is used a number of times
throughout my writing. A great many of the things that have to
do with personal liberation or freedom, it seems to me, involve
labouring mightily against a door which actually is not locked.

And again the business of the ladybug is simply just to use another talent, as it were . . . in that your characters don't . . . I mean, they have the talent, but they don't use it until they succeed.

It is partly a lack of realization that this is possible.

Yes, and the intriguing thing of course is that it is the ladybug's own wings; it isn't done from outside.

Of course.

A rather interesting, and this is a real generalization — your books seem to move from some . . . almost from Africa to a sort of increasingly personal book. Hagar is older, and in your writing you seem to be closer and closer to a personal statement, by that, I mean fictional. . . . What do you think is going to happen with this?

I know what's going to happen with it, but I can't tell you. It is the statement I'm trying at the moment to cope with in the novel that I'm writing right now.

Right. I won't ask you about that one. But is there any way I could ask generally about the technique of the book, whether any questions — any way in which you can talk about it or . . . leave it.

Well, with this present novel, I've got the first draft done and it needs a great deal more work. I've found the form of it extremely difficult, to discover what its own true form is, and I'm not sure I've got it worked out properly yet. I always have this difficulty, because the sort of shape a novel takes is extremely important, but it certainly isn't anything that can be divorced from content. It isn't just something that you sit down and think, Ho Ho, what form are we going to have this time? You think about the characters, about their dilemmas, about what you want to convey, and hopefully out of this grows some kind of a form. It's just a question of trying to find the form which will convey the material you want to convey.

Yes, right. . . . One last question. In what way is writing important to you?

I've been asked this question in a variety of ways many times, Graeme. I don't think it's a question I can answer. It is simply the way I live. It is just something that I have to do, and I really don't know why.

JACK LUDWIG

FICTION
Confusions
Above Ground

NON-FICTION
Recent American Novelists
Hockey Night in Moscow

JACK LUDWIG was born in Winnipeg in 1922.

You have two novels published and a third one almost finished. What about it? What can you tell me about it?

Well, it's a novel which grew out of a short story I wrote about ten years ago, and published in the *Tamarack Review* and then published in the States, called "A Woman of Her Age." And after I had written the story, I sat with it for a while, and I never really did accept it as strictly a short story, though I felt it was a complete short story as it was. There were too many things that sort of opened off it, and I've been thinking about what those things might be. But not till I got the Canada Council grant and went to England did I have the leisure and the ability to really sit with it and contemplate it. What I did was sit with it and contemplate it and sort of sketch a few things out, but when I returned to Canada, I began to write it, and it went just the way I hoped it would because it was a kind of game in one way. It opened up all the characters sketched, say, by names or by a sentence or by some short little episode, they became major people, and I have to do something with them and still keep the action going the way I thought it should go.

Is this "opening up" the difference between a short story and a novel for you?

Yes. I've always known or thought I'd known the difference between a short story and a novel. For instance, the story itself has to do with the lament that the old lady is making over the fact that her genes are dying, and that one son has been killed and the other son obviously is not going to get married. But that just won't hold as a theme for a novel, and so it became a kind of paltry theme for the novel and the novel had to look at things in a much greater perspective. I think that the Quebec political fervour is the only real motion in Canadian politics that I have witnessed in my lifetime. The FLQ disaster is of course only a small part of what Quebec is about these days: my Mrs. Goffman, an old European radical, would have to be stirred by what was moving young Quebecers. I hope that something about the phoniness of a generation gap emerges in the new book. Even the contempt she had for nostalgia and sentimental reminiscence in the short story turns out to be not tough enough for the political realities of the 1970s. I wrote that story in 1957–58 and it would have been reminiscent for me to have expanded that story into a novel. Instead, I would like to be loyal to the character and grant her the independence from time her snappiness deserves. I wanted, in short, *not* to write a historical novel. So what she does is look upon the theme of the short story as a paltry view of what she should be doing in life.

Going to the other end, was Confusions *the first novel you wrote?*

No, I wrote a novel that's really a kind of tour de force, and it sits and I haven't shown it to anybody at all. It's called *The Iron Net*, and it's about an illiterate guy who starts in the freight yards in Winnipeg during the Depression and is hitchhiking his way into a kind of sugar beet area during the harvest time in order to make money harvesting, and gets all involved in what's going on, and the place is extremely — symbolic.

Does it still trouble you?

Yeah, it's the sort of thing that, you know, at some point, if things don't pile in as quickly as they have been in the last little while, it's something I'd really like to come back to. Then I wrote a very long story, parts of it have been published, before I wrote *Confusions*. It's about a loser who makes his family, whether the family knows it or not, support him in all his losing ventures. The family becomes existentially defined by this loser, and everybody's life stops while this guy is going on. That one has just been sitting too.

Are you writing more or fewer stories as you develop as a writer?

I think that what happens is that . . . for instance, I've got about five stories at the present time that really were taken out of *Above Ground*. They had their own integrity, and they really couldn't stay in *Above Ground*. One of them — one or even two of them are so involved that they may become novels on their own too. So that I still think in short story form about certain kinds of experience.

So that it's almost a probe, almost an examination in many cases.

Yeah. Yeah, and if it runs away with itself, then it can't be a short story; it has to be a novella.

So the novel defines itself for you rather than you deciding ahead of time?

Right. Oh, I haven't a clue what anything is going to be when I start to work on it. I don't know whether it's going to be a novel or a short story. As a matter of fact, I switched to a play with something that couldn't have been a novel or a short story, and then some of the things that happened when I was in Europe have turned into long poems, because they are neither play or short story or novel.

That makes the next question almost irrelevant. I was going to ask why the novel, rather than movie scripts or whatever?

Yeah. Actually, you know, the novel is still the form for the sort of total immersion in experience with all the richness of the inner life and the outer life. I mean, it's made for that. And as long as that's what I'm interested in doing, the novel would be the primary form for me.

What do you think of films?

I would never, say, do one of two things: that is, I would never, I think, want to be involved with something of my own that had been written in some other form being turned into film, nor would I write a script and then turn it over to somebody else for processing. That is, the only way I would ever become involved in this thing would be if I were to write a script and do it with someone I admire, with some director I trust and somebody I could work with, because the whole commercial process, the hack working-over, is not interesting from my point of view. I know you can make money doing that kind of thing, but I handled the money thing a long time ago when I decided not to be a shoe salesman or a car salesman or a broker or a doctor or something like that.

But what differences do you think movies make to the novelist, or do they make any difference?

They make a great deal of difference. For instance, I think that fiction is being tremendously affected by cinematic devices of suspense, mystery. I think that the way the film can move easily from one place to another, from one thing to another, the montage technique, have by analogy or sometimes by direct imitation been used by novelists, by short story writers, and to very good effect. There is a story of Elizabeth Bowen's called "The Cat Jumps," where she describes what happens during a very eerie moment, when wind comes in under a door, and someone who was very very frightened watches the edges of a rug sort of creep and ruffle. Now that is obviously Hitchcockian stuff and it comes right out of the movie.

Great. At the end of Confusions, *Joseph Galsky-Gillis says he wrote the book to change his own life, and he also says that he wrote it to change the reader's life. Now the whole question of writing for self and writing for a public — how do these things balance out for you?*

Well, I think the point of view — he's quoting, incidentally, or he's referring to Rilke — and I remember several years ago there was an old girlfriend of Rilke's who turned up in Williamstown, where I was living, and she read that poem of Rilke's, which is the poem that is called "You Must Change Your Life," and I was just shattered by it, I mean, I just found it a tremendous kind of arrogant statement, and my first reaction of course was who was he, who's this guy to say if you read me you must change your life, and then I came to understand what he meant, and also to believe that this is probably the only premise that a serious writer can have about what he is doing, and what is there is the idea of change, and there is the idea of the turning. In the novel that I'm writing now, the theme that recurs is the theme that to *shuva*, which is the turning to the Hasidic notion that one may have encountered in Buber, and that is this turning; and towards the end of the novel Mrs. Goffman, who has heard the story from the Book of Jonah, for instance, over and over and over again, and she always thought about Jonah, and Jonah being swallowed by the

whale and then being spewed up again, and Jonah's gourd being
smitten, and suddenly she thinks, My God, that story isn't about
Jonah at all, it's about the King of Nineveh, because the king, who
was old, very old and wicked, when he had the truth brought to
him, put on sackcloth and ashes and started to lament and really
changed his life. That is, in the eleventh hour of his existence he
did something about it. And I think that this is a theme that comes
back over and over and over again, and as such there's no real dif-
ferentiation between what you believe, what you write, and, you
know, how you try to live, with all the contradictions involved.

*Do you look at your readers, then, rather like the wicked king who should
change his ways?*

I mean, I think that this is a very bad world that we're in at the
present time, and without at least some recognition, some ability
to name the world as it is, that, you know . . . there's too much
trouble coming on us.

*Right. Do writers know something special about the world, life, or what-
ever, say, like physicists or anthropologists or sociologists?*

I don't think so. I think that particular people, who tune in
through compassion and through a perception of things which
will not be coerced by majoritarian views which say the opposite
is true or something else is true, will insist on that vision and will
insist on the privacy of particular things and particular feelings
and particular values.

And that comes out of themselves?

Yes. I don't know how you would ever train anybody to do that or
to be that. Presumably one could take a guy and — well, particle
physics, for instance, and if he was bright, do something with him,

and he'd be able to see the world in a particular way, so you could more or less reproduce a Yang or a Dirac or somebody like that, an Einstein, but I'm sure that you can't do that with the novelist.

What sustains you as a novelist?

I think just the magic and the unexpectedness of the next thing that's coming. It's this sort of unbelievable confidence and faith that when you write this, something will follow from it. I haven't a clue what that other thing will be, and I think that that's probably the most important thing. In other words, it's the work itself, and the relationship that you have with the work. And when that's finished, it really is finished; that its publication and reception and distribution, which are all great and marvellous and terrific, are not up to the excitement of the thing as it's being done, and the openness for other things that might lead out of it.

It's a process — I mean, is writing a process?

It's an experience. I mean it's an experience which is one of the . . . one of the greatest experiences.

How do you work? How many words do you write on a good day?

Oh, I could write fifteen thousand words on a good day. I don't know whether I keep them all, but I work and have been working in the last little while — it's when it's possible and there aren't other things interfering — I've been working steady for fifteen to eighteen hours a day, seven days a week. Not on just one thing alone. And this sometimes involves an enormous amount of rewriting, that is, when something is done in one huge jet, and then you know, later on, of course it has to fit into something that has gone before, something that is going to come after, but it does sort of prepare lots of things at one shot.

Going back to what you said earlier about finding things as you write, then in this sort of gush as you say, is that the process of discovery?

That's part of it, yeah, the process of discovery, and then to let it go and not feel bound by what I'd written before. You see, this is the thing. Here was the short story, for instance, the short story has a theme, and as I started to write the novel, it became clear to me that either I was going to be limited by the theme as it was stated in the story or else she herself would have to undergo some kind of change, and this is what happens, she does undergo a change. As a matter of fact, her undergoing a change makes it almost mandatory that the theme of the novel become changed itself.

This seems almost facile now: do you enjoy writing? You obviously enjoy writing. . . .

Oh, yeah, yeah. A fantastic thing.

Do you find it difficult to begin in the morning or during the day?

No, never. (*laughter*)

Do you find it difficult to stop?

Yeah, I think I do.

What sort of feedback do you get from your writing?

This is a good time to ask the question, because this very story that I'm talking about now produced the most amazing kinds of feedback that I've ever had. There are all kinds of letters and, you know, you meet people and things go on, but I got a letter, and the letter had been chasing me around in Europe, and it was all sort of stained and the handwriting was the sort of handwriting I associate with the undergraduate, and I thought some ex-student of mine was looking for a letter of recommendation to go to graduate school or something like that, and I opened it and found it was written by a kid in a foxhole in Vietnam. The story, "A Woman of Her Age," had just been put into an American paperback, and these things had been brought to the front lines, and this kid was reading the story, and started to write in the context of the Vietnam War, in the context of his revulsion against what it was he was involved in, and while he said he was up to his hips in rainwater and mud and everything, what that story meant to him, and this, from my point of view, was the greatest thing that had ever happened to me as far as writing went, because he couldn't understand how anybody could face these existential questions, and particularly an old lady, you know, who's in her seventies, when all these questions seem to have been taken away from the guys who were in Vietnam themselves. Now I have corresponded with this guy and invited him, he's out of the army now, invited him up to Toronto, and we spent about three, four days just talking about the whole thing, and he's terribly involved, terribly moved still with that story as an indication that somebody can keep going, somebody can be involved with something other than, you know, politics, gross national product, and the rest of it.

That must be very exciting.

And so it's really, to generalize, it's really the young people's response that I care about, much more than I care about literary critics or reviewers or anything like that.

Talking about young people, what about your teaching, your teaching and your writing, how do they go together?

They go together very well. There's never any difficulty. Most of the time, of course, I teach the things that interest me, and a very strange thing happened in the course of teaching, where say I'd be teaching Yeats or I'd be teaching Joyce, and when I'd been paying particular attention to a subject and yet, as a writer, something else might be happening and, that is, this might lead into a metaphor; it might lead into a thought, an idea that I wanted to develop. And so there's this kind of two-tiered existence that you have in the classroom. That is, you're always there as a writer, and you may enrich the particular work that you're teaching by bringing in your own involvement with your own work, but at the same time there may be something, not just in the work but in the dialogue between you and the student, that introduces the possibility that it will go back into your work.

Is there any danger of talking ideas out in the classroom and consequently losing them for your fiction?

I think the difficulty is in teaching a creative writing course, and that's why I really don't involve myself in that kind of thing, because that's where you really lose it, that is, by getting involved in somebody else's work, and there's only one way to do it, and that of course is through your own imagination. That is, you can't be a critic when you're talking about somebody else's work from the inside.

Okay. A mercenary question: have you ever made or do you ever expect to make any real money from your writing?

I've made, you know, real money, not huge amounts. . . . No, I really don't think so. Obviously a book like *Above Ground* can't become a bestseller. It's too complicated, it's much too involved. If something like that were to happen, I'd be delighted, it would be just great, but that's, you know, the difference really between this kind of writing which has a commitment to a view of things, and another kind of writing which is much more public in its involvement, in its commitment. I mean, I would always run the risk, for instance, of finding somebody who wouldn't want to publish a particular thing that I'm doing, and that would just be too bad. I mean, one can certainly do that. It's one of the risks of my particular kind of trade.

So that the money to buy the time to write, you have to get elsewhere?

More or less. Right, and that's why — this is one of those decisions that I referred to earlier as on the money bit, that I made a long time ago, and that is that time was the important thing, and the arrangements that I could have at a university, having to do with what I did in the classroom, my relationship with administrative people and with students, these were the important questions, and that the money would be secondary to them, and as a matter of fact that's the way it's all worked out, with grants, and the Canada Council has been helpful. I had a full grant from them and a couple of little things first.

I was just going to ask you about the Canada Council. Do you think it's a good thing for a writer to have this kind of financial support?

Oh, I think it's absolutely essential.

Is there enough of it in Canada?

Well, I don't think there's enough of it. I think, for instance, that the provincial granting outfits could do a lot more than they're doing with writers. And I'm also concerned with magazines and with publications and the difficulties that some of them are having, and I think that this is probably an area where the Canada Council and the provincial councils should take a hand.

What about the private sector of the economy, you know, insurance companies and banks, they buy sculpture or paintings sometimes. Should they patronize writers?

I think they should. I think what they should do is set up a buffer organization that has some kind of foundation, something like the Advertising Council in the United States, for instance. If you had an analogue of that, where everyone was contributing, and yet the control or the running of it — for instance, the Advertising Council hires somebody like Harold Rosenberg, who is the art critic for the *New Yorker*, and a really far-out guy, and in a sense he has jurisdiction over what is going to be done. Small foundations have been set up by people interested in writing, where they've made the foundation almost independent of where the money is coming from. And this, I think, is all to the good.

Do you know of anything like this in Canada?

There's one out in B.C., that's the only one I know of. As far as I know, there is no other one in Canada. But there are a lot of them, incidentally, in the United States, very small foundations, and it is possible, if you're doing a particular kind of thing, to get a grant from these people, no strings attached whatsoever.

And they give you somewhere to live too sometimes.

Yeah. Of course there are also the writers' colonies like Yado, and I spent one winter at Yado. There's the Huntingdon-Hartford Colony out in California and the MacDowell Colony too; that's three things that are going in the United States. People are totally supported in the sense of their board and their room, and all they have to pay for is their laundry. But they have working space and living space, and that's provided for, you know, three months to six months of the year.

Did it work for you the time you were there?

Very well, yeah, it was marvellous. It came at a great time, and I did just an enormous amount of work. As a matter of fact, I did the first draft of something that ran into 633 pages.

Okay. I'd like to talk more specifically about some of the things that emerge in your novels. I have a feeling that after Confusions, *the particular confusions of that book seem to end; that is, your Ivy League devil seems to vanish, the black tongue, the bitterness, maybe even the guilt-free consciousness that he spoke about, it seems certainly to fade, if not to die out. I mean, the Hasid's concern with compassion and life and the speaking of good news seems to be more of a preoccupation. Do you think that's fair?*

Yeah. I think that's probably true, if you just add that it isn't that the black tongue disappears, it's that it is translated into something else. It's not translated into compassion, it's not translated into good news, I think it's translated into character, and that it becomes a much more novelistic matter than it is in *Confusions*. *Confusions* is not a novel in that sense. It really is a verbal game that is played, though as usual with this kind of satiric thing, it's a very serious book, from my point of view at least.

So you think that. . . .

I think that a character like Mavra, who is talking about things like the defence intellectuals, just offhandedly, is probably doing it much better than Joey Gillis.

Yes. Mavra is in some ways like Devereux Peterson in Confusions. *I detect a kind of madness in her which is another reality that Joseph talks about when he looks at Devereux and says: "Dev made our imagined griefs play acting. It was reality, irreversible, stark, not subject to whim or game." And Devereux is. . . .*

But hers is, you see, here is again the novelistic version of the same thing, and it's there and at the same time it is subject to whim and game, and it's also capable of being changed, and she, unlike somebody like Devereux, has self-awareness and is living in this incredible way; that is, the explosions come at the time she feels she would like to be somebody else, she would like to do something else. And of course what she wants is a different past and a different present and a different possibility. It's sort of a yearning to bust out. Devereux of course is really stark because he is two-dimensional, there is no way of dealing with this at all. There is no reversibility.

Right. Perhaps you've already answered this question, I'll ask it again, would you say that where the enemy, using that word in the most general sense, in Confusions *is a way of thinking, that the enemy in* Above Ground *is more the fact of physical death and what to do in the face of this?*

Yes, and not so much what to do in the face of it, but if that is so, then involvement on a lesser level becomes a form of madness. In that sense *Confusions* and *Above Ground* are really two versions of more or less the same theme, and that is, very early in the book, when Joshua sees a man die, and really believes that love can stop that, one has vitality and strength and a certain kind of power, and therefore death is just another one of these obstacles that one overcomes; and then he finds out that it isn't, and finds out with his father where even more is at stake, you have the experience of Lazarus, and that is, I keep coming back to Browning's poem "The Epistle to Tarsish" where the notion of Lazarus having been in the other world, how can he come back, how can he look at this stuff, how can he possibly face it; and in a sense this is what makes Joshua look at the world in such a strange way. And that's when he gets away from Mavra, for instance in the third section of the book, and he comes down and finds that the sun is still shining and the pavement is there and the policeman sounds like some great prophet; this is the reality that you're rooted in, that you're grounded in; you always come back to it.

Yeah. Galsky-Gillis said at the beginning of Confusions: *"Ten years from now I'll write a book set in a morgue." Is* Above Ground *that book, or to what extent is* Above Ground *that book? Because the presence of death in the book is almost palpable, isn't it?*

Yes. No, I think that Gillis there is of course being facetious, but at the same time he's talking about the direction everything is taking; that is, if dehumanization proceeds to a certain point, then only the computers, only the hardware will be significant, and the absolute equivalent of dehumanization is death, and therefore. . . .

One writes a book.

One writes in a morgue, right. No, I would say that though *Above Ground* is rather a dark book, and of course the end of the book is a kind of incredible lament, that it still is in life and addressed to the possibilities of life.

Set against all this, there is the role of—well, the dramatic and effective assertion of life comes through sexuality, through fucking, in fact.

Yes, and one of the ways is the constant affirmation of physical existence, and sexual embrace is sort of the highest form that this takes, so that when you're talking about life, it's not some kind of abstraction. I mean, it has to do with birth, it has to do with death itself incidentally, and it has to do with this sort of incredible union between a man and a woman: that is when Mavra knows that if she's ranting and raving, if she gets into the sack, she'll stop it, and Joshua knows that all this other stuff can just be shunted aside, and at the same time knows that what takes place in time is not a victory over time, and you cannot fuck out of time, and therefore a sexual embrace which takes place in time is a pyrrhic victory over time.

Lila and Nate, in Above Ground, *reveal one of the central and very practical applications of sexuality, of assertion of life, because when she makes him believe he's great in bed, she can make him believe that he can deal with the mob, he can deal with the Mafia.*

Exactly. Yes, this is one of those little parable things almost, but very realistic, that is dropped into things in contrast to Maggie's situation. Here is this woman, and incidentally, she really is there for herself, but she's there for Philip Roth too. And I had a conversation with Philip Roth a few years ago and we were talking about his attitude towards New Jersey ladies and, you know, the whole sort of middle-class crew, and I asked him if he had ever met anyone who looked like all the others and turned out not to be, and he vowed no, and of course if you've read *Portnoy's Complaint*, you know bloody well that he never had, which is too bad for him. (*laughter*) But the point is that again there are all kinds of ways of deluding yourself, and any time a novelist loses the freshness of his involvement with what is before him, he's gone, and one of the sad things is to see a really brilliant writer and a very, very funny gifted guy like Roth repeatedly, you know, book after book, fall into a cliché. I mean, he really has fallen into a cliché about middle-class people. Now, I have run into characters who are something like Lila — I've never met anybody exactly like Lila, but I have met these people — and then, as you look at them, there is nothing about them that would lead you to believe that they have really grasped something significant and important and done something about it. And so she's there, and you know she's. . . .

She's very convincing.

Yes, she's very convincing.

What that little parable really implies is that if you believe you're good at life, you can handle what it throws at you.

Exactly. Or at least, if you can't handle it, you can handle something. I think that the metaphor that comes through *Confusions* and comes through *Above Ground* — and of course it will be even more obvious in the new book — is the metaphor of the mastery of something, and the mastery of something may be even the mastery of illusion. For instance, I have one whole chapter in the novel that I'm writing now where a character is contemplating the rape of his secretary, and as the chapter goes on, you realize that this has been going on every week for sixteen years, and that it's obviously never going to take place. And yet it is all there, he becomes terribly excited and the whole thing builds up, and he keeps looking at the secretary, and timing it, and when he times it, all the character qualities which made it impossible for him to do it sixteen years earlier of course crowd in again, and the disclaimers follow one after the other.

Is there any virtue in being able to sustain the excitement even of the illusion?

Yes, because obviously this is really what has kept this guy going, though it's not like an Ibsen type of illusion. It's not a political illusion or a *Wild Duck* kind of illusion. I mean, it's an illusion that is a great involvement and where the fantasy becomes the equivalent of what happens in real life. A friend of mine, we were talking about some hypochondriac, some guy who went around with great, great headaches and, you know, just involved in millions of dollars of medical investigations and nothing ever found, and the guy himself finally came to realize that he was a hypochondriac, and this friend of mine, who was an internal medicine specialist, said one thing that's never been properly understood is that imagined pain and real pain are exactly the same in their intensity, so that fantasy has reality which may have all the qualities of reality for those who are unable to reach into reality. That's the significant thing.

Yes. You've partially answered my next question, but I'd like to ask it anyway for elaboration. What's going to happen to Joshua when he gets old, when he gets too old for fucking to be the metaphor of the assertive . . . ?

That's one of the things that one cannot conceive of, that one absolutely cannot conceive of. (*laughter*) I mean, I really can't. You know, all the grey octogenarians, you're not interested in the octogenarians who cop out and fall to the side, but you know, guys like Hans Hofmann, the painter, Picasso, these are the guys, you know, who are affirming life, and there's just no end to it, so that . . . I think that the metaphor still exists.

Yes. Well, I'll ask what is almost a by-product of that: to what extent can writing or is writing an equivalent kind of metaphor for assertion, for the control that you're talking about, the mastery?

If we remember what I said about the sexual embrace, that is the irony of the sexual embrace which withstands time and withstands death while using time; and that writing, serious writing, which affirms something counter to time still exists in time. I think that one of the good illustrations of this is, you know, Proust's *À la Recherche du Temps Perdu*. Here is the book that is supposed to crystallize all experience and keep it away from destructive time, but the book is written in destructive time and all the characters, while he is writing this long, long book, are growing older, so that he may have them in jars at the beginning of the book, but if he's going to keep them in jars at the end of the book, the people in the two sets of jars have obviously undergone tremendous changes, and that of course is the irony. And in that sense, of course, one of the tough things that you accept is that writing is no compensation — at least, I don't believe in Shakespeare's notion of literature or poetry being something immortal, withstanding time. I really believe with Yeats that it's in the work itself that everything exists, and in the affirmation to the work, through the work, that things mean anything at all, and that you accept the fact that they die and may die or just fall to the wayside.

There's the figure of Uncle Vim in Above Ground *who suggests an alternative way to Joshua; he's described as "waving his arms to discount the finite"; a very attractive and a very impressive figure who gives Joshua considerable strength from that first, almost magical assertion. How does he fit in?*

Well, he's somebody who comes with the seasons and he is almost like time, and because of this superior attitude towards clock time, he waves aside the insignificant, he waves aside pain, and he waves aside any kind of restriction and he doesn't even believe in the actuality of the finite, and therefore he is always talking about, you know, you will overcome and you will become this and you will do that, and there is no question in his mind at all, and of course the way he dies is the way you would expect somebody like that to die: he dies with his hat on, with his shoes on, in bed and sort of stretched out, with a cigarette in his mouth.

Yes. There's the question of — I think madness is perhaps not the best word for it, but I can't think of another one that isn't clinical — but throughout both books there are characters like Jarvis, the naked kid with the table legs who runs berserk and all; there's Gersh's sister in Above

Ground; *there is obviously Devereux Peterson, in* Confusions. *I'll ask you: is Mavra mad in the same way?*

No, no, she's not mad in the same way. They are mad and they become metaphors for something that she cannot become a metaphor for. The word that's used, I think, in connection with all of them is the word *reversible* or the word *irreversible*; and the toughest thing to accept, I think, in existence is the notion of irreversibility. I think that we can't believe, for instance, that if we spill something, we can't wash it out, or if something is ripped, we can't sew it up. I mean, everything has to be repaired, and one of the really hard things to accept is there are things that happen that cannot be repaired, and they just stand there. And of course it's really part of the shock of involving one's sensibility in life to confront the things that are not reversible, and so somebody like Devereux or somebody like Evvy — I mean, here is someone you look at and suddenly, you know, the interstices of space part and you're looking at a different kind of thing, you see it is totally changed, and how can you accept that?

Mavra, then, is reversible; she can if she wants . . . but she can't give herself a different past, though, and you suggest. . . .

No. The thing is, she probably isn't reversible, but she's capable of, you know, a million kinds of sort of emotional moments. We are dealing with the difference between a neurotic person and the kind of pathos that attaches to that, and the kind of pathos that attaches to a psychotic, and it is there where the hopelessness has been accepted.

Okay. A final question: does being a novelist, an artist, if you like, demand a particular kind of selfishness?

Oh, it demands the selfishness of time as like, you know, if I'd been working as intensely as I have been, say, over the last six months or so, that time has to come from something, and it has come from — well, there are friends of mine in Toronto, for instance, whom I haven't seen for, say, three months or something like that, and if anyone had told me that I would come to Toronto and not see close friends of mine for that long, I just wouldn't have believed it.

Does this selfishness appear anywhere else except in time? If the novelist's province is his own experience and his own feelings, does his concern with these have anything to do with that selfishness?

Well, it's a self-fullness. I mean, what it is is, when something is buzzing, when you're in the middle of your work, you can't believe that there is anything outside of it, and it's impossible. It's not just that the freedom of field that the existentialists talk about has been restricted to a page and the page's blankness is disappearing, it's that something is growing out of there, and you feel that it's just obliterated everything else. And how can, for instance, this other kind of paltry thing be going on? And of course the paltry thing might be the Vietnam War. Particularly today.

This kind of — I come back to the word selfishness *— how does it complicate your relationships with people, or does it?*

Well, you know, it's a difficult business. That is, the same amount of imagination and concern and sort of emotional commitment that's needed for writing is needed in the day-to-day existence. And from my point of view, life proceeds in that way too. I mean, it proceeds on an hour-to-hour basis and it's something that you work at, and if you do, for instance, at a particular time have to cut out from something else in order to keep your work going, you have to remember that you did that, and at some point make up for it or do something else. Now, children, of course, have a terrific amount to put up with, when a father, for instance, is a writer and is involved in this particular way.

I was going to ask what happens with family, with children, with members of your family that you write about or not. I'm not suggesting that it isn't fiction, but surely there are people whom you know and who have in some way contributed towards characters in books —

This, of course, is one of the toughest things of all. I don't know how it is possible for one to write fiction without drawing on the experiences closest to one, and as a result, you know, you really have to take a stand on it. And it's — of course it is, I suppose, selfish, and it may even be murderous on a particular level. The demands that the book may make are the demands that are met, and, you know, it is very difficult for you to believe in the fictional thing which you believe in as a work of art having a human effect which is not in the realm of art, but I'm frequently just terribly shocked. Somebody came up and told me that there was a reference in *Above Ground*, a very, very minor detail, a reference to the hue of someone's face, and evidently someone out in California thought that this might have referred to someone that she knew, and she was terribly, terribly distraught by this thing. And of course my feeling was that, considering all I have to answer for, this is very slight, but at the same time I just couldn't believe that this could or would be an issue.

ALICE MUNRO

FICTION
Dance of the Happy Shades
Lives of Girls and Women

ALICE MUNRO was born in Wingham, Ontario, in 1931.

I'll begin with a general question: do you think writers know something special, in the way physicists or anthropologists do?

You mean probably that writers are . . . have just seen something special. I don't think they *know* something special. I do think that they, perhaps, just perhaps they see things differently. Well, I know to me, just things in themselves are very important. I'm not a writer who is very concerned with ideas. I'm not an intellectual writer. I'm very, very excited by what you might call the surface of life, and it must be that this seems to me meaningful in a way I can't analyze or describe.

Now, when you say it's not that they know something special but they see something special . . . what kinds of things?

Well, for me it's just things about people, the way they look, the way they sound, the way things smell, the way everything is that you go through every day. It seems to me very important to do something with this.

Yes. I mean, perhaps one of the most exciting things I found in reading your stuff was an incredible kind of recognition of how things are.

It seems to me very important to be able to get at the exact tone or texture of how things are. I can't really claim that it is linked to any kind of a religious feeling about the world, and yet that might come closest to describing it.

A slightly different kind of question: in what way is writing important to you?

God . . . do you mean why do I do it? I don't know if I can get at that. I always have done it. It's . . . do you mean is it important as a kind of therapy? No, that's not it. I don't know why it's important. I don't understand this. I know that I'm never not writing, so that I'm not just sort of turning out one book and then taking a rest and then turning out another book. I'll never live long enough to deal with all the ideas that are — things that are working, because I write very slowly and things, with me, things sort of jell very slowly. But there are always things there that just — well I'm thinking of a thing I'm working on now which I haven't really begun to write much of at all, and it just, it exists and so I'm going to have to put it down or forget it. If I can.

You say it exists. So then is your writing a response to something that is simply there?

Not there in the external world. It's there in my head, this story, if you want to call it that, the characters, the relationship, the lives of these people. I can now see it in my mind, not very well, rather dimly, and things will change as I work it out, but something is there that I'm probably going to have to deal with. Though other things are also there that I have failed to deal with. Often I fail to deal with things several times before I work them out successfully.

But it's all there, and of course it comes from the external world. Where else would it come from? But I'm not the kind of writer that says: Now I've got to do something, I've got to write something about this existing problem or this relationship or this experience I've had. I don't work that directly.

It's not problem solving them?

No.

Dell, in Lives of Girls and Women, *says: "How contemptuous, how superior and silent and enviable they were, those people who all their lives could stay still, with no need to do or say anything remarkable!"*

Yes, I do feel that about those people, don't you?

Yes, but presumably one of the things that drives Dell is the need to do something remarkable.

Yes, I suppose that does, it certainly drove me when I was a child. I always planned to be famous before I was quite sure which direction I would go in. Now I would like to say that drive has left, but. . . .

To do something remarkable and to be famous are different things, aren't they? I mean, the desire to be famous is. . . .

Yes, is the reward for doing the remarkable thing. No, but you can do something remarkable in order to be noticed partly, can't you? Not just to achieve the thing in itself, and I think as a child I always wanted very much to be noticed.

One of the things she also says is: "To be made of flesh was humiliation." I want to make the distinction here between your desire to write and what motivates Dell, but perhaps her need to do something remarkable has something to do with this sense of humiliation. Do you think that carries over at all into writing?

With me it has something to do with the fight against death, the feeling that we lose everything every day, and writing is a way of convincing yourself perhaps that you're doing something about this. You're not really, because the writing itself does not last much longer than you do; but I would say it's partly the feeling that I can't stand to have things go. There's that feeling about the — I was talking about the external world, the sights and sounds and smells — I can't stand to let go without some effort at this, at capturing them in words, and of course I don't see why one has to do that. You can experience things directly without feeling that you have to do that, but I suppose I just experience things finally when I do get them into words. So writing is a part of my experience.

And the way of really coming to terms with your experience is to write.

Yes, and I can't imagine living any other way.

Dell also says there's no protection unless it is in knowing.

That's talking about death, specifically. Yes, it could be something to do with writing, couldn't it? But it doesn't protect you really. You know when you're writing, and I think people think of a writer that he or she is someone who knows, and yet in one's ordinary life this doesn't carry over.

And the thing is, presumably, that if you put it down so that you really did know, then you'd stop writing.

Yes, I think perhaps . . . *(laughter)* You know, when I'm in the really hellish part of a book, I think, This is the last book, when I finish this book, I'm going to stop and live like a sensible person. And even now I think maybe after the next book, though just a little while back I said to you I can't imagine living without writing, I think possibly that I could attain some level where I would have done enough and where I — maybe as you say, I would know, and then I wouldn't write anymore.

What is the knowing, just what it is like to be alive?

Yes, and it may be a way of getting on top of experience; this is different from one's experience of the things in the world, the experience with other people and with oneself, which can be, which is so confusing and humiliating and difficult and by dealing with it this way, though, I don't mean that I deal directly with personal experience, though I do but after quite a long time has elapsed. I think it's a way of getting control.

Imposing order?

Yes, but it's control by hindsight in a way, isn't it? And as I said, it doesn't mean you have control over what is happening now.

Dell also says, they are talking to her about writing, she says: "They were talking to somebody who believed that the duty of the writer is to produce a masterpiece."

Well, that is indeed what I did believe till I was maybe thirty years old (*laughter*) and I realized that the choice I had was not between producing a masterpiece and producing something else, but between producing something else and producing nothing at all (*laughter*) and I became more realistic.

You said you've always been writing. How really did you start writing?

I started writing things down when I was about fourteen or fifteen, and earlier than that I made up stories all the time. But I think they were the things that — I think many children do this, and I don't know, maybe loneliness in adolescence is one of the things that makes it persist.

And insisting on your own view of the world too, I guess.

Yes, perhaps it helps to grow up feeling very alienated from the environment you happen to live in, which is another thing that happened to me.

Where did the alienation come from?

Well, I grew up in a rural community, a very traditional community. I almost always felt it. I find it still when I go back. The concern of everyone else I knew was dealing with life on a very practical level, and this is very understandable, because my family are farmers and they are two or three generations away from being pioneers. In order to survive it's necessary to be very good at making things with your hands, and always to think practically, and not to see more than is obviously there, not to see what we call beauty or — oh I'm not doing very well here, but I always realized that I had a different view of the world, and one that would bring me into great trouble and ridicule if it were exposed. I learned very early to disguise everything, and perhaps the escape into making stories was necessary.

It's an extremely impractical kind of a thing to be doing.

To most of my relatives the work I do is still a very meaningless, useless type of work.

A frill, if anything.

Not even a frill, almost a wrong thing to be doing, because it is so — if I were hooking rugs, though, it would be all right, you see, because you put the rugs on the floor and people walk on them, but what do you do with books? In the community where I grew up, books were a time-waster and reading is a bad habit, and so if even reading is a bad habit, writing is an incomprehensible thing to do.

Dell's Uncle Craig, with the two sisters — when they were younger, when she first knew them, they were really admirable and attractive people, but you make a great point of her seeing that one of the real virtues for them is hiding one's own personal light under a bushel.

Yes, this was certainly true in my family, and with many people of this sort of Scotch-Irish background in that part of the country. One doesn't try because one may fail . . . the personal revelation is also something that isn't understood at all. It's a shameful thing.

Another general question. Given that writing is a lonely thing, have you felt isolated as a writer on top of the personal loneliness?

You mean because I haven't known other writers, and because I've been working alone for so long? Oh no, I don't think I've suffered any unnecessary loneliness at all.

What about being a Canadian writer? Or do you think in these terms at all?

No . . . I'm beginning to feel guilty that I haven't, because it's being borne in on one that one should (*laughter*) but — no, I haven't.

Do you think there are any obvious advantages or disadvantages in being a Canadian writer?

I think there are some fairly obvious advantages, that a lot of the ground hasn't been ploughed before, and that — I don't really think in competitive terms — the words I'm choosing are not quite right, I was going to say the competition is not as stiff. I don't quite mean that, but I can think of so many very, very good short story writers working in the United States whose names are hardly known, I would imagine, even to Americans. It seems to me that in Canada, if you are doing good work, recognition comes pretty readily.

Any disadvantages?

I suppose it's possible that you don't reach as wide an audience as quickly or something like that, but no, I don't really feel there are disadvantages. I feel damn lucky to be a Canadian writer.

That's good, and it's curious because that's been the kind of response I've had from most people. . . . Okay. It struck me, I guess partly because my writing, like yours, comes out of Southwestern Ontario, that Southwestern Ontario might become a kind of mythical country, like the American South for example.

Yes, I've thought of this, yes, probably because the writers who first excited me were the writers of the American South, because I felt there a country being depicted that was like my own. I can think of several writers now who are working out of Southwestern Ontario. It is rich in possibilities in this way. I mean the part of the country I come from is absolutely Gothic. You can't get it all down.

Also I think the culture there is a prevailing culture, which is a nice thing. They really do have a sense of tradition. They really do have a sense of how things have been.

Yes. It's a very rooted kind of place. I think that the kind of writing I do is almost anachronistic, because it's so rooted in one place, and most people, even of my age, do not have a place like this anymore, and it's something that may not have meaning very much longer. I mean this kind of writing.

Okay. A different kind of question again. What is the writer's role in a society? Do you think the writer has any responsibility to society?

I never think about this at all. I have all my life just thought of doing my work and sort of surviving in society. Now this is a very selfish point of view perhaps. I don't feel anything about responsibility or a role, but I think this is partly because I grew up having to feel so, so protective about this whole thing, about writing, and then, you know, I married young and I was a suburban housewife in the fifties, and I went through the whole thing again, of having to be very — having to protect the real thing I did, so that I suppose I function as if I were cut off from society, and I'm always even rather surprised when, well, when a book is published, that it exists, when people say I read your book. *(laughter)*

Right. This then would be a good time to ask have you found that there are any particular problems as a writer in being a woman?

Yes, I think there are great problems — it's almost impossible. But then there are problems for a man in this country too because you have to be a wage earner, and I'm not sure that a woman's problems are any greater. But there are tremendous, you know, emotional demands made by children.

Yes. You have three children, and that in itself is, as you say, an incredibly demanding thing. What kinds of problems does a woman writer encounter, do you think, even before children? Are there any in the — in coming to be a writer, knowing what your role is as a woman or what the role expected of you is?

Yeah. I think there's a problem in that when you become — it's a way of observing life that is not, that perhaps doesn't work well with one's role as a woman. The detachment of the writer, the withdrawal is not what is traditionally expected of a woman, particularly in the man–woman relationship. Most women writers I know are very ambivalent this way. There's the desire to give, even to be dominated, to be — at least I, in many ways, want a quite traditional role — and then of course the writer stands right outside this, and so there's the conflict right there. And then when children come, well, some of the problems are practical. It's getting enough time, like in twenty years I've never had a day when I didn't have to think about somebody else's needs. And this means the writing has to be fitted in around it. I've read about myself, you know, Alice Munro has produced little, and I think it's a miracle that I've produced anything.

How do you find the time, say with young children, to write? Did you find the time when they were young?

Yes, I've always found the time except for a few years when my confidence failed me completely, and it wasn't the children, it was my own problems. But I just found it through incredible stubbornness and really through fighting the children, which may not be a good thing.

It seems to me a hell of a lot harder for the woman writer than for the man writer, because at least the man can leave his office. But the house is there all the time.

Yes, the problem is when you're young, when you are a young wife and mother as I was, it's awfully hard to say: Well I'm going to — well, not neglect — but withdraw from this child to do my work, because at that point you have no confidence that your work is ever going to be any good. And you have to get very tough.

There is some of that suggested in the short story where the character gets an office . . . she needs an office and it begins with an apology. . . .

Terrific apology.

Yes, that one is going to do this at all. What about before, say before one is married, even? The kind of image that a woman has of herself, a girl has of herself. It's quite all right for a young man to think, well I'm going to explore the world, write books, go on and on forever, you know — have fantastic sexual adventures all over the place. But a young woman has a very different image of herself, doesn't she — or does she?

Yes. Well, she doesn't have a different image of herself. . . . I think the generation growing up now is entirely different. But if I go back to when I was growing up, I always operated in disguises, feeling if I do to a certain point what the world expects of me, then they'll leave me alone, and I can do my work. I never did feel that in order to write I had to go to Europe, go to North Africa, go round the world, or do any damn thing at all, but just have a room with a typewriter in it, that was all I needed. And so I put the world off by hiding this as much as possible, but getting on with it.

Is writing a secretive thing for you then?

Yes, I still can't write if there's another adult in the house. I don't quite know why this is, but it must be that I'm still embarrassed about it somehow.

How do you work when it's going well? Do you write quickly, do you write slowly?

When I start the first draft I write fairly slowly, I write about seven hundred words a day; and then when I get on to the second draft, I write maybe twice that many, and so on until when I'm doing the final draft, I just work twelve, fourteen hours a day and rip very fast.

Do you enjoy writing?

Yeah. I like it when it's going well — why shouldn't I? That's the only thing I can do. I can't play tennis. (*laughter*)

Okay. A couple of questions which may or may not be of interest. What do you like best about your work, about what you've done?

You know, what I really like, I like when it's funny and I love it when someone laughs, when the pre-pub copies came out and my husband was reading it and he was lying in bed and laughing. I would be looking over his shoulder and say: What are you laughing at? To me it was great to have brought this off, because I think when you have made something funny, you've achieved some kind of reality. That's what I'm trying to get.

All right, the other side of that question is what do you like least about the work you've done so far?

I think it's sometimes too wordy. I think my approach is slow sometimes. I don't know if there is anything I could say I like least, but there are failures all through that I can see, and that I can't do anything about. They're not failures that I could have gone back and changed, I knew they were failures when the book was finished. They were things that I just couldn't do. I feel that the last section of *Lives of Girls and Women* is a failure, and I did the best I could with it. But what else do I like? Some of the stories I don't like at all anymore, but that's because they were written so long ago.

Whom do you write for?

Well, is it the constant reader, the ideal reader? (*laughter*) You know, we all have an ideal reader. I can't say I write for myself, though it has to suit me and when it suits me I'm not moved, no matter what an editor or a critic or anybody says. So in a sense I'm writing for myself.

Do you have any sense that you want to reach a lot of people with your writing? I mean apart from what you said earlier about the desire for recognition.

I want to reach as many people as possible, yes. But when I'm writing I don't think about that. In fact I find really the only way I can write is to forget about it being published and reaching people at all. Otherwise the sense of self-exposure or something would be too — I couldn't stand it.

Does being a writer demand a particular kind of selfishness?

Oh goodness yes. Well, yes. Yes, of course, you have to think that your work is more important than almost anything else, and you have to start thinking this when you're very young. And I can't understand quite where this selfishness or confidence or — where it comes from. You have to believe it the way you see it, and perhaps this is what makes the difference between all the people who sort of have talent and write stories for the university magazines and the people who go on writing. I think it's a matter of selfishness and this irrational inner confidence, and I don't know where it comes from.

It isn't need, is it, because a lot of people who write good stories, people who want to be writers, have as much need to be a writer as the people who succeed . . . so you think it's probably just a kind of icy confidence.

Yes, I think this is the way I see it — is it that you want to get across to people how you see it or . . . No, just that you think it's so important.

Given the assumption one has, we all have it, that if we write, we assume that some people will want to read us . . . what you feel you have to give is your image of how things are?

Yes, but actually when I'm writing, I don't think of it as *my* image. I am so far gone that I think of it as *the* image, as a kind of revelation coming from . . . you know.

You succeed very well at it, I might just say. Does the selfishness — do you find your selfishness complicates your relationships with people?

Well, I try to hide it pretty well, (*laughter*) but if it gets out. Yes, I think it does and then to go back to what we were saying about the specific problems of being a woman, and a writer, I think it complicates a woman's life much more than a man's, because men are expected to be selfish in a way about their work, to have faith in themselves.

And insist upon their work.

And it is disturbing if women do this.

Because it's an assertion of self which is not expected.

Yes, which is outside the whole relationship to men and children.

Your stories are very personal. I use personal *as opposed to* autobiographical. . . . *Do you find yourself wanting to use people, wanting to use people in situations, but feeling you shouldn't because in fact they would recognize it?*

Oh yes, I have this problem. There are a lot of things I can't use because of this, but I've been going through a very personal kind of writing which I think may have culminated in a book. I never particularly wanted to do this kind of writing, I fought against it for a long time. I told somebody the other day I really want to write stories like Frank O'Connor's stories in which, you know, there are all these people living at a distance, going through lives. But when I try to do things like this it doesn't work — it isn't for lack of trying. So I ended up doing all this very personal stuff. I'm not sure whether I'll go on doing this.

At the end of "Images," a really nice short story, the girl encounters the. . .

Yes, I like that short story the best.

. . . not a madman or anything, but the eccentric, and she comes home and what she has discovered out of it all is that "our fears are based on nothing but the truth."

Yes, well that's what I believe. (*laughter*)

I mean the whole force of your writing seems to be on that. The fears and the triumphs are just out of what is in fact there.

Yes.

Do you see yourself as trying to record things, like a representational painter?

Well, I see my technique as being very traditional, very conventional. Yes, sometimes this worries me, because I see other people making breakthroughs — it's not — maybe it is in a way a thing like, well — I'm not doing the current thing, but it isn't really that. It's that I seem very slow to pick up these ways of doing things which are really so good, so effective. But I suppose, I don't even know the terms in which one talks about painting, but I suppose what I admire is a kind of super-realism anyway, like I'm crazy about Edward Hopper.

Andrew Wyeth?

Yes. Jack Chambers too. So it may be that I'm trying to do this, this same thing.

You talk about people doing things that you admire and breaking through; are they things that you want to do?

Well, I wish I had thought of them. (*laughter*) They mightn't work for me, because I don't think you can superimpose anything on your writing. You can't say: Well, I'm going to chop up these sentences or some damn thing, you know. You just can't do it that way; it's got to come from you, but nothing like this does come from me. I tend to work, as you know, in a pretty traditional way.

It really is a very human and a very compassionate kind of way that you write. It's almost as if there is no style. I mean that as a compliment.

Yes, I know what you mean. But you see that I don't write about, I can't write about states of mind. I have to write about — I can't have anybody in a room without describing all the furniture. (*laughter*) You know . . . I can't yet get into people or life without — it's really what I was saying earlier — without having all those other things around them, and God knows that isn't the way most people live anymore.

Yes, all right, in some sense your characters aren't alienated in the modern traditional sense of alienated. They react against something, but they are always part of something, aren't they?

Yes. But up to now I've only written about Western Ontario, and I've mainly written about — well, my personal stuff has been about childhood and adolescence.

You say you started writing at fourteen, and at some point you presumably settled into writing very seriously. Do you have finished books, novels, which haven't seen the light of day yet?

No, no, no no. I just have boxes full of abortions. You know, things that haven't fully developed.

Do you find yourself writing with no end in view, no particular story or novel? Do you find yourself just simply writing episodes?

No, no. I'm fairly controlled. This is another thing I wish I could do; I wish I could just write and see where it was going, where it would take me, but no, I have a pretty well-defined pattern. I don't know whether I'm going to be able to bring it off, but I don't sit down without it.

At what point do you recognize that it's not going to be a long short story, but it's in fact going to be a book in itself?

Yeah. Well. I think I'll really tell you about this because — (*laughter*) — it's a bit damaging in a way, because some people said, of course, *Lives* is only a collection of long short stories. This doesn't particularly bother me, because I don't feel that a novel is any step up from a short story. When I began to write *Lives*, you see, I began to write it as a much more, a much looser novel, with all these things going on at the same time, and it wasn't working. Then I began pulling the material and making it into what are almost self-contained segments. I mean, the sections could almost stand as short stories. They're all a little bit too loose, but this seemed to be the only way I could work, and I think maybe this is the way I'll have to write books. I write sort of on — like a single string, a tension string — okay? That's the segment or the story. I don't write as perhaps — as some people say a true novelist does, manipulating a lot of strings.

All right, a question that may be a difficult one: where do you go from here? It's almost as if — I mean, is there any danger that you will have exorcised all the ghosts?

It might well be. You mean, when I started — you know, about half the stories in the first book are sort of beginning stories and then they start getting closer and closer. The first one I wrote, "The Peace of Utrecht," I didn't even want to write, because it's the most autobiographical story I've ever written. It was very close, and from then on this was the only kind of story I wrote, and then I began writing the book. Okay. I've gone, yeah, I've gone as far as I can go in this direction.

What you've really done is perhaps just exorcised the ghosts of child-hood, you know, there's. . . .

Yeah. But dealing with the ghosts of one's maturity is more difficult. (*laughter*)

They're more persistent.

Yes. They're still there.

Okay. There's another intriguing area, and that is the relationship between men and women. And there are two quotes, I'll read them both, because it seems to me they give two emphases. Dell is talking about the bright young man whom she is in high school with — they are competing for marks — and she says about him: "He was truthful in telling me what he felt about me, apparently. I had no intention of being so with him. Why not? Because I felt in him what women feel in men, something so tender, swollen, tyrannical, absurd. I would never take the consequences of interfering with it. I had an indifference, a contempt almost that I concealed from him. I thought I was tactful, even kind. I never thought that I was proud." And then she also talks . . . that's one side of a woman's relationship with a man. Then there's the other when she talks about her Uncle Craig, and she says: "Masculine self-centredness made him restful to be with." (laughter) Now. . . .

Well, it does. I was remembering how I felt about men when I was a child. They never wanted to do anything with you. I mean to change you to . . . What was the question?

I'm not sure exactly what it is. It had to do partially with the kind of — and maybe I ask this primarily as a man, you know, I'm not sure, but it intrigues me, the kind of secretive world that is suggested, particularly in the first quote about Dell's perception of the young man, and also the sense that — and the two aunts have the same thing about Craig, when he's away typing. All he has to do is go in there and type and they're impressed on the one hand, but at the same time they find him — what? Childish?

Yes.

And there again is ambiguity.

Yes, I do feel that that's what women have felt about men and about men's work. On the one hand, men have to be built up so that they can fill this role of lover, leader, dominator that we have been taught to require, or that perhaps we do basically require, I'm not even sure it's all what we're taught. At the same time, there's a feeling that they're children who have to be protected from the knowledge of how meaningless their endeavours are. (*laughter*) I think this is true because women particularly are concerned with the very basic things about life, the food, the physical life, and what men do then seems almost like an indulgence.

Is it because they're more social in their ego in some sense?

Women?

Men. I mean they're out there in this society which on the whole your characters have found alien and hurtful and in many ways absurd; and men's egos are much more concerned with those kinds of things? Whereas the women basically are much more concerned with making jam. I don't mean that in a derogatory sense, but in the sense that they are just actual practical things. . . .

The women are concerned with taking care of the men in a physical sense. Okay. So the men have to be doing something to make taking care of them worthwhile.

But there's also . . . she then meets the guy from the farm who is much more fundamental, I mean the whole sexual exploration, the sexual discovery, but he also has in his church an equally — it's a crutch, isn't it?

A crutch. And something that she doesn't question.

Except that she wants no part of it at all. Within this logic, is the male activity, say in the work, for example — are kinds of crutches that men depend upon?

I wonder if they appear this way to women. I don't know if women go so far as to think of them as crutches. But there's a feeling there that maybe I was trying to get at, a feeling I have that women are much tougher than men, that they can take far more, and that for instance you mustn't criticize men, you mustn't tear them down beyond a certain point. This may be a simple sexual thing, that if a man's confidence is destroyed, the whole function is going to be lost. I can't get at it too well.

We were talking earlier about where you go as a writer. There are worlds to be explored in post-adolescence, you know. Just in terms of Lives of Girls and Women, *say "Lives of Men and Women" or something. I mean, that whole ambivalence, or whatever, is a very rich area. Is that the kind of thing. . . .*

That is the kind of thing I would like to deal with. When I was writing, it interested me tremendously to try to get down these . . . these feelings that women have about men.

The thing is, your whole rendition, dramatization, whatever it is, all the condescension which girls and women have towards men, is something I always suspected as a young man when I was growing up.

Also fear. I think I said something in the book about the way boys, little boys, your pre-adolescent boys, hate girls, and I've always felt this too, that there's a kind of a hate there that you can tap in men. It has no equivalent in women's feelings for men.

And you think it carries on beyond the pre-adolescent?

Yes, in adult men too, yes.

Do you have any sense of what it is based on?

Well. Hatred of sex, I think. I'm not sure at all, but most of the terms in which this hostility is expressed are sexual.

Yes, right. Then most pornography has to do with the humiliation.

Yes, yes. So fear of sex . . . and women are responsible for sex. I think that's probably it. But this condescension, as I say, is a very different thing and it has to do with, oh, it may be very compli- cated and it may be something to do with the need to have men like you too. It may not be so much a condescension thing, because you can't criticize men. You can't go too far or they won't approve of you; they think you're a castrating bitch, you know. This very frightening thing.

Do you think men demand or expect from women a kind of admiration or a kind of unthinking support?

Yes, I think they assume their pursuits are more important and their gifts are too, probably.

But in a sense, if they have to go to a woman to have them agree with the importance of their pursuits, they can't totally believe in, can they?

No, I suppose not. You mean if they have to put women down?

I mean the effect of, as she says: "I would never take the consequences of interfering with it," and that is. . . .

No, I think what I meant by that, I think really what I meant is the consequences of any destruction of a male, which is a frightening thing to happen to a woman.

But then when you say it's a destruction of a male, all he was doing was assuming that he was more important than she. I mean, he puts her down for her interest in the humanities. . . .

Yes he puts her down, okay, but she doesn't really. . . .

She doesn't accept that.

She doesn't accept it.

But she simply avoids it.

Yes. Okay. Why can't she put him down? It's a fear that he might just be too crushed, that he wouldn't have the resources that she has to survive being put down, because women have been in this position for a hell of a long time, and they have the strength of any subject race to survive.

Do you think that basically one of the problems women have in coming to terms with men is that they're afraid of destroying them?

It's a problem I have, yes. Yes. But then this is all dealing with, you know, a generation ago. I wonder how things have changed. They may have changed a great deal or maybe less than we suspect. I don't know.

I suspect less, actually. (laughter) This is the area that the book you're working on is concerned with?

Yes.

Wow. You've got no shortage of material.

MORDECAI RICHLER

MORDECAI RICHLER was born in Montreal in 1931.

Well, the first thing I'll ask is whether you think that writers know any-thing special in the sense that physicists do or anthropologists do.

That's a very intricate question. First of all, it's not an exact science; it's hardly a science at all, it has to do with intuitions. Possibly it's not so much that they know any more as that they're compelled to tell what they do know. I can't generalize. I don't think I know more, and this is not a modest statement. I feel compelled to be an honest witness to what I do know. Involved in this is a recognition of death, a kind of desire for vengeance, I guess, and a need to be known as well. Somehow there's a mixture of motives, but there are a lot of easier ways to earn a living, as you know. . . . Well, I certainly have a lot more questions than answers. I don't think I have any answers.

Then the questions presumably are questions that anybody could feel but not necessarily articulate. Or do you have a province or a kind of area where you function, say, where other people don't, where for other people it may simply be recognition of something you show them?

Well, I have a need to deal with an ordered world. I find the one we live in very disordered, and so when I'm alone in my room writing, I'm ordering my own world. I make all the laws (*laughter*) and it's exacting, it's not always enjoyable, but obviously it's the only thing I really do enjoy. I'm not trying to slide off, but it's very difficult. I don't believe in special privileges for writers, or that they're a special case, or that any kind of artist is a special case, and anyway, when you're not writing, your problems are the same as anyone else's. In fact, when you're writing, they're related to your craft or trade or art or what have you, but everyone has one. So I do not believe that there's an artistic temperament or that artists are — well, to take the worst clichés, absent-minded, or bad about handling their money or any of that crap. They're all different. But there's also a kind of arrogance involved. Yes, I feel I have something I want to say, and what I have to say may be a lot of crap, but that's for someone else to decide, to pronounce on.

How much of your writing is for yourself — and I'm not talking in terms of therapy, I'm just talking in terms of personal satisfaction and then a working out of personal things? How much is for the audience, whoever they may be?

Well, it's a very subtle, I guess, mixture of — there are days when I enjoy it, let's say one out of ten, and there's an enormous satisfaction, or pleasure, what I think of as bonus days, when the writing goes well. It would not be complete if I then tore it up and said: Well, I did that and that is fine, nobody has to know about it. I'm not that pure, and also there is a relationship between yourself and the reader. But when I think of the reader, I really think of my friends, and I can sometimes, after such a day or rereading passages I've been working on, think that, Well, X, someone I — a friendship I cherish, or someone I enjoy — will like this and I want him to or her to, but that's . . . One is involved with ten or twelve people in this world and not more. Now on a coarser, or

on a trade level, the more people who want to read it, the happier
I am, but there is nothing in the back of my mind that this will go
over or people won't like that.

*But when you talk about not liking the disordered world, when you order
it in your room, are you ordering it primarily for yourself or do you in fact
want people to learn from you?*

I don't want people to learn so much, although . . . I mean, I do
think the difference between a serious writer and a commercial
writer — and I don't despise commercial writers — is fundamentally a moral one. An artist also tells a story, which is Forster's
distinction, and I think that writing is within a moral tradition,
and so however apolitical you may be, you're making moral
choices and judgments, and I write out of a kind of disgust with
things as they are, certainly, and I get relief out of this. Now if it
were mere ranting, there would be no point in it at all, so it must
be informed by a level of wit and style and so forth.

*But if you're writing out of a sense of disgust, then if you are moral, you
would presumably want people to change on the basis of what you see.*

I'm not the kind of writer who can change or expects to change
anything. What I do hope to do is set down a sort of honest
record of things of our time and our place, to balance . . . I don't
know if you've read something I once wrote in a *New American
Review*, where I spoke of the writer as a kind of loser's advocate,
as a witness to injustices in this world, and said that the writer
should speak for those people who are not getting a fair share of
the sun. I don't mean social justice really, although of course I
want to see more social justice. I mean other things, wider rami-
fications of injustice.

266   ELEVEN CANADIAN NOVELISTS

Okay, a slightly different kind of question. You have a great deal of experience with all kinds of writing. What is there specifically about the novel that you like?

Well, I'm naturally a novelist, or so I think, and when I try and write short stories, for instance, they end up overcrowded, really like chapters. A writer whom I respect enormously in this country, and there are very few, is Morley Callaghan. However, I think Morley is fundamentally a short story writer, and unfortunately there's some misplaced idea that there's something larger about being a novelist. . . . Anyhow, my talent lies in the novel, I think. I prefer writing novels or short stories or essays to film work, in that I don't naturally or happily come to group activities. You write a novel — it's entirely your own. Of course, the jacket may help or the attention or the binding, but it really doesn't matter. Whereas in a film, you are another part of a machine, an important part, but there are too many factors beyond your control. There are other compensations.

What difference do you think film has made to the novelist, to his craft and to his way of working?

Well, I'd like to answer that on two levels. I think, like any novelist in my generation, I've been enormously influenced by film, and it's a large part of our culture experience, so that we've absorbed certain film techniques into our novel writing. Now, by that I don't mean that we write a novel to be made into a film. I don't mean that at all. I mean we were accustomed to the quick dissolves and time changes, we were all brought up on film, and so part of the storytelling technique in film has become part of our novel-writing technique. I think the films today are somewhat overrated, more than somewhat overrated, even the best of them, and are largely seen by a young audience with very little experience of literature, and they come across things well seen but don't recognize them as being stale or as having occurred in novels or in Joyce years and years ago. But I am interested in films as well and I don't despise films.

What kinds of things do you think film can do better than the novel? Has film liberated the novelist or . . .

No, I do think you reach a much larger audience with a film. It's part of the idiom, whereas novel reading is not. In America, writers tend to be pigeonholed and you're either a film writer or a critic or a novelist, and each group deprecates the other, has contempt for them. In England, it's a lot looser, and, you know, I'm all for that, in that one should not be too arrogant about novel writing. Ninety-five percent of the novels written are written for profit anyway, so I don't see why film is a lesser craft. And there are some very serious film writers about now, and the conditions of film writing have changed. As a writer I'm interested in trying all sorts of different things. Also I haven't got so fertile an imagination that I can go from one novel to another, and so I like breaking it up. I wouldn't like to adapt again, which I have done in the past, like take someone else's book, work on what is really a traditional film project. If I had to, I'd do it, but what I am going to do is an original film, actually with a very good director, and that interests me enormously.

Do you enjoy writing? Do you enjoy sitting down and actually writing?

I don't know anymore. I find it increasingly difficult. I'm more critical of my work and it displeases me more often. Now I think most good writers, and I think of myself as a good writer, are fundamentally in competition with themselves, and your next book is your best book. And I'm harder and harder on my own work. It's no longer a pleasure just to be published, and there was no novel as pleasurable to publish as my first and it's not my best novel by far, but that was a great pleasure. You know.

Yes. Do you find it hard to begin in the day, whatever the routine is?

Well, some days I find it impossible to begin, but I always spend my four hours down there and I may read magazines, I may do a crossword puzzle or check all the baseball averages or get some work done; there are days when it goes and days when it doesn't go. But I think I have to go every day in order to earn the good days.

Right. What sustains you as a writer?

Well, a certain compulsion, a degree of ambition, and an enjoyment of that office.

It's just the fact of being a writer, is that what draws you and holds you there?

Yeah, I can't conceive of myself as doing anything else. I've been lucky; I've had a certain amount of recognition and success, which makes it easier, and you doubt yourself enough without it, so it's — (*laughter*) — I mean, you doubt yourself enough with it, is what I was going to say. But it does make it easier. There are gratifications.

Does being a novelist demand a particular kind of selfishness?

It demands a particular kind of arrogance, yeah, because what you're saying is that your experience or your vision is more interesting than others'. You're saying I'm going to write you a story which is better than any you can tell me in a bar, or more interesting than anything you have to say. And packaging it and saying,

Okay, buy it — there's an arrogance involved in that transaction.

This kind of concern, you know, with self, with the ordering of your views of things — that's what I think I mean by a kind of selfishness.

It's a kind of egotism, certainly.

Does that complicate your relationships with the people around you in any way?

No, it probably makes them easier in that there are these public gratifications or recognitions which maybe make you more generous in personal relationships. This is just conjecture.

Okay. Looking at the stuff you've done, the stuff you're doing now, what do you like best about your work?

Well, I find it unnerving to reread things I've done, and I try not to do it unless I'm driven to it. However, on one level the two things that have satisfied me most are *The Apprenticeship of Duddy Kravitz* and *Cocksure,* and as a matter of fact my book of essays — I'm sorry, I've lost the thread, what . . .

Taking a look at the writing of Mordecai Richler, what do you think are its strengths, the best things about it?

Well. In defence of even my unsatisfying work, it was always what I felt at the time. It was never bent to commercial uses or to any other kind of corruption. Whatever failures of vision or ideas there were were my own failings. What is distressing is that a lot of things you regret are there on the record and can be quoted back at you, (*laughter*) but I'm not displeased with what I've done.

Good. This question is more specifically concerned with the content of your writing. There have been some suggestions that in Cocksure, *at least in that book, that you're a satirist in a kind of conventional way, that is, behind or underlying your criticisms there is an established or small-c conservative view of the world; and yet it seems to me, in looking at your early books, that there is much there to deny this. In one sense the major concerns of your books are the sense of loss, the kind of despair, really, that seems to run through an awful lot of the books. There is reference to honour and to courage and to virtues, but in the families and in the past of nearly all the characters these never seem to be present. Now there are obvious exceptions. Norman's father in* A Choice of Enemies *was a man who made it, who did embody something which Norman, you know, really envied. . . .*

No. I mean, there is a lack of consistency in it. There was always, from *The Acrobats* on, I think — you say I'm concerned with honour and virtue and with the right way to live, which does lead you, I guess, or can lead you into satire and into what seems like conservative reaction, saying let's not destroy what's good.

Yes. But my feeling was, say in The Acrobats — *we will come back to this later, but it seems to me as desperate, as savage a book in some ways, as unrelenting a book as* Cocksure. *I mean, the ending is ostensibly a kind of resolution, but as a reader I didn't think that was particularly convincing; the impact of the book came from the brutalizing of this innocent, and the real virtue somehow in that book was innocence rather than any kind of social or civilized. . . .*

Yes, if I can just interrupt you for a minute, I agree with you, and I think that in almost any writer's work you can find all his ideas and everything he is going to write about in the first book, and the rest are variations or hopefully deeper scrutinies of the same kind of concerns, but most writers have one or two concerns, and I think you can say of *Cocksure* again that the brutalization of innocence. . . .

But, no, the satire thing is that I don't feel that you've ever really drama-tized what this world is that everyone has lost; the fathers and the uncles of most of your characters are very similar, they are weak men, emascu-lated men in a way, so that the immediate predecessors of your heroes, you can look there to find where the world....

... Sort of lost decency or fallen from grace....

Yes, and I've the feeling that there isn't that world which you expect from a satirist, who can turn back as, say, an old Tory would be able to do and say the good old days when, you know, when women weren't allowed into clubs, he could be very specific about the world that he is bemoaning the loss of. Whereas you're not doing that; there is from the very begin-ning a sense of nowhere to turn, of a real Fall. Innocence is brutalized in your books by guys we can't really blame, you know, Ernst killing Nickie, you can see that Ernst can't be held totally responsible for this....

Yeah, well ... Ernst and there's a continuing concern to take ostensibly unsympathetic characters, such as brash, coarse Duddy Kravitz, or....

And Roger in the first book.

Yes, and explore them and say, yes, they are sympathetic and have a case, and....

What I'm trying to get at is this sense of there not being any kind of a clear-cut world for them. Now the enemies were there. They were for Norman's father. He made a choice of enemies and he was a man who could act, and a man who chose a side and was a hero. But he's the only person I can think of who did have that kind of simple instinctive world.

But of course there is no simple world, you know.

Okay. A general question: what writers do you like to read?

Well, I think that the greatest novelist in the English language in our time was Evelyn Waugh. Now, I don't know if that's startling or not, I mean his attitudes or political postures are abhorrent to me, or were, but he was a masterful writer. Faulkner again was a terrifying reactionary and racist, but what a marvellous . . . I know we're stuck with those things. And I also came very early to like Céline enormously — again a mad anti-Semite. I think there are a lot of talented people about today — in England, I don't know. The last novelist I read with a real sense of discovery was Muriel Spark, whose *Memento Mori* I like. I read, you know, Roth and Malamud and Bellow, of course, and other American novelists, all with enjoyment. But I think I've passed the age of being influenced by them.

You mention three writers whom you admire as novelists but whose world view you find unacceptable or at least. . . .

I have to find all their world views unacceptable in order to continue myself.

Do you find as a writer that you have a problem reading other people because of this?

No. I like to know what the shop across the street is selling, but if I thought somebody else was writing my books or, you know, the books I . . . there would be an enormous depression and very little need to go on, so again the arrogance comes in. No, I'm writing what somebody else can't or isn't. But I like also to know what other novelists are doing.

Are there any kinds of writing that you really dislike in the novel?

Oh, I think there's nothing as boring as a seriously meant novel which is bad. I find that more objectionable than an Arthur Hailey, for instance. But I'm not going to name any. (*laughter*)

There's the whole question of influences. I don't know how to ask it or how you want to answer it, but you mentioned Céline and you mentioned Waugh. Do you see them as influences or models?

I guess to some extent. Now when I was a kid, I wanted to write like Malraux and Jean-Paul Sartre and Hemingway; in some ways I guess *The Acrobats* is a pastiche of that kind of writing. I don't think I really found my own style until *Duddy Kravitz*, and then it all became easier in a way because it was all my own. I felt confident then; for better or for worse, this was the way I wanted to write. Until then I was all hit-and-miss and groping around. Possibly I began to write too early and I often think about that, because I left university when I was about nineteen and went off to write, never thinking for a minute that maybe I couldn't, and I regret that unlike, let's say, Brian Moore, who is a very good friend of mine, I haven't had a lot of nasty jobs and that sort of background to fall back on. I've been circulating among other writers and painters almost all my adult life, which is not a very good thing really, because it's a very special sheltered world. There are a lot of big competing egos and other things like that, but fundamentally it's a decent, easy, generous, civilized community to move in, but it can distort your vision of what other people's lives are like. I mean, most of us have jobs we hate and every morning is agony, and that's what life is about, I think, in many ways. And you tend to forget that amidst all that, your friends are having good or bad luck but are doing what they want to do.

Do you feel that you're part of any kind of — school is a lousy word — any kind of recognizable group of writers? Do you associate yourself with any kind of style of writing?

Not really, I think, but I associate myself certainly with feelings that are in the air which we all have or people of my generation have about the way the world is run, and a kind of shared sense of humour, and disgust with politics and impatience, but that belongs to everyone who shares the intellectual life, to readers as well as to writers.

Have you ever been lonely as a writer? Not necessarily as an individual, but as a writer, or in moving off when you were nineteen, moving among this group, did you find a kind of almost social support for what you were doing?

Yes, I found friends and a social support for the first time in my life, and here were people who felt as I did, and who disliked many of the same things I did, and there was a shared pleasure in other things, so for the first time I moved among a community of friends with a taste for books and. . . .

And you feel that's important for a writer?

Well, it was certainly important to me at nineteen, because I was a damned unhappy kid when I left and it was necessary to know there were other people (*laughter*) . . . I mean, Canada was a big and lonely place. I don't know, it is probably not the case now, and everything has shrunk anyway and people move about so much more, but then it seemed like you were at the end of the world.

And that's why you went away, is it? Did you go away with the expectation of a kind of Paris of. . . .

Yeah, I guess there was a lot of romanticism involved, but also I wasn't going somewhere as much as I was getting to hell out of Montreal, which I found suffocating and excruciatingly boring and provincial.

Okay. What sort of feedback do you get as a novelist, you know, letters or personal contacts? Do people recognize you and so on?

Well . . . you get a very varied kind of feedback. You get letters from people who have enjoyed your work and they tend to be very short and shy and the kind of letters you like getting. And you get, you know, kind of nut letters, more from my journalism than from the novels, because you get a much bigger audience, just picking up things accidentally, where somebody who has bought your novel has made a choice. He's read a review or someone has told him about it or he's read an earlier novel. But I get a different kind of feedback here, where a lot more people know you or recognize you and who have not read your novels at all, but have heard that they're nasty (*laughter*) and they can be quite rude, but most of them have not read any of the work at all but have only heard about it third-hand; and it's largely the Jewish community here, you know, who object to it so much. It has its engaging side. They think they have a claim on me. Here I am writing about their village and what in hell do I know about it that they don't know, and what right have I got to do this. Of course, they have never even read it, they just know I say bad things about the Jews in those books. Anyway, it doesn't bother me.

I was going to ask whether feedback is important, whether you like it.

Well, you like it when another writer or someone whose work you may admire, or a critic, writes you about your work privately, or even publicly. I was, for instance, you know, thrilled by Anthony Burgess' review of *Cocksure*. I've never met Burgess, and he understood the book better than most people and liked it and that pleased me.

You said, and it's obviously true, that Canada was a difficult place to grow up in as a writer. Do you think it was a particularly difficult place to grow up in as a writer?

Well, yes and no. It seemed difficult at the time, and it was when I was a kid, but here we are mining the ore for the first time, so you've got a certain advantage in that if I were sitting in London now writing novels about London, there've been a lot of people there before me, and to be blunt, there are not very many people here and you're kind of creating the mythology, if you like, for the first time. And so it's somewhat easier. You're not burdened by the weight of all the good stuff that's come before. And then, in very real terms, this is Bonanza country for a writer, with writer-in-residence jobs going everywhere, there are all sorts of graft and perks, and that's nice.

Has it been a good time over here? How long has it been here now, a year?

I've had a marvellous time, but it's rather like . . . it's been an endless party with just enough time between for hangovers. I haven't got much work done, but it's been a lot of fun, you know.

Would you like to come back again?

Well, we are thinking of coming back. I still vacillate. I'm frightened of becoming a "thing" here. No, I enjoy it, I'm just as corrupt as anyone else, but there is a large part of me that doesn't like it at all, and people become personalities here too quickly . . . and I think a writer is best served by anonymity, but it's nice to come over and have it every few years. (*laughter*) And then get back to England where your work is taken seriously but you aren't.

When you say that your work is taken seriously but you aren't, does that mean that the critics or the readers or the kind of public is more sophisticated than here in Canada?

Yeah, a writer is not such an unusual thing there, and there's more sense of competition as well. I don't feel — I don't know whether it may sound awful or not — that five guys are going to bring out better books than me this year here. It's worrying in New York and it's worrying in London, and I think that's rather good for a writer. It's quite, you know, you can relax a bit here. (*laughter*)

But still and all, if you write here, you'd still publish in New York and London.

Yeah, yeah. But then you can fall back on, well I'm a big wheel here, what do I care about decadent London or brutalized New York. So there are dangers here. Too much attention is paid, as opposed to Willy Loman.

Okay. I'd like to talk about your books more specifically. Some of the questions may appear presumptuous, if so just. . . .

No, but I must warn you I have a very unretentive memory for what I've written, but I'll give as much. . . .

Okay. A kind of major theme, we touched on this earlier, is the death, often the brutal death, of innocence. Not innocence, but innocent people. There's Nickie in The Acrobats, *there's Sallie in* A Choice of Enemies. *She dies while they're talking about politics. These are the beautiful people in a way, who die like this. Norman speaks at one point of a necessary sacrifice of the Nickies and the Sallies. Norman, who is one of the good men, virtuous failures as he calls them, he's obsessed by this business of the child's balloon, you remember when he has amnesia in the railway station and the balloon goes up and it's really a. . . .*

You make that book sound better than I remember. (*laughter*)

And he wanders around and he's really obsessed by the thing the child has lost.

Yes, that's right.

Would you say this is almost an axiom in your early novels?

You know, I just leave that for other people to work out (*laughter*) . . . I bring in the meat and it can be stamped any way you . . . I don't know.

This is the question I was asking earlier, you know, on the business of the satirist, this again is something not only lost but brutalized. When André is thrown off the bridge by this enraged but very sad. . . .

Yes, but in *The Acrobats* it was a somewhat facile system imposed on people, which would embarrass the plot, but in *The Acrobats* I was in a very world-weary disgust system. But okay, it was a concern and remains a concern.

But it's a concern that seems to me also present, certainly, in A Choice of Enemies. *It's more sophisticated there because in fact it becomes Nickie's fault that he lets Ernst kill him, partially.*

Yes, but everything is about the destruction of innocence and the death of beauty. I mean, that's what we're enduring all the time.

But it's a spiritual thing rather than a social thing, isn't it?

It's a many-levelled thing. I don't try to find out. (*laughter*)

Anyway, it seems to me you have, set against these innocents, you have generally two kinds of people. One of them is the virtuous failures, as Norman says, the good people, and you're very hard on them; the kind of emasculated liberal who wishes for good things to happen and. . . .

Yes, you're always harder, I guess, on your friends than on people or things you have contempt for. Like Stalin's crimes are much more important than Hitler's, which were to be expected, but Stalin murdered in the name of life. Hitler didn't.

Yes, that's true, but it seems the liberals in your books, there's no hope from them for change. They're good people and they're in many cases sympathetic people, but one certainly can't expect them to do anything about what has been lost.

Yeah, that's true, I guess it is, you know. There's a lot of flabbiness in liberalism, I find, and liberal people, but most of my friends are liberals. (*laughter*)

Okay. Then you have a second class of characters as a kind of alternative, and these are the tough, experienced people, the men who have survived. Norman says to Carp in A Choice of Enemies: "The Best ones were killed, Carp; only the conniving evil ones like you survived." This is true. Ernst has survived, and this is what makes him so different from all the liberals in London, and the same thing is true of Roger Kraus in The Acrobats; he's a very vulnerable man, but he has survived, and survival, as you say at some point, is a virtue, there's a kind of premium on it. I wonder whether . . . You have these two classes of people, and in between you have the innocents, who are brutalized, and there doesn't seem to be anything else. Excluding Duddy Kravitz and also Hersh in that novel — both of them are intriguing characters because they suggest other possibilities. It seems to me that one could see Duddy as the tough, experienced one, something like Ernst. He has survived and he has survived in a way that. . . .

So far. . . .

So far. But I wonder what happens to poor old Ernst at the end. In a way the Star Maker is the worst of them all, you know, of these tough, experienced people . . . the Star Maker survives.

Yes. He is it.

But then this figure becomes more powerful as you go through your books. At the beginning it was Kraus in The Acrobats, who had this hang-up with his sister, and he has survived too, in a way, because he went back to a good post in Germany, but he's a much more sympathetic and more understandable and in some sense a more human . . . in every sense more human than the Star Maker.

Yes, but *Cocksure* is a satire dealing with caricatures and extremes and not with people.

But in a sense there has been this progression in your work. As early as Duddy Kravitz, *where you have this section, the parade of the Fletcher Cadets in the wonderful newspaper, and the happy Bar Mitzvah film. So this is already that style. . . .*

Yes, what happened was, I'd had enough of the realistic novel and went off on a satirical tangent, if you like. I'd now had enough or gone as far as I could go, and was hopefully trying to gather all the strands into one . . . disaster of a novel. *(laughter)*

Okay, another thing I'll try on you. Women, at least certain women, seem to represent a possibility. I'm pursuing something which perhaps is too specific, but in Son of a Smaller Hero, *Melech's, the grandfather's, dancer, this beautiful, you know. . . .*

Well, I'm afraid I've never written very well about women. I think my feminine characters tend to be one-dimensional.

But there seem to be two kinds again: they are brutalized or wishy-washy liberals. But at least in three of the books, specifically in The Acrobats *and in* A Choice of Enemies, *there's Tony, who says to André at one point, "There's something rotten inside you; together we shall fight it." Now she fails, but in a sense she seems to be on to something, you know. She can't do it, but it is almost as if she does represent a kind of . . . And Sally in* A Choice of Enemies, *her kind of faith and love and her commitment to Ernst. Again she fails, and she becomes brutalized as a result, but she does seem to represent a kind of capacity for humanity which is outside of that rather too neat kind of triangle set-up.*

But the women in my novels tend to be rather idealized creatures, and not written about with the greatest confidence, I'm afraid.

You don't see in any of them some element which isn't present, say, in your male characters?

Well . . . to put it at its most critical, I'd say they have been used to eliminate the masculine characters in the novels, to put the poorest face on that. But I can't think of any female character I've created that pleases me or is satisfying in that respect.

Is this because of the conception of them, you haven't seen clearly what you wanted to do with them, or. . . .

It's a failure of some kind.

Yes. Okay.

There are areas in novels which we — which writers sometimes seem to cover up more than eliminate, and every novelist, I think, has these bad patches. I guess.

Funny, I don't think it's necessarily a bad patch from the reader's point of view. I, on the contrary, felt — perhaps incorrectly — that there was some possibility here, that if André could have seen his way clear or the situation allowed him to. . . .

Yeah, but if I may . . . women, intelligent women readers would disagree with you, and reasonably so.

What does an intelligent woman reader object to?

They just don't believe it.

Maybe they didn't believe there was anything to be done.

Well, they can tell where . . . where I have guessed rather than where I wrote with confidence.

I'm still really focusing on the first three novels, where one of the problems seems to result from freedom, and Noah says at one point: "No God, no ethic; no ethic, freedom. Freedom is too much for man." And the main thing that Noah achieves, paradoxically, at the end is some kind of freedom, at least from the fetters of his immediate environment where he grew up. Now, is this freedom going to be too much for him? Is it the kind of thing that hassles poor Norman?

Yes, it's probably . . . all our freedom is, you know, moves this into chaos . . . and . . . we do live in chaos without any agreed-upon system of values which we can refer to, and so the more we disentangle ourselves from the hypocrisies of our background, the more chaotic our life becomes. Now possibly too much was thrown overboard, and even with its built-in hypocrisies there was a system of some kind in the past. Even the bourgeoisie had certain values, I think. We've had such contempt for them and for the world they built that we've discarded everything or attempted to discard everything, and maybe it's necessary to look again. There are certain small decencies, and we may, you know, possibly have to re-examine some of these. You know, we can no longer hope, or only a fool can hope, for revolution as a solution to anything. Increasingly we know each system contains its own injustices, and any of that social justice which I presume we're both for only solves superficial problems. If you can't get a decent girl, if you're physically ugly, no political system is going to make life delightful for you. A man with cancer at twenty has had a bad deal no matter what. I mean, there are all sorts of things we hadn't calculated. We were too glib, I think, and made things too easy.

Duddy, talking about the scorn that one has, at least one "fashionably" has, for the bourgeoisie — it's in that real denunciation of Benjie when he says: "Are you saying I should be chasing after something else other than money? Tell me what," and Benjie has no answer, because again he is one of the lost good people.

A character like Duddy Kravitz possibly has enormous strength in that he's not, in that book, sufficiently perceptive or sensitive to believe in his own death, and that does give acquisitive money-making people a lot of strength and energy and vitality, which I both despise and admire.

In some sense he's not free in the way that Noah is, because he has an ethic, and like it or not, you know, it's there and that's his strength. And that's why he's. . . .

He has the strength of his lack of knowledge to act with confidence and . . . possibly he has more pleasures.

Again, starting with The Acrobats, *André says: "All gods dead, all wars fought, all faiths in men shaken," and again he says: "Love is one of the words that is no longer any good, like courage, soul, beautiful, honest. . . ."*

I'm afraid there are a number of slogans of the period in that book, not sufficiently well examined, of which I was very proud, having that currency, that kind of change to bring to the market. I would not be so sure about such things any longer. There seems to be too much presumption in those flat and dogmatic statements. But writing is a continual process of trying to find out what you think about things and about living, and I don't really know until I sit down and start writing and working it out.

Still and all, Noah says in Son of a Smaller Hero: *"There is no longer anything that one could wholly belong to, this is the time of 'buts' and* parentheses," and Norman, in A Choice of Enemies, *is clearly without conviction. We feel that there is no longer a "choice of enemies," that one is denied even that kind of thing, and the thing we were mentioning a few moments ago — Duddy, when he denounces Benjie's superiority, says: "You think I should be running after something else besides money, good, tell me what, tell me, you bastard." There is no answer there either.*

Remember that what I was trying to get at there was the narrow and ugly contempt groups of intellectuals have for the intellectually unwashed, if you like. We have our own trade in idiom and pieties and conventions. And we don't really bother with the larger group of people, and it's a tendency, especially when we are younger, to dismiss them as subhuman, so that when someone like Duddy Kravitz comes searching and looking, he's too garish to even be considered. So I think there are uglinesses within the intellectual community, that I was trying to. . . .

I think one of the great strengths of Duddy Kravitz *is how well in fact you have involved the people who are normally scornful, of people like Duddy, and really involved them in his working, in his motives and in. . . .*

I don't think of him as fundamentally unsympathetic. And yet there are readers, they're mostly Jewish, that find him . , . It looks like I've failed in connecting with them, probably because of the baggage they bring to the book. But he is supposed to end up, in spite of all the ruthless and rotten things he's done, so that you think, well, yes, this is another human being.

Yes, and who has accomplished something, inasmuch as he's accomplished a self, even if that self may not be the most. . . .

Yes, and not without barbarian insights.

Sure. It seems to me that even given this facet of Duddy's denunciation of Benjie, it still is in keeping with these insights, though much more sophisticated. It's the kind of thing that you're saying in The Acrobats *about there being no alternative.*

Yeah, but what I would get back to was what was stated simply and with such confidence in the first book, about the problems that continue to preoccupy me, but hopefully I deal with them with more grace and insight now. Yes, all the concerns are still there.

So in one sense Cocksure *is the only possible result of at least this thematic development in your book, this kind of exploration. I mean, what other people can you follow? Where can you turn, what other characters?*

Well . . . there's a long thing I've been working on for years now, it really takes up with Hersh, and it's Hersh's story, but as I'm still working on it, I can't really go into the book, because I'm rather superstitious that way. But it does take up Hersh's story.

Yes, he's an intriguing figure. One of the things that did intrigue me about him is . . . he is an innocent, at the beginning, say, the business with MacPherson, he is the only one that hangs back and says: "Come on, he's not that bad." He comes into Duddy's life again for that period and all his friends hang around Duddy's apartment and Duddy really likes him. Hersh is an unusual figure in your books, for that reason, you know, a guy who is a king of human potential. He is not an innocent who is destroyed, he is not an Ernst, nor does he appear to be — at this point at any rate — a wishy-washy liberal.

It does represent to me a return to the novel of character, which is really the novel which I guess interests me. Oh, I've enjoyed writing satirical novels, and . . . again I hope we'll be more subtle than in things that come before. But yes, he is a complex character.

Do you feel that the savagery of Cocksure *is a kind of natural extension of all these preoccupations of* The Acrobats *a long time ago?*

It's one possible extension, yes. There are other (*laughter*) nuances, tunes one can play on it, but it's one, you know, and it's as far as I can go in that direction.

What characters other than Hersh, in those novels, lead away from the conclusion of Cocksure?

Well, I wouldn't know how to answer that. I guess others do. I don't even know where Hersh will ultimately lead me in this one that I'm working on at the moment.

But another way of seeing this thing I am worrying here, I mean, I feel more and more like a terrier, is the sea of silence that . . . it's Norman who talks about it at the end of A Choice of Enemies, *where this section of the ocean off Vancouver Island, where there is no sound, no siren or bell that warned ships of dangerous reefs, and consequently it's strewn with wrecks, and he says: "This is an age of silence. Faith, honour and courage have become the small change of crafty politicians, but it's a time to persevere."*

I don't remember that at all.

There's a very striking passage at the end where he feels himself suddenly surrounded by . . . I don't know whether it exists or not, but an area where. . . .

Neither do I. (*laughter*) It must, I'm sure.

. . . there are no warnings. It's another way of saying we live in an age without standards, we've snuffed them all out, the good ones with the bad, and consequently everything is strewn with wrecks. Up to A Choice of Enemies *your novels tend to be strewn with the wrecks of individuals*

who, because there were no warning bells or sounds, and the premium is on perseverance . . . and this is another thing which I find central to all of your novels.

Yes, that's true, it's a continuing thing. I guess I have an increasing regard for old men, because they have survived . . . which implies grace and wisdom even if it's unrecognized.

Well, Ernst, again, this Hitler Youth kid who kills. He can be really crass and pragmatic, and he has to be because of his past, but he does end up partly redeemed and saving the life of the merchant or whoever it was that he was working for, and so presumably in his persevering he's accruing virtue in some sense. He is an unattractive figure in many ways.

Yeah. But that was a novel that also dealt largely with left-wing bigotry, which at the time concerned me a lot. It was written during that whole McCarthy period, when it was assumed that all bigotry was a ring-wing monopoly.

Yes, and you're effective too. It's curious that that's one of the books of yours I like the most.

Well, I liked it. I haven't . . . you know, it's the first time I've talked about it in years. It did not have a good reception. It's out of print, and no one thought that highly of it, I think, which doesn't help.

Is there any way in which one can say that in the major characters up to Duddy Kravitz, in some sense Duddy is the best you can be, given the time?

Oh, I wouldn't say that at all. I mean, I think there are a lot better people than that. More gentle and gracious than Duddy Kravitz.

You're very hard on those people, though, in the rest of your novels.

Well, hardness has always been like a measure of my concern or regard, maybe a very perverse measure, but that's the way it is.

I've taught Duddy Kravitz *a number of times to business students, and they really wonder, all the secretarial science students say: Of course, he will live without love, you know. (*laughter*) But the business students are deeply troubled by him, because they see in one sense that he has made something, but they again are very troubled about what is going to happen to him, whether he'll be like Cohen, who is kind of — it is Cohen, isn't it, who is haunted by the guy who died in his scrapyard? — that Duddy will forever be haunted by things that he has done. Hersh again — and I'm interested to know that the book you're working on now is a kind of investigation of this guy, he is an intriguing one and extremely important to Duddy. You say at one point that Duddy gets more pleasure from Hersh's crowd than he ever got before. Why is this?*

Oh, I guess he felt a freedom or a lack of competition with him, but we all feel this about crowds outside our own, our different métiers; there is more liberty with strangers or in another society, and we can enjoy ourselves when we're not with competitors in a similar world, so I often enjoy myself more in the company of businessmen than with writers, and it's an entirely different world, quite romantic to me. And so I think a perceptive or an easy or complex businessman would rather enjoy an evening with a writer in that he's not out to get anything from him or to make any sort of deal, because no deal is possible. There are other possibilities of exchange, of contact.

He seems to need him more. I mean, need him as well as in this other way, because he spends a lot of money on booze and —

Yes, he probably wants his goodwill or regard.

Because somehow Hersh was innocent of the thing that was done to Mac-Pherson too in a way. He says to him at one point; he said, "You weren't involved in that," you were good or something. . . .

I think he probably feels his presence is an accusation of some kind.

It seems to me, again coming back to the alternatives that I see in the novels, right up to Cocksure, *that there are two obvious possible ends for Hersh. He's going off to England as a kind of creative . . . he may end up like Norman, who is a totally disillusioned man, who is cut off from his own background, he feels very strongly that he's a stranger in England, he doesn't know anything about the people who are living there . . . they end up then as weak good men, the lost virtuous people; or he could end up like a kind of André, not in the melodramatic sense —*

Yes, I understand. . . .

. . . but as an innocent man who is again somehow brutalized. He obviously is not going to be an Ernst, but he could conceivably be an André or a Norman. These are the two obvious paths that seem to emerge in your books so far. Do you think this is fair?

Well, I just feel a sort of discomfort talking to you on that particular. . . .

Okay. Well, just a couple of very general questions. Do you worry about your critics?

We think about them, or I do, on about two or three different levels. As I said earlier, there are certain critics whose approval or respect fills me with delight, and among them I include some friends. Beyond that, I . . . of course I'm outraged by ignorant or bad reviews, but beyond that the good and bad reviews are somehow interchangeable and you read them, like the Morning Market

Report, well, this one will help to move the book in Detroit and that one will do some good in Montreal. One way or another, they don't understand the books. I'm troubled again if someone whom I admire seriously dislikes the book for a good reason. You tend to remember that. But critics, because I'm also a critic, and spend a good amount of my time writing about books, I think a critic's office or relationship is really with the reader, not with the writer, in that you should bring admirable books to the reader's attention and condemn bad books, which is a way of celebrating the good ones. But they tell the writer very little he doesn't know, because you know where you fumbled or what you got away with, and you usually get away with a lot more than they know, and it's gone by the time it comes out, and you're involved happily in something else. But I don't go up the wall because of critics. I think this is a very honourable office, and I don't even subdivide writing into creative writing and non-creative writing. There's good writing and bad writing, and that's all there is.

Here's a question that's going to be very difficult to even come to any kind of agreement on. What is the novelist's role? Does the novelist have a role?

Well, I can only speak for myself, I guess we're a kind of unfrocked . . .or I'm an unfrocked priest, if you like, or a frustrated . . . I think it's a moral office, and if I leave one book behind, then that's the most I can hope for. If it can be said that I was an honest witness to my times, I would consider I've done my work well, but these are very large demands.

It's funny when you say unfrocked priest, one of the characters said that, André in the very beginning. Someone asked what was the matter with him, and they said in fact, "He's a kind of priest manqué, but none of the existing churches will do. . . ." (laughter)

I guess that's a general feeling we all share.

Well, that's it. Thank you very much.

Well, thank you. I really never have been interviewed so intelligently before.

SCOTT SYMONS

SCOTT SYMONS was born in Toronto in 1933.

Scott, what do you like best about your work?

Well, that's embarrassing because there's so much about my work I just don't like at all. But I guess what I hold most successful in what I've written, or the quality I hold most successful, is that it's not extrinsic — it's intrinsic. I don't deal with the clevernesses and the concrete wit. This external eye, professional literature, which is so much now of modern Canadian writing, where you feel that they're so competent, they're so able, they're all lining up to be competent and able, I don't write like this. I write — oh, I suppose I'm an amateur, but my approach is intrinsic — it's from within. I'm learning from my emotions, no matter how bad my emotions are, no matter how frail they are or may be. I'm writing from inside myself.

Do you think you're in the tradition of literary confessions?

This seems to be true. I've never thought of it that way, but let me say this, that increasingly in the past three or four years I have found myself reading the great religious writers, not just the *Confessions*, say, of Rousseau, but going back to the early Christian fathers, reading what are essentially in the nature of confessions or professions or affirmations. They're not pretending to be great intellectual statements, they're not pretending to be clever poetry, they're just a guy opening up and saying these are the difficulties I have in celebrating life. So that yes, your point, I think, is right. I belong in that tradition of the confessions, and I'd push that even further, Graeme. I'd say that the evidence comes in on me increasingly, it almost upsets me, that fundamentally I'm a religious writer.

Well, can you elaborate on that, why does it upset you?

Well, because I never thought of myself as being a particularly religious man. I hated most of the damn Presbyterian-Anglican religion that was dumped on me as a kid, and I went to a school where I was forced to go to chapel twice a day. None of those memories were in themselves very attractive, and I suppose I was brought up at the tail end of successful occidental liberalism, therefore intelligent people didn't admit to liking religion or having one, really, let's face it. And increasingly — I've been writing four hours a day for twelve years now — and increasingly, the evidence comes through as I go back into my writing that I'm a religious writer. I gave a lecture at McGill a few weeks ago, and just reading my stuff, and at the end of it someone said she didn't mean it as an insult, she said it all sounded like a prayer, and I had to admit that, yeah, that was it.

This is what you mean by being a religious writer?

Yes. I don't mean I'm writing about religious ideas or the Church or — good God, no. No, no, no. The people who have been turning me on, the people I've been reading in the last years, are, say, Saint Francis or Saint John of the Cross or Julian of Norwich or the Greek and Roman classic writers who essentially are religious writers.

All right, that's one side of it. You began by saying there are so many things about your writing that you don't like. What kinds of things do you like least about your writing?

Well, I don't think I'm a professional writer. I'm not a novelist.

Would you like to be?

No. Couldn't care less. I don't think I can even put two sentences together. I don't like my writing when I get into the bad situation of trying to think of myself as a writer, that is, I get into the position of accepting the fact that for some reason or other I make my living out of writing and that my books are published and the people ask me to come and speak at $100 and $200 an hour about my writing, and I keep on scratching my head and saying, well, I'm not a writer, and then I get thinking in their terms about writing and I realize how bad all my writing is, because I'm a professional writer. I write diaries; I write letters; I write morning songs; I write Magnificats; but I don't belong to any of these classes, for example, that line up for the Governor General's Award, this sort of thing. I can't associate with professional writing.

Is it because of their competence? I mean, you've said you have a great suspicion of mere competence, a hatred for mere competence.

Yeah, I always think that competence is Methodism-on-the-make in Canada. I feel it is, I know it is, and people who have sold out their spiritual right merely to acquire competence are a great enemy in English Canada. I'm one of the new incompetents. You know, I laugh at my four university degrees. I laugh at my professorship; I laugh at all that, you know. I won the National Newspaper Award and then screwed off, I couldn't care less. These things don't matter to me. What matters is that when I get up in the morning, I feel joy, and I'm able to enter into it sufficiently that after a while, maybe in an hour or two, I can write it down, and then maybe, if I'm lucky, there's a friend I can send it to, and he'll have joy from what I've written, and that's when I'm happy. And as you know, most of that never gets published at all. It's all with my friends. Out of the blue, they're sitting in an Ottawa civil service meeting and a letter comes from Scott Symons written in the tundra in northern B.C. looking at, you know, spring lilies with grizzly bears trotting around and I'm drawing a picture of the lilies and just sending it off to my friend, and he gets it at the civil service meeting at Ottawa and he just starts to chuckle and feel happy and, you know, that gives me joy.

Do you think that writers, or yourself as a writer, know something special, say in the way the geographers or physicists do?

All right, the blunt answer to that is yes. Or as Leonard Cohen says, we have a secret. But here again, I'm not a writer, I don't think I know something because I'm a clever guy who has a genius as a writer. I know something because, as a human being, I am accessible to the gift of Grace. I will use Christian terminology here, and then I will try to explain it in my own terms. My secret isn't something that I create. It's not my wit, not my mind, not my will, nor my Canadian citizenship which gives me my secret. It's God, which sounds corny, and we don't use those words anymore, words like *God*, at least the more clever of us don't use those words anymore. But when I wake up in the morning, I can't say that it's *me* that's given me this insight of sunshine and joy. It's something that's come into me. I've been born, and insofar as I am open or humble, insofar as I'm almost like a maiden, I have what

I call my morning maidenhead, and the morning comes into me, I have a secret.

Which comes from the conjunction of. . . .

Of the new day and the fact that I can open up and say: Look, I'm stupid, I'm weak, and hope comes filling in. You know, the cleverest things I've ever produced by thinking or by being witty, and I'm supposed to have a good wit, you know all that sort of junk, but the cleverest things I've ever produced with my wit or my mere mind aren't worth anything compared with feelings I get when I'm . . . if you want, in a state of prayer. I have to go back to those old metaphors because our new culture has no words for them. The new competence, the new *willed, concerted, conscientious* Canadian, almost committee-concocted culture, this culture has no word for the things that I am describing.

Do you consider yourself a mystic?

I'm in trouble again because the answer appears to be yes. This is a very disturbing interview. It's disturbing because the answer appears to be yes; the evidence comes in that this is so. I'll give you a very concrete case. I'll be walking along the street anywhere, I'll be on the route to the CBC studio, than which, for young guys on the make, nothing could be more important in life, and I'll see a flower or I'll see, much more important, somebody's eyes, and I'll just stop. I'll stop and I'll stand there. I'll stand there fifteen minutes later, just gone, and I don't blow my mind. My mind is there like a lucid beam of light inside a field of flowers; or my mind is there like a butterfly in a field of flowers going to each centre of nectar, and I presume again that that experience, described to people who don't take it as a normal thing, is mystical.

If you did not live in the twentieth century, what century would you like to live in most?

Oh, I live in a whole lot of centuries anyway. I wouldn't live in the eighteenth. I'd be very happy in Laud's England. I'd have loved to have had a hand in translating the Saint James Version of the Bible. I'd have loved to have been there when More, Sir Thomas More, was martyred because I think I would have gone with him. That is, I'm a Catholic who has become English — that's what happened to all of us in our psyche — and I'd have gone with More, and I'd have said: Yeah, may the king rule well, God bless him, but I'm going to mine. So that's the seventeenth century, at the beginning, and the sixteenth century. I'd like to have been one of those people who carried straw for the cathedrals in the thirteenth century. I'd like to have been an assistant for, say, Giotto in his studio in fourteenth-century Florence — I'm sure I would like that. I like the century I'm in, but I don't live in it; that is, the century I'm in is only livable in if you live outside of it, because within it it's gone nuts. We are now between two minds, the same way that Michelangelo's life straddled two kinds of mind, the Medieval and Renaissance, and you get that torture in his later sculpting. We are now between two minds, which is all that McLuhan is telling us about. He's telling the squares what way we're really living although he's not living it. He's just sending messages to the academics about it. And we're living between two minds today, and the result is the best of us go nuts. Therefore today is very exciting, but I don't want to live in it.

Yes, you say in Civic Square *we've got the schizos on the one side and the Blandmen on the other. . . .*

That's right. And the best of us are schizo! You have what I call the Blandman, who is really the dead end of occidental liberalism.

Trudeau is an example of the end of occidental liberalism, and so is Women's Lib, and the Gay Front, and all this new socio-political stuff is dead-end Western liberalism. It's the mere mind trying to think itself out of its own deadened end, its own cul-de-sac. I think the "with-it" phrase for this dead end of liberalism, of glib-liberalism, is "creative disintegration." This is the phrase I've heard used since I've come to Toronto recently. I just sort of flipped when I heard it. And I wanted to shout at the people using it: "Why don't you just say that you're sick? Why don't you just say that your society is falling apart — and high time that it did . . . ?" But I've lost your question — where were we?

We were talking, I think, about the century and being between two minds. Is it the schizo and the Blandman, or is it — is there a more constructive alternative to the Blandman?

Yes — I'd better try to be clear about this — I'd better not let my own mind get caught between schizophrenic and bland! The two minds we are between today are the traditional three-dimensional mind, the square occidental mind, of which the Blandman is simply the decadent end — the Blandmind, on the one hand; and on the other a completely new kind of mind, which is far from medieval, but for which a medieval landscape is visual correlative. We are caught between the square mind and some kind of neo-medieval mind, if you will. The square mind sees everything in simple, detached, objective, three-dimensional terms. He sees things in terms of subject and object. But the new mind sees things in multiple terms — it sees many things at once, all intersecting, conjugating, interrelating. And there is no such thing as merely subject or object. Of course, the square mind, the mind of the Blandman, confronted with this neo-medieval mind, considers it "split," considers it a divided mind. And the fact is that a square mind which has lost its own centre, and which hasn't simply fallen apart, but is en route to this new kind of mind — this mind "en route" does seem merely split, does seem merely "schizophrenic." And, insofar as it does not reach the new centre, the new form of mindfulness, it does remain merely schizo, merely "divided," merely lost. So I would say that we are in serious transition. And to many people we are literally in a world which has "lost its mind." But the fact is that we are en route from the old, square, liberal mind, which is a product of the Renaissance, to a new mind, which is a cousin of the medieval world, or let's call it a great-nephew of the medieval world. And many of those who have left the world of the square mind, and are caught halfway to the new mind, are truly "divided," are truly schizophrenic.

Can you give any concrete example of this transition, Scott? I mean, how would you show a Blandmind what you are talking about?

Well, the obvious way to alter the square mind is drugs — marijuana and LSD. But I don't particularly like these. I don't need these. What I would do is take the square mind, the Blandman, into a medieval cathedral, and tell him to start responding. I'd watch that overall body of the cathedral take the liberal, the square, over. For one thing, his own body would start to move differently, as he started to move in terms of the space of the cathedral. For example, the square would slow down! And then I'd watch him realize that objects in the cathedral aren't simply things which are set outside of him, and detached in three dimensions at the end of a vanishing point — like looking down life at the wrong end of the telescope, which is what the Blandmind does. His is the civil servant's eye, the eye which labels everything. But in the cathedral, everything — subject and object — are harmoniously linked. Everything is one, and many. You can't simply "square" the Gothic medieval cathedral. And if the Blandman responded sensitively to being in the cathedral, he would have to come out

with what is truly "a new kind of mind." And with a new kind
of body — a body that was in relationship, palpable relationship
with everything it saw. A body that was in coital relationship with
everything it saw. . . .

The thing that intrigues me in all this is that it is clear that for you your
writing is at once a "confession" and also the profession of a very strong
world view. For example, in Civic Square *you are really telling us some-*
thing about our culture, as you see it. Are you trying to get to as many
people as possible with this world view? Do you think you can make a
difference to people through your writing?

Now I'm going to answer that indirectly. First of all, my writing
was my life-saving kit. I knew that my culture was not going to
allow me to flower, was not going to allow what the French call an
épanouissement, an opening, a budding, a coming out. So I started
my diary in 1958, which was my spiritual survival kit, and I ended
up writing three and four hours a day for ten years. So my writing
was first of all spiritual survival, though I didn't know that at the
time. And then, as what I was writing entered into greater and
greater conflict with the world that was being created around me
and which was being called the Canadian Identity, as this conflict
grew, I realized it wasn't just a question of spiritual survival for
me to write, but also I'd better get some messages out, because I
knew that the Canadian Identity was what I call a Black Mass, it
was a Black Eucharist, it was evil. I know. To me, the Canadian
Identity is evil. This is a people that has concocted, out of its own
will, an evil culture, because it destroys Grace. Therefore, first
my writing was spiritual survival, and increasingly it has become
spiritual fulfillment and spiritual plenitude which I want to share
with a few people, but I have no desire particularly to become a
popular writer, and I notice that increasingly as you and I talk,
the word *writer* is going out the window. We're just not talking

about writers as writers. I ain't, so God help me, a writer. God protect me from it. I ain't. If I could consolidate my own sense of Grace, and if I can share that with the one person I love, that will already be a miracle. If I can share parts of it with ten or twenty or even twenty thousand people, I should be joyful, and that's about where it is for me. And the best medium I have for sharing my sense of Grace — of joy, if you will — is what I write, daily. And because our culture is so inflexibly glib-liberal in its modes, I have to write what people think are novels. They have to put my writings into categories such as, This must be a novel, so plunk, it goes in as a novel. *You* know it's my diary, but they have to call it a novel because they can't think that one publishes one's diaries, so it's called a novel. And then I write some letters to the reader. Well, one doesn't write letters to the reader, so they publish it as a novel, which it ain't. But my publisher knows the facts of life. It's literally letters to the reader.

Are there any specific or unique problems or advantages in being, and I use the word writer *in the way that you want to use it, in being a writer in Canada or becoming a writer in Canada?*

Well yes, indeed. We have the advantage over the Americans. We're still a great literate culture, for example. I've had experience of this recently, and increasingly I understand that the Americans are more sophisticated than we are, but we are more civilized. This is an advantage to being Canadian as a writer. There is an excellent tradition in our culture of letters. One of the great cultural vehicles of early Canadian society is letters, and it comes through a tradition which of course we've rejected as being non-Canadian, and that is the genteel tradition, the tradition of the British upper class in Canada. We've rejected that because it seems un-Canadian, but the fact is that for fifty years at the beginning of the nineteenth century, this tradition of letters, of which Mrs.

Moodie is an excellent example, this tradition was the vehicle for something fine in being Canadian, and it helped me write. That's an advantage, for example. We still have this vestige of British civility. We used to be called British North America. We have this vestige of gentility, even though God knows we're systematically destroying it, because it bothers those that ain't got it, and those who've got it tend to use it badly as a snobbery. So there's that advantage of vestigial gentility. There's another advantage to being Canadian: one is bilingual. I'm bilingual, *je parle français comme je parle anglais. Je parle français, je dis, comme français.* A civilized guy is bilingual, that's all. Anybody in the world who's civilized tends to be at least bilingual. You know, in Europe there are probably more than a hundred million of them. You don't have to be Lord So-and-So or *Le Compte de Quelquechose*, you just have to be an average guy with a high school education and you're bilingual. You have access to another world — that's a great advantage to being Canadian. An advantage which of course most English Canadians, feeling so superior, apparently don't have to use. There is another advantage — one that I adore — to being a writer in Canada. That is that we're not just WASP — not simply Protestants. There are two million Anglicans in Canada (there are only four million in the States) — that is, there is an Anglo-Catholic culture here — not just WASPy Protestant, eh? And the fact that we're thirty percent Roman Catholic, so that there are areas of Grace which feed into us, areas of celebration, areas of palpable liturgy, which mean that our writing can be, if we use these things, warmer, richer, less merely cerebral — that's an advantage to being Canadian. Of course, none of the writers use it — they're busy fighting it. They're busy pooh-poohing it. They're busy being clever about the IODE and showing how ridiculous it is, and so on and so on. Well, it doesn't take great courage to do that, and that's what they're doing. There are *dis*advantages too, to writing in Canada. You know, this is God's frozen people, you know, the WASP English Canadian who is not the Anglican, not the upper-crust Anglican that one thinks is the great enemy. The WASP English Canadian is the Methodist, Presbyterian, lower middle class, you know. No one has got around to teeing off at that, but that's it. The WASP Canadian is the lower-middle-class Methodist Presbyterian, and this is the bad little bee in our bonnet. This is the definitive Canadian disease. That we've all been Norrie Fryed! That we've all been bitten by such a little WASPerie! I mean, how in the name of Christ did we end up with the Moderator of the United Church as our national intellectual barometer? As — for so many years — our surrogate prime minister? We must have had a heinous spiritual blind spot somewhere. The brute fact is that the Methodist-Presbyterian Canadian culture is against us being civilizedly articulate and sentient and sensual, if you wish, and palpable. I touch on such things as this: that in Methodism or the United Church, there is no concept of the Real Presence in Holy Communion, the body and blood of Christ is not there, and now you say: What in God's name has this got to do with the discussion of literature? Just this, and it's very important: that a culture which has as its central religious metaphor, not the real presence of its God in this case, Christ in Holy Communion, but has only the memory, it's too busy explaining there's only the memory of the presence of Christ. Such a culture has the same limitation in its writing and in its touch. If Christ's presence isn't really there in Holy Communion, then I can assure you that correlatively and anthropologically this can be proven, the writer's touch isn't there in his writing, and it isn't there between him and his wife, and it isn't there between him and his kids. And in such a culture, people pat their cats more than their lovers or their children, and this affects our writing in English Canada. You will laugh at me, but it's true. It's true. Anyway, I don't mind being laughed at — I just don't mind. I use these metaphors here because we need to step outside the tiny tight little categories of Canadian writing. Our writers are so small, they're so constipated, they're so busy climbing up the Canadian vertical mosaic, they're so busy getting the next little job at the CBC; they're so busy getting the next little editorial job with *Saturday Night*. They're so busy becoming the next guy who does the clever article for *Maclean's* magazine, and I just want to vomit, just vomit — they're so busy making a career out of Canada.

What should they be doing?

Touching themselves. Getting in touch with themselves. They haven't gone on to be in touch with themselves. How in God's Own Name do you make yourself into a writer if you start out by a kind of formalized schizophrenia that puts yourself out of touch with yourself, so you don't feel anything, just so you can get on creating your career. Figure that out and then think of the CBC, and think of the mass media and think of our magazines and so on, and realize that this media, these media are predicated on that concerted willed self-schizophrenia which allows you to be out of touch with yourself so you can get on with your career.

Surely one of the problems always of the mystic is to explain or to convey the nature of his experience.

Well, I would say that anyone who sat down with my three books could have no doubts at the end of the three as to what it was I was going through. Anybody could see that I was negotiating my way through a series of secular experiences — of blatantly secular experiences — and trying, through them, to find the spiritual. I was trying to find sacramental reality. And my effort — again this is where I'm not a writer — my effort is not to explain these experiences to the reader, but rather to put the reader through them. I inhabit the reader, and the reader is not, to me, a "he" or a "him" or an "it." The reader is a "you," and very often when I'm writing, as you know, Graeme, the reader himself becomes the hero.

Yes, really then what you are saying is that when one of your books works, the reader, and it's always a single person for you —

That's right.

— experiences what you've experienced.

Yes — and he has the right to reject it, and he has the capacity to reject it or not do it, but something is being offered that he may participate in should he wish so to do. I'm not trying to put anything over on the reader. I'm not trying to sell him a bill of goods about me. I'm palpable but not concrete, I'm not one of the concrete poets' writers. The concrete poets or writers take their emotions, divorce themselves from them, and make them concrete on the page extrinsically. I don't. I'm palpable. I'm there palpably.

Is there a difference between life and art for you?

No. Just life. Let me throw this back at you now. For example, we have these books in which I've come to the surface, as it were. But also I've written you letters and to your wife and to friends that are close to you, I've written letters which come through and which often are better than the things of mine which are published. What do you feel I'm doing when you get letters from me? What is occurring? What is going on when you get those letters? What — ? Let me shoot it at you.

A letter from you is very much like sitting and talking to you here, less artificially than we're sitting and talking now; but you also said to a mutual friend, when she said she had not read your book, you said, "It is not necessary now because you have met me." I don't know if you recall that.

A letter would say exactly what *I* would say.

Does that reveal your basic attitude towards your writing? That your books are for the people that don't, that can't, meet you?

Yes. My books are auxiliaries, for myself. For people I can't meet, but with whom I'd like to talk. And I can add that insofar as I'd like to see any of my writings published, I would like to see a book of my letters published.

At the end of Civic Square, *you say, "secular hymns, there's a kind of sadness in them all, that is a longing after non-secular hymns perhaps?" Have you moved, then, from the secular hymn to non-secular since the publication?*

That's right. I was talking there about the kids, wasn't I, all their mod music sounded like psalms and hymns without the Real Presence, without an understanding of what God and Grace and joy were, and I would say yeah, that between 1965 and 1970 I had moved from a secular society into a sacramental society, and I am concerned, not with this Mod glib revolution which effectively is a de-sacralization of everything. I am concerned with a re-sacralization of everything. I am concerned with re-sacramentation; a restoration of things we have wilfully lost — rather the way there was a formal "Restoration" in seventeenth-century England. And I may just add here, I don't care what goes on any longer in the secular city. I am concerned with the City of God. I've just made a decision about that. My decisions must be similar to the decision,

312 ELEVEN CANADIAN NOVELISTS

say, of Christians in the second and third centuries AD when they observed the Roman Empire in full decadence around them, and they knew they could not save that empire, but they knew that there were people — they used the word *soul* — we no longer know what that word means — but they decided they were going to save their souls and the souls of their friends; and I would simply say today that I don't care what happens in Ottawa, and I don't care what happens in Washington, maybe they will blow themselves up, though I doubt if they're going to blow up the whole world, they're too selfish to do that — but I'm concerned about the life in the eyes of my friend or my friends, and how they smile and whether when they walk there's an extra bounce of kinetic energy which makes their walk more akin to a skip. And I'm concerned with the fact that you went walking before you saw me today and you saw a kestrel, a sparrow hawk, in Craigleigh Gardens. Now that gives me joy, and it will probably give me spiritual energy for the rest of today, knowing that my friend Graeme saw a sparrow hawk in Craigleigh Gardens.

You talk about Christianity, and yet your metaphors tend to be almost pantheistic.

Yes, this is the thing. I'm stuck with the language of glib-liberal Western society.

Which after all is a Christian society, or the remnants of one.

Yes, we've jumped into a lot of difficult things in these last two or three sentences. Let me see if I can sort something through for ourselves. English as a language is born of the Reformation. It starts to take form under Henry VIII, let's say — for example, and with the sonneteers, such as Wyatt and Surrey. The point I'm making is that our language comes of age at the very moment we break from Catholicism. English is a creation of the Reformation and the Renaissance. It is a "square creation." A creation, in a sense, *against* millennial concepts of joy and Grace — and in favour of material utilitarianism. Thus the language I use as the very vehicle of my personality is *against* certain traditional elements of rejoicing and celebration within me. The language I use is in considerable measure Puritan and pragmatic. I am happier speaking French, believe me, and I am happier living in French, and I shall be even happier when I learn Spanish, as I intend, or — or Aztec . . . Understand me. It isn't the old Catholicism which interests me as such — though I happen to be Anglo-Catholic, as against High Methodist. It isn't just the verbalized tradition of millennial Catholicism, which we have so largely lost in the process of making the English language. It's the fact that so much of our language is predicated on a disintegrative mind and a division of subject and object, and, as well, upon three-dimensional perspective. My language is against me, against my very being. My language is predicated upon ontological erosion.

Why didn't you stay in Montreal?

I should have.

Why don't you go back?

My wife wanted to come back to Toronto and we lived out that last five years of English-Canadian smugness and comfort from 1960 to 1965, but I became more and more upset because I knew that the Canadian Identity was predicated on the systematic destruction of potence.

Why don't you go back, Scott? Why don't you go to. . . .

I can't go back to French Canada now. Too much has happened

and I've grown too far. The political area that I'm in does not any longer preoccupy me. I'm happy in the mountains of Mexico living with the Indians. I was happy working in the Yukon. I've been happy living with fisher folk in Newfoundland for this past year. My country is other people's eyes and. . . .

We were talking about language. I mean, if the language you use in some sense represents the enemy, why do you still write in English? Why do you still presumably think in English?

Well, because it's my culture, and because there's some very great things in it. It produced the St. James Version of the Bible again, to hark back to something. And it can be used to celebrate, though it hasn't much been used to celebrate since 1640, say since John Donne and Crashaw, but it's part of me. I have a commitment to my Anglicity, as well as to my Canadianity, and also I'm moving out of language, I'm doing a lot more drawing, and this summer I shall spend my time hooking rugs. Frankly, I'm moving out of language. Language to me is auxiliary now. The great influence of my life in the past year has been Saint Francis, absolutely. When *Civic Square* came out, I went down and took a copy of it, the first copy that came off the press — there were only five hundred copies — and I — you know, I drew pictures of flowers and birds and flowering phalli in every single one of them by hand, to the amazement of my publisher, and I went down and took the first copy of that to St. James Cathedral when they were having their Communion and I gave it in as my offering in memory of my father, with the written comment on it that it was for the church and it was a recognition of the fact that I loved my father too late, and it was interesting because that Sunday when I gave the book in on the offering plate, the sermon from the pulpit was about Saint Francis, and if Saint Francis came in amongst us today from a wealthy family, and he took his clothes off in public, and he left his family, and he went to live with the flowers and birds and told his friends about this, people would say that he was insane, and try to put him in jail. And that moved me terribly. What do you think, Graeme, that I *can* do? Obviously this interview has been important — oh, it hasn't been an interview, but they call it that. It's been a conversation. What do you think I can do to get more joy to my friends and the people around me? Now that's a very concrete question, not a silly mystical one. It's like my letters. I share things. I have a book coming out — it's called *Heritage* — on early Canadian furniture. But really it celebrates the faith of our fathers. And in it I discuss the relationship between the Christian concept of the Real Presence and Canadian sensibility. So in *Heritage*, as in my letters, I share a lot of my deepest feelings and emotions. And much of my joy.

In Civic Square *you wrote that "Joy is my real, my hidden, my forbidden identity."*

Yeah. I remember having had to confront the fact that in our culture, in Canada, joy — like tenderness — is a rare reality. Well — one day I simply had to recognize that there was a real fountain of mirth and wit and joy in me. And that Canada was suppressing these things within me. And there was no longer any way that I could deny this fact. There was no longer any way that I could keep my joy, my vehemence of joy, suppressed and hidden. It simply had to come out. And of course when it did — in the process of letting my joy and celebration loose from within me — I found myself, willy-nilly, at war with my society, because I was breaking all the rules of middle-class Canadian respectabilitarianism. And I lost my job, and family, the works. Because, as my doctor said — "Scott, you're addicted to joy." He said it as though I had some disease! And according to my society I *did*. So I was exiled — because I demanded the right to celebrate.

Presumably, then, joy is linked to tenderness.

Joy, orgasm, and tenderness are all linked. The blockade of my orgasm was the blockade of my joy, was the blockade of my tenderness. I wasn't willing to accept the kind of psychic hardening of the arteries, of the heart. I finally, simply, wasn't willing to accept such false elements in the Canadian Identity.

So what's next, what are you working on now?

Well, I have been planning a book on *objets d'art*, Canadian silver and glass and carving. I want to celebrate these. But the more I get into it, the more I find the people themselves climbing into me — presenting me with their concerns and fear — and tears. Everywhere I go in Canada, I find people deprived of their traditional values and beliefs. I find a people cowering behind their loss of history. They keep up a mask; but underneath I find despair now in Canadians. It's often reflected in an amateur cynicism, a timid, self-apprenticing cynicism. And I must write about this. Because it gives me pain. I find it almost impossible to write with joy about our history and our culture when my — our people are so torn, so mutilated in their beliefs now.

Does this mean a novel, I mean in any regular sense?

Maybe. What it really means is a soul-probe. A probe of our collective and personal soul. A "post-mortem" on a nation which has destroyed itself, wantonly, for the sake of mere material and social advance.

GRAEME GIBSON is the acclaimed author of *Five Legs, Communion, Perpetual Motion,* and *Gentleman Death.* He is a long-time cultural activist, and co-founder of the Writers' Union of Canada and the Writers' Trust. He is a past president of PEN Canada and the recipient of both the Harbourfront Festival Prize and the Toronto Arts Award, and is a Member of the Order of Canada. He lives in Toronto.

MARGARET ATWOOD is the author of more than fifty volumes of poetry, fiction, and nonfiction. Her novels include *The Edible Woman*, *The Handmaid's Tale*, *The Robber Bride*, *Alias Grace*, *The Blind Assassin*, *Oryx and Crake*, *The Year of the Flood*, *and Madd Addam*. Her most recent works of nonfiction are *Payback: Debt and the Shadow Side of Wealth* and *In Other Worlds: SF and the Human Imagination*. Her most recent children's book is *Wandering Wenda and Widow Wallop's Wunderground Washery*. Ms. Atwood's work has been published in more than forty languages; a number of her titles have been adapted for theatre, opera, television, and film. She is the recipient of numerous awards. Margaret Atwood lives in Toronto with writer Graeme Gibson.

AUSTIN CLARKE's *The Polished Hoe* was awarded the Scotiabank Giller Prize, the Commonwealth Writers' Prize, and the Trillium Book Award. His work since 1964 includes eleven novels, seven short story collections, and three memoirs published in the United States, England, Canada, Australia, and Holland. In 1998, Clarke was invested with the Order of Canada, and since then he has received four honorary doctorates. In 1999, he was the winner of the W.O. Mitchell Prize, awarded to a Canadian writer who has produced an outstanding body of work and served as a mentor for other writers. In that year, he also received the Martin Luther King Junior Award for Excellence in Writing. Austin Clarke lives in Toronto.

MATT COHEN won the 1999 Governor General's Literary Award for Fiction for his last novel, *Elizabeth and After*, which was also longlisted for the International IMPAC Dublin Literary Award. He was born in Kingston, Ontario, where he lived for part of each year, not far from the fictional setting of many of his novels, including *Elizabeth and After*. Since 1969 he published more than twenty books, including novels, short stories, poetry, translations, and several books for children under the pseudonym Teddy Jam. He is a recipient of the Toronto Arts Award and the Harbourfront Festival Prize. His penultimate novel, the critically acclaimed *Last Seen*, was shortlisted for the Trillium Book Award and 1997 Governor General's Literary Award. Matt Cohen died in December 1999 at the age of 56.

MARIAN ENGEL was a Canadian novelist. Engel's best-known novel is *Bear*, and her other novels include *No Clouds of Glory*, *The Honeyman Festival*, *The Glassy Sea*, and *Lunatic Villas*. She won the Governor General's Literary Award for Fiction for *Bear* in 1976, and was made an Officer of the Order of Canada in 1982. Marian Engel died in Toronto in 1985.

TIMOTHY FINDLEY's acclaimed novels include *Spadework*, *Pilgrim*, *The Piano Man's Daughter*, *Headhunter*, *Not Wanted on the Voyage*, *Famous Last Words*, and *The Wars*. Findley was a two-time winner of the Governor General's Literary Award: *The Wars* won the 1977 award for fiction; *Elizabeth Rex*, a play, won the 2000 award for drama. The recipient of many accolades for his fiction, non-fiction, and drama, including the Chalmers Award and the Edgar Award, Findley was made an Officer of the Order of Canada, and a Chevalier de l'Ordre des Arts et des Lettres in France. Timothy Findley died in Brignoles, France, in 2002.

DAVE GODFREY is a writer, publisher, and academic. Godfrey's books include *The New Ancestors* which won the Governor General's Literary Award, *Death Goes Better With Coca-Cola*, and several other collections of short stories. An activist in Canadian cultural politics beginning in the late 1960s, he was cofounder of both the House of Anansi Press and New Press, and ran Press Porcépic with his wife, writer Ellen Godfrey. He studied at the University of Toronto, Iowa, and Stanford, and has taught creative writing and publishing at the University of Victoria.

MARGARET LAURENCE was born in Neepawa, Manitoba, in 1926. From 1950 until 1957 Laurence lived in Africa, the first two years in Somalia, the next five in Ghana, where her husband, a civil engineer, was working. When Laurence returned to Canada in 1957, she settled in Vancouver, where she devoted herself to fiction with a Ghanaian setting: in her first novel, *This Side Jordan*, and in her first collection of short fiction, *The Tomorrow-Tamer*. Her two years in Somalia were the subject of her memoir, *The Prophet's Camel Bell*. Laurence moved to England in 1962, where she wrote five books about the fictional town of Manawaka, patterned after her birthplace: *The Stone Angel*, *A Jest of God*, *The Fire-Dwellers*, *A Bird in the House*, and *The Diviners*. She complemented her fiction with essays, book reviews, and four children's books. Her many honours include two Governor General's Literary Awards for Fiction and more than a dozen honorary degrees. Margaret Laurence died in Lakefield, Ontario, in 1987.

JACK LUDWIG is a former novelist, short story writer, and sports-writer. He published three novels, *Confusions*, *Above Ground*, and *A Woman of Her Age*. His other books include *Hockey Night in Moscow* (later expanded as *The Great Hockey Thaw; or, The Russians Are Here!*), *Five Ring Circus: The Montreal Olympics*, *Games of Fear and Winning: Sports with an Inside View*, and *The Great American Spectaculars: The Kentucky Derby, Mardi Gras, and Other Days of Celebration*. Ludwig also wrote essays, adapted several classic plays, and edited anthologies of poetry and fiction.

ALICE MUNRO grew up in Wingham, Ontario, and attended the University of Western Ontario. She has published fourteen collections of stories as well as a novel, *Lives of Girls and Women*. During her distinguished career she has been the recipient of many awards and prizes, including three Governor General's Literary Awards and two Scotiabank Giller Prizes, the Rea Award for the Short Story, the Lannan Literary Award, England's W. H. Smith Book Award, the National Book Critics Circle Award, and the Man Booker International Prize. In 2013 she was awarded the Nobel Prize for Literature. Her stories have appeared in *The New Yorker*, *The Atlantic*, *The Paris Review*, *Granta*, and other publications, and her collections have been translated into thirteen languages. She lives in Clinton, Ontario, near Lake Huron.

MORDECAI RICHLER was born in Montreal in 1931. He published ten novels, numerous screenplays, children's books, essays, and journalism. His novels include *The Apprenticeship of Duddy Kravitz*, *St. Urbain's Horseman*, *Solomon Gursky Was Here*, and *Barney's Version*. The recipient of many awards and honours, including the Governor General's Literary Award, the Giller Prize, the Commonwealth Writers' Prize, the Paris Review Humour Prize, the Stephen Leacock Award for Humour, he was made a Companion of the Order of Canada in 2001. Mordecai Richler died in Montreal in 2001.

SCOTT SYMONS was born in Toronto in 1933. He attended a number of private schools, the University of Toronto, Cambridge University, and the Sorbonne. His first two novels, *Place D'Armes* and *Civic Square*, are among the first works of LGBT literature published in Canada. He published a third novel, *Helmet of Flesh*, and a book about Canadian furniture called *Heritage: A Romantic Look at Early Canadian Furniture*. He was a professor at the University of Toronto, a curator at the Royal Ontario Museum, and a visiting curator at Winterthur and The Smithsonian. Symons is the subject of a documentary film, *God's Fool*, by Nik Sheehan. He died in Toronto in 2009.

LIST

The A List